From the Athenian Tetradrachm to the Euro

From the Athenian Tetradrachm to the Euro

Studies in European Monetary Integration

Edited by

PHILIP L. COTTRELL, GÉRASSIMOS NOTARAS
and GABRIEL TORTELLA

Co-editors

MONIKA POHLE FRASER and IAIN L. FRASER

Routledge
Taylor & Francis Group
LONDON AND NEW YORK

First published 2007 by Ashgate Publishing

Reissued 2018 by Routledge
2 Park Square, Milton Park, Abingdon, Oxon OX14 4RN
711 Third Avenue, New York, NY 10017, USA

Routledge is an imprint of the Taylor & Francis Group, an informa business

First issued in paperback 2018

A Library of Congress record exists under LC control number: 2006018632

ISBN 13: 978-0-815-38910-1 (hbk)
ISBN 13: 978-1-138-61970-8 (pbk)
ISBN 13: 978-1-351-15792-6 (ebk)

Contents

List of Tables

List of Figures

Notes on Contributors

Michael Artis

Previously Professor of Economics at the European University Institute, Michael Artis now holds a Chair at Manchester University where he directs the Machester Regional Economic Centre. He has published widely in the areas of macro and monetary economics and especially in the area of European monetary integration.

Marcello de Cecco

Professor of Monetary and Financial History at the Scuola Normale Superiore di Pisa since 2003, having previously held chairs at the University of Rome 'La Sapienza', European University Institute, the University of Siena and the Giannini Chair of Italian Culture, Faculty of Economics, University of California, Berkeley. From 1997 to 2000 he was a member of the Italian Prime Minister's council of economic advisers and, presently, is a member of the board of the Istituto dell' Enciclopedia Italiana. He has for many years been an editorial writer for the Italian daily newspaper *La Repubblica*.

Filippo Cesarano

The head of the Historical Research Office of the Banca d'Italia. A visiting professor at Siena, Florence and other universities, he has published articles in various British and American journals in the fields of monetary economics and the history of economic theory. He has been a member of the advisory board of *The European Journal of the History of Economic Thought.*

Vítor Gaspar

Currently, Director General of Research at the European Central Bank in Frankfurt; has published extensively.

Paul De Grauwe

A full professor at the Catholic University of Leuven since 1982 and has been a visiting professor at various American and European universities since the late 1970s. He has been a research fellow of the CEPR since 1990, and in 1991 he became a member of the Belgian Parliament. His research interests lie in the fields of international monetary relations, monetary integration, theory and empirical analysis of the foreign-exchange markets, and open-economy macroeconomics.

Lars Jonung

Research Adviser at ECFIN, European Commission, Brussels, previously professor of economics at the Stockholm School of Economics. His research focuses on monetary and fiscal policies, on monetary unions and exchange-rate arrangements, and on the history of economic thought. He served as chief economic adviser to Prime Minister Carl Bildt in 1992–4. He has been on the board of a number of listed Swedish companies.

Pablo Martín-Aceña

Professor of Economics and Economic History at the University of Alcalá (Madrid) He has been the Secretary General of the (Spanish) Asociación de Historia Económica and former editor of Revista de Historia Económica. He is the author of numerous contributions to the fields of business, financial and monetary history.

Juan Carlos Martinez Oliva

Deputy Director of the Historical Research Office, Banca d'Italia; has been a Visiting Professor at the Universities of Genoa and Perugia and University Guido Carli of Rome; Economic Advisor, International Monetary Fund. He is the author of many contributions in the fields of economic history, international economics, monetary policy and applied economics.

Cécile Morrisson

Directeur de recherches émérite, CNRS, former director of the Centre d'Histoire et civilisation de Byzance, Collège de France-CNRS and Keeper of Coins and Medals in the Bibliothèque nationale de France. Past President of the International Numismatic Commission. She is, presently, the advisor for numismatics, Dumbarton Oaks, Washington, Center for Byzantine Studies. She has written extensively on the economic and monetary history of the Byzantine Empire and made frequent use, in collaboration with the physicist J.-N. Barrandon, of activation analysis for investigating the metal composition of the coinage and its economic implications.

Richard H. Tilly

After having taught at the University of Michigan, Ann Arbor and Yale University, New Haven, was appointed in 1966 as the Director of Institute for Economic and

Social History, University of Münster, a post from which he retired in 1998. He has published widely in the fields of German business, financial and monetary history.

Ioannis Touratsoglou

Director Emeritus of the Numismatic Museum in Athens, having been Director of the National Archaeological Museum in Athens, 1999 to 2001, while having published in the fields of numismatics, ancient epigraphy and archaeology.

PREFACE

From the Athenian Tetradrachm to the Euro

Theodoros B. Karatzas†

It is now October 2001; we are destined, within less than two months, to enter the era of a common, circulating European currency in the real and not just the virtual sense. This is a brave new reality for the peoples of Europe, but one which has, nevertheless, been preceded by similar endeavours over the course of past centuries and millennia. After browsing through some of these historical examples, I will try to describe what I consider to be some of the main features surrounding the adoption, use and decline of common currencies, and what lessons can be drawn which may be of relevance for the euro.

The idea of a common currency, or of widely accepted currencies, is not unfamiliar to the history, tradition and practices of Greece and its neighbouring geographical region. During the seventh century BC, coinage emerged as currency in the area of the east Aegean. It was the need to expedite and systematize commercial transactions that turned the small, metallic disc-shaped plates into carriers of monetary value. Money became an instrument of communication for peoples of different geographical areas and civilizations, a stimulus and measure of financial success, and a weapon of economic and political dominance. Trade within, and between, different cities in Antiquity was a crucial driving force for the birth of the currency. Thus, and virtually simultaneously, emerged the notion of an 'international' currency.

By the mid-sixth century BC, city-states such as Aegina, Corinth and Athens, then major trading powers, were producing the first coinages. A policy of monetary aggression was employed by each city-state, seeking to render its own currency the predominant means of exchange. From the late sixth until the early fifth century BC, the famous 'turtles' formed the coinage of Aegina, circulating in Persia, Egypt, southern Italy and the wider Mediterranean. However, Aegina's rivalry with Athens proved disastrous, diminishing its influence as well as that of its currency in the Hellenic affairs.

As Athens rose as a regional power so did the influence of its currency. Its coinage, featuring the distinctive 'owl', introduced in the late sixth century BC, was maintained iconographically for more than two centuries. Athenian tetradrachms, bolstered by the Athenian naval force, became a true international currency. They were accepted all over the Mediterranean world, while various imitations travelled all the way to Persia and Arabia. The Peloponnesian war at the end of the fifth century BC depleted the silver resources of Athens, eventually destroying its supremacy.

In the fourth century, Philip the Second of Macedonia was the first to introduce bimetallism in Europe, issuing massive quantities of silver tetradrachms and golden staters. After defeating the southern Hellenes, Philip formed a pan-Hellenic alliance against the Persians. Through Celtic and other Balkan soldiers employed as mercenaries in his army, large amounts of silver and gold coinage were transferred to central Europe and the Balkans. Philip's son, Alexander, extended Macedonian rule from the Danube to Egypt to India. The international coinage he introduced served to instil at least a semblance of unity in his vast kingdom. During the centuries following Alexander's death, a wide number of Hellenic cities continued to mint tetradrachms in the name, and coin types, of Alexander. These posthumous coinages remained an international 'strong' currency *par excellence*, which dominated markets from southern Italy to the Middle East.

It was the Roman world that managed to establish a truly homogeneous currency, the first common European one. It followed the Roman legions across the vast Roman Empire – from England to the Middle East to the edges of Sahara. War and trade proved to be the main avenues for the international diffusion of money in Antiquity. Later, the Byzantine golden currency, the 'dollar' of the Middle Ages as historians called it, acquired vast distribution and reputation. Trade, diplomatic and military exchange carried Byzantine currency across an enormous area stretching from the North Sea to the Indian Ocean.

From Antiquity to modern times, a common currency was typically the culmination of an effort to affirm a unity of tribal, religious, national or political features. The survival of the common currency, however, was predicated on the strength of political, economic, and military unity.

In the modern era too, Greece, along with France, Belgium, Switzerland, and Italy, participated in the Latin Monetary Union. The Union, which operated from the second half of the nineteenth century until the 1920s, has been considered by some as the first international effort to regulate exchange rates. It was finally dissolved following the contradiction between a common currency and the lack of a common monetary policy.

Modern world history has known several monetary unions, from colonial New England during the seventeenth and first half of the eighteenth century to the Scandinavian Monetary Union in the nineteenth and early twentieth century. And a number of active monetary unions between European countries endured during the twentieth century, such as those between Belgium and Luxembourg, or Switzerland and Liechtenstein.

A set of shared features more or less underpinned the adoption and use of all common currencies. The basis given by geographical proximity or regional integration was one. A strong, outward-oriented economy, engaged in international trade, was another. Political might, if not elements of imperial power, to a great extent also underpinned the use of a common currency. Finally, some degree of a broader cultural stature was also present, if only as a derivative of politico-economic clout.

Similarities also exist as to the conditions of decline of common currencies. More often than not, the disuse or obsolescence of a common currency followed the economic and political decline of the issuing state authority, or the monetary union's breakdown under the disruptive impact of opportunistic national economic behaviour. Monetary instability and prolonged inflation, adulteration of the coinage and systematic monetary depreciation were the dismal harbingers of the abandonment of a common currency.

The concept of 'one international currency', and the struggle to achieve and maintain it, is as old as the use of money in human civilization. No example, however, of a monetary union in modern history has come at all close to matching the significance, scope, and ambition of the European Economic and Monetary Union. This time it is not war as in Antiquity, but a commitment to peace, globalized trade and widespread prosperity that underwrite the bright prospects of our single currency.

EMU is unprecedented in both the number of national currencies it involves and the magnificent share it represents in the world economy. National currencies are soon to become an irrevocable part of history; there is now one single monetary policy for the entire euro zone, and one effective exchange rate between the euro and external currencies. The EMU project has required brave vision, technocratic sophistication and enormous political capital to come to fruit. It is a reality thanks to the persistence of Europe's leaders, but the benefits are to be reaped by all the peoples of Europe.

Already from its formative steps, the euro zone is experiencing the beneficial effects of the euro in the form of remarkable transaction efficiency, and a monetary stability unseen on such a scale since the Bretton Woods era. This is important for all members of the euro zone, and it is multiply important for those of them, like Greece, which have suffered high rates of inflation in the not too distant past.

Most notably, the European Monetary Union represents a seminal political decision or, if I may say so, a new political culture. Past historical efforts at monetary unions (and indeed several decades of sub-optimal experience with the European Monetary System) have demonstrated the tremendous difficulties and the failures resulting from each member state pursuing its individual interests over the common good of the union. EMU comes with an armoury of institutional guarantees, aimed to prevent disruptive economic nationalism or irresponsible macroeconomic management by the Union's member states. This, indeed, brings about a 'win-win culture' and a new technology of political cooperation towards the common good. For all member states, the longer-run benefits of such cooperation under EMU exceed any short-term advantages that would have been derived from individualistic economic strategies.

What are the lessons that past monetary unions and common currencies can offer for the euro? First, the euro needs to remain a strong and credible currency. For now, inflation has been curbed but neither has it, nor can it, ever be beaten. Second, the euro zone economy must remain a growing, thriving, dynamic economy. Such words may sound misplaced given the difficult moments the world has been facing during September 2001. However, we should keep focus on the broader longer-term economic picture, and that remains promising indeed. Third, the political cooperation and union between euro-zone partners must be strengthened – towards the 'ever closer Union' our European founding fathers envisaged. This means both an inward and outward political strength of the Union. And, finally, as euro-zone countries comprise some of the world's most advanced democracies, the public's support for the euro must be sustained. Under all these preconditions, our Economic and Monetary Union may prove not only the most inspired but also the most enduring of all similar experiments undertaken in the course of history.

From the Community's early steps after 1957, Greece has asserted her determination to be an active participant in the European integration process. Greece's entry into EMU from 2001 was the culmination of a long effort, which included the 1960 Association Agreement and the 1980 Accession to the European Communities.

Throughout that long process, the National Bank of Greece has been a central pillar of the Greek economy and a champion of European integration. The National Bank was the first credit institution to operate in the modern Greek state, and held the privilege of note issuing for 87 years, from 1841 to 1928 – until the country's central bank was established. This historical record, *inter alia*, affords the National Bank a key role in the Greek economy's transition to the new monetary era.

The National Bank group controls a major share of the domestic financial market, possesses the largest banking network in the country, and plays a crucial role in the south-eastern European region. We in the National Bank have chosen to implement a strategy of active internationalization, not simply via integration in the existing international networks, but by directing our activity to selected world markets where we possess the knowledge and the ability to succeed. The National Bank is committed to contributing decisively to Greece's effort for the success of the EMU project. Our bank has undertaken to inform the public through ad hoc and periodical publications, training its cadres and personnel and implementing structural changes in its operation.

A new era of monetary union, cooperation and stability in Europe lies ahead. With one of the most strongly pro-EMU societies in the European Union, Greece will continue to play its role in bolstering the common effort, and the National Bank will do so as well.

Introduction

In his contribution, Ioannis Touratsoglou comments that the coins first likely to have had an 'extra-national' circulation were the 'turtles', struck by Aegina from the second half of sixth century, BCE, until the opening decades of the fifth century, BCE. Their wider place within the Mediterranean world was soon taken by the 'owls' – the Athenian tetradachm. These became commonplace on eastern markets, which led to imitations being minted in Arabia, Egypt and the Levant during the fourth century BCE. Consequently, it was very fitting that the international symposium, from which this volume's contributions originate and which was held to mark the European Union's adoption of the euro as a common currency, should have been convened at Vouliagmeni, just to the south east of Athens on the shore of the Saronikós Kólpos. This very well attended meeting was organised and very generously hosted by the National Bank of Greece in conjunction with the European Association for Banking History.

The symposium's aim was to place the euro's introduction within its historical perspective by considering past pan-national currencies, both European and global. Consequently, the 11 papers presented and discussed collectively covered developments over a time span of two-and-a-half millennia. In their revised versions, they fall within four broad chronological sections. The first comprises three contributions considering aspects of the European monetary experience from Classical Antiquity until the High Middle Ages. The discussion then leaps forward chronologically to the Modern era. Its initial focus is given by three contributions addressing nineteenth-century European developments. These are set within a wider spatial framework by two essays that review, first, the classical gold standard, primarily in terms of peripheral economies' experience, and, second, the Bretton Woods system. Fourth and lastly, the euro's origins and launch are explored in three further contributions.

Touratsoglou's review has a very broad chronological perspective in order to secure its objective – that the euro's introduction was, in essence, a step 'back to the future'. He points out that the euro is but a further international currency in a long historical tradition that within Europe had previously embraced the Athenian tetradrachm, the Spanish silver peso, the Maria Theresa thaler and the French franc.

The innovation and further development of coins fuelled the expansion of trade in the eastern Mediterranean. The growth of international dealings led to both the wider circulation of particular coins and the general adoption of particular national and federal monetary systems. However, commerce and economics also joined aesthetics, beliefs, culture, politics and traditions through the images stamped on coins and, much later, printed on bank notes. Touratsoglou traces these developments through a consideration of the mints of the eastern Mediterranean from the mid-seventh century BCE, to the first century BCE. His outline indicates that the coins that came to be more generally used were either struck by the mints of cities and states linked within alliances and federations, or imposed through the power exerted by a centre of trade and/or political empire.

A common currency arising from conquest is the theme of Juan Carlos Martinez Oliva's contribution, which considers monetary integration within the Roman Empire. As he emphasises, this unity was imposed by military victory, which he explores by taking a core/periphery view of the 'Roman world's' political economy. After reviewing the core/periphery approach, Martinez Oliva shows how Roman monetisation between 200 and 300 BCE was taken further forward by the Punic wars and involved 'learning by doing'. These developments set the stage for the Augustan monetary reform, which reinstated the standards of fineness for the aurei and the denarii that had been introduced by Julius Caesar in 47–46 BCE. The re-established monetary system supported the growth of trade with areas bordering the Empire and, through Arab intermediaries, with China and India. However, the Empire's dynamics led to the onset of its metropole's wane from about the second century CE, marked by Italy's depopulation and decline of its agriculture, compounded by fiscal mismanagement. The imperial power reacted by debasement, coupled with compulsory labour, requisitions and supplementary levies.

Debasement was used by Marcus Aurelius to meet the costs of frontier wars waged against Germans and Parthians. This war-finance policy was subsequently followed by Septimus Severus and Caracalla, who also employed debasement for mounting ambitious building programmes. Their approach involved exploiting the Roman currency's long-established reputation for stability through deliberately maintaining the physical appearance of the coinage system established in 64. However, this sleight of hand could only be temporary, and transactions increasingly took place in moneys of account, with payment made at current market rates. Moneys of account were to persist even after Diocletian tried to bring about in 293 a thorough reform of the imperial currency and, again, following the Tetrarchs' two attempts to regulate prices. Debasement and inflation resulted in the collapse of commerce and finance, which accompanied the Empire's general depopulation during the third century CE.

Cécile Morrisson considers the Roman heritage in a contribution that reviews Byzantium's currency from 324 to 1353. Its gold coinage circulated as far and as wide as north-western Europe and the Indian sub-continent, while occasionally reaching China. It was the 'dollar of the Middle Ages'. The Byzantine solidus/nomisma retained its original standard from the fourth until the tenth century, with early issues probably aided by a new, Balkan source of gold, as suggested by trace-element analysis.

Byzantium's growing economic and political problems, particularly during the seventh century, may be reflected in the decline and value of the follis, the bronze coin, and the issue of light-weight solidi between 537 and 687. Clear and greater pressure came from Arab expansion during the seventh century, which resulted in the Empire losing its wealthiest provinces to the disruption of its economic system. Nonetheless, the gold coinage was retained, albeit with some very limited debasement during the late seventh century. It remained the resurgent Empire's currency at the end of the tenth century, but was the subject of 'a slackening of the standard', or 'creeping' debasement during the eleventh century, undertaken through not refining the gold prior to minting. The lack of accompanying inflation suggests that the aim of debasement, as has long been argued by Morrisson, was to meet the needs of monetisation arising from trade expansion and state expenditure.

War-induced debasement occurred at the end of the eleventh century until halted by the establishment of a new monetary system in 1092. The new gold coin, the hyperpyron ('fire refined') was employed in international trade, where it was known as the bisantius, which became the generic term for gold coin and the model for the bezant and augustale. The international use of the hyperpyron (as in the Mediterranean trades), was maintained from the 1220s through issues by the Greek Empire of Nicaea until, during the late thirteenth century, it was superseded by the Venetian ducat and the Florentine florin.

With the benefit of a perspective provided by hindsight, these three contributions show two principles that seem to apply at all times but which are more clearly apparent in Antiquity. First, commercial integration greatly benefits from, and stimulates, monetary unification. In the Greek case, where there was only ephemeral and incomplete political unification, solely market integration tended to favour and foster the predominance of one type of coin, most often that of Athens, the paramount commercial metropolis. In Rome and Byzantium, where commercial unification was reinforced by political unity, this was, of course, even more so. Second, and most clear in the Roman and Byzantine cases, political, military and fiscal overextension produced inflationary financing of the (notional) budget deficit and currency depreciation.

These two principles seem to apply equally in the modern world. Clear examples are: commercial and monetary integration (gold standard) during the late nineteenth century; commercial and monetary reconstruction after the Second World War; American overstretch at the time of the Vietnam war and fall of the dollar; and, of course, the European Common Market and EMU euro.

The opening three contributions also collectively provide an example of the fruitfulness of melding the approaches of numismatists and economists, especially when arguments can be supported by the results of new advances in metallurgical analysis and wider theoretical constructs. A multi-disciplinary approach is less overtly marked in the contributions concerned with modern and contemporary developments, yet their authors are all imbued with a wide perspective of their particular theme.

In his consideration of German monetary union, Richard Tilly builds upon the revisionist approach current since the mid-1970s. His contribution not only acknowledges the importance of the Zollverein's establishment but also points to the roles of prior Prussian monetary unification and the wider monetary environment set by the policies of France and Great Britain. He also emphasises the actions of private agents, as opposed to those of the German state governments, with the wide take up of Bank of Prussia notes from 1856 and the growth of bank deposits.

As with the contributions that explore the Classical world and its Medieval heritage, one of Tilly's concerns is the relationship between trade and money, hence his attention to bills of exchange and the codification, as in 1847, of related commercial practice. A quantitative examination of exchange rates displays greater stability for the mid-nineteenth century, particularly with regard to international, as opposed to inter-German state, rates. His results, he suggests, indicate only modest gains arising from the early stages of German monetary unification. He concludes with five possible lessons from this historical experience but of which only one directly bears upon Europe of the early twenty-first century – that small states outside monetary unions have limited policy autonomy because of the pressures exerted by capital flows in particular and economic globalisation in general.

Tilly's contribution on 'national' monetary unification is complemented by two considering Europe's monetary unions of the second half of the nineteenth century. Marcello de Cecco revisits, as he puts it, the Latin Monetary Union. He introduces his subject by contrasting the monetary system of the *ancien regime* with that subsequently established by the market, which he argues was brought about by the arrival in Europe of New-World silver. Within this perspective, he sees LMU as being a product of a transition phase when silver was being increasingly supplanted by gold. This revisits, in turn, a sub-theme within Tilly's contribution but de Cecco frames his subject in terms of nineteenth-century Europe having, from 1815, two alternative monetary models for possible imitation or perpetuation (both themselves also alternative to a silver currency): Britain's gold standard or France's Napoleonic bimetallic system.

Widely adopted bimetallism came under pressure as a result of the 1849 Californian gold discoveries, and the states represented at the 1865 Paris conference sought extra-national solutions to the consequent monetary problems. Instead of moving onto gold, Belgium, France, Italy and Switzerland maintained bimetallism through a coinage treaty that had an initial duration of 15 years. However, LMU persisted until 1927, joined by Greece in 1868, while Chile, Colombia, Spain and Venezuela accepted the Union's system albeit without the inter-circulation of 'small' silver coins.

The second part of de Cecco's contribution analyses the problems that LMU soon encountered, beginning with the fiscal problems of unified Italy that resulted in the Banque de France coming to hold Italian and Papal coins in some quantity. This difficulty, which caused Belgian and Swiss statesmen considerable concern, was soon followed by another, and much graver: the fall of the (gold) price of silver from 1873. This shock could not be fully absorbed by LMU, being only met by the suspension of the free coinage of silver in 1878, which resulted in its 'limping' standard. Paradoxically, silver's continuing price fall relative to gold maintained LMU. The Union's liquidation clause, insisted upon by France, was rendered inoperative through the fall of silver making it prohibitively expensive for each of its member states to redeem their respective silver coinages. LMU probably managed to shield 'Latin' Europe against the full effects of the late-nineteenth-century secular price fall, while it made the Banque de France a buffer between bimetallic Europe and the developing international gold standard.

The onset of monetary integration within 'Latin' Europe took place almost in parallel with that in Nordic Europe. There the weight of international relations resulted in the adoption of a 'domestic' solution to monetary problems: the Scandinavian Monetary Union, which became fully fledged in autumn 1875. This northern monetary block is the subject of Lars Jonung's contribution. SMU instituted a Nordic gold-based common monetary area, involving the free circulation of 'small' coins and, later, 'small' notes. It further developed in 1885 through an agreement between the three signatory countries' central banks that introduced mutual drawing rights. SMU reached its highest stage of development in 1901, when the Danish central bank agreed to accept other members' notes to any extent, and continued until the outbreak of the First World War.

Jonung's analysis strongly suggests that SMU had a positive real impact through aiding the deepening of Scandinavian financial markets. However, SMU's real and nominal effects are difficult to establish with it being gold-based and, therefore, open to the wider influences of the developing international gold standard during the late nineteenth century. As with the gold standard, SMU was ruptured de facto by the outbreak of war in 1914, but the arising consequences were not fully addressed. Although there was a post-war growth of cultural Nord-ism, SMU was unable to survive, despite attempts by Knut Wicksell. Indeed, he recognised, as Jonung suggests in his contribution, SMU's Achilles' heel – the lack of a common central bank to co-ordinate monetary policy. Unlike LMU, SMU did not encounter serious problems before 1914 and was not forced into an early 'hibernation'. Yet, its achievement suggests, in Jonung's view, that currency blocks were easier to establish when monetary policy was not the subject of politics.

LMU and SMU operated within the context of the emergence and maturation of the classical gold standard. This is considered by Pablo Martín-Aceña, who concentrates upon the experience of the periphery and, thereby, in part continues a theme first raised by Martinez Oliva. Martín-Aceña's contribution explores what has been largely monetary terra incognita through assessing the experiences of Brazil, Chile, Colombia, Italy, Portugal and Spain. Their economies, particularly those of Brazil, Italy and Spain, found it difficult to adhere to the 'rules' of the 'gold standard club'. This was in part due to their dependency upon exports of primary products and their consequent exposure to macroeconomic instability. A related factor was their reliance upon imports of capital from the 'centre'. Common difficulties could be augmented within each member of the periphery, depending upon the composition and character of its respective financial system. Overall, the 'Latin' European components of the periphery fared better than their counterparts in South America with regard to exchange-rate instability and the vicissitudes of the export cycle. Furthermore, the government's need for finance led in general to the emergence of a privately owned bank of issue, which resulted in an institutional context producing a direct link between the balance of payments and the monetary base. Martín-Aceña concludes by putting flesh on the bones of collaborative research through reviewing the Spanish experience from 1902. This is undertaken to find an explanation for why peripheral countries, when they left the gold standard, chose to follow stringent monetary policies, involving a proxy gold-standard norm, but not to return to gold.

Whereas de Cecco strongly suggests that LMU was an institution of the transition phase from a silver-based monetary regime to a gold-based monetary regime, Filppo Cesarano argues that the Bretton-Woods system marked the last stage in the transition from commodity money to fiat money. Furthermore, whereas past monetary orders either had been imposed by conquest (the Roman-Byzantine order) or had developed organically (the classical gold standard order), the Bretton-Woods order was designed by experts. This unique situation leads Cesarano to examine the context for the establishment of the Bretton-Woods system, namely the development of economic theory during the inter-war period. As he terms it, the 'state of the art' had experienced a watershed with the onset of the Great Slump. The 1920s had been marked by efforts to reintroduce the classical gold standard, or at least a variant of it. Nonetheless, departures from orthodoxy were encouraged by an increasing scepticism of the 'metallist' doctrine, whereas the severity and duration of the post-1929 slump resulted in a fading belief in the gold standard's ability to induce equilibrium. This major change resulted in an increasing acceptance of 'managed' money. The extent of the shock administered by the Slump caused policymakers, as well as academics, to look away from the gold standard when trying to find solutions that stabilised not only exchange-rate parities but also prices and employment. Critical in all these discussions was the contribution of Keynes, and he was also to play a major role in shaping the international monetary regime of the third quarter of the twentieth century.

The origins of the Bretton-Woods order lay in experts' plans designed to counter German autarchic proposals for replacing the gold standard and displacing London as a prime financial centre. In order to allow the operation of a liberal international commercial and monetary regime in conjunction with states having independence over their domestic policies, the Bretton-Woods order maintained capital controls and permitted exchange-rate flexibility in the long term. However, it became a pseudo-gold standard system from 1949 through the unintended institution of what were to be fixed exchange rates (in part, the result of the over hang of older orthodoxy amongst policy makers) – to allow both European reconstruction and the maintenance of anti-inflationary policies. However, the rules of the resultant 'pseudo-club' were doomed through the incompatibility of retaining a (resumed growing) link to gold with the independence of policy making. Policy clashes with the 'rules' eventually arose when capital controls were progressively lifted and the United States' gold reserves began to diminish markedly.

The last three contributions consider European monetary developments from the early 1970s until the present. Michael Artis presents an analysis of the development of the European Monetary System – from a crawling peg to a counter-inflationary framework to a greater Deutschmark area. By 1990, it appeared to be an 'ideal' monetary system, enjoying low inflation while being flexible and sustaining this flexibility. Furthermore, it allowed relative smooth realignments amongst its members, and was robust in the face of the liberalisation of capital controls. Yet, in 1992–3, it experienced a sequence of major speculative exchange crises that led, first, to its major modification and, ultimately, to the establishment of the European Monetary Union.

The Exchange Rate Mechanism was the successor to the European 'snake', and previous experience led to great caution being exercised over any outward reference to monetary union. Other problems arose over competitive devaluations within the Mechanism, and from the conjunction of a weak dollar against the Deutschmark. These mapped onto the Mechanism's evolution, with a major turning point reached with the inception of the 'franc fort' policy, an important part of the transition to the 'hard ERM' that fully emerged from 1987. As such, the Mechanism was a stabilising institution (culminating after 1987 from when there were no further realignments amongst its members), through progressively inducing credibility in its objectives and achieving nominal rates close to purchasing power parities. The Mechanism also involved exchange-rate targeting as a counter-inflationary policy, and adherence to the Deutschmark was not diminished amongst the Mechanism's members by German unification in 1989.

Most remarkable, whereas the Mechanism was gravely affected by crisis from 1992, it provided (unlike the previous 'snake'), at least a clear signpost to the route by which European Monetary Union could be achieved. The impact of the crises of the early 1990s led to the formal adoption of much wider currency bands within the Mechanism, yet in practice the resultant shift proved largely to be very close to the original band of +/-2.25 per cent. The re-cementing of the Mechanism was completed by, first, the adherence of the Finnish markka and the Greek drachma; second, the re-entry of the Italian lira; and, third, the inception of European Monetary Union from May 1998.

The last two contributions move from contemporary history to analysing the present. Paul De Grauwe considers the factors that allowed the inception of European Monetary Union, and postulates what further measures might be required to secure its longevity. He stresses the greater political will to achieve monetary union during the 1990s, as compared with the 1970s. This increased commitment arose from a change in macroeconomic policy, the possibility from the early 1990s that the full unification of the European market might be stymied by exchange-rate crises and the growing perceived need to have an institution to replace, or displace, German monetary hegemony. However, De Grauwe puts forward that EMU can, through intensifying centrifugal forces, increase economic disparities within Europe. Consequently, he maintains that there is a need for a risk-sharing institution that may come about, in part, from total European financial market integration. Yet for risk sharing to be complete, it will also require an institutional mechanism that embraces Europe's poor as well as its affluent.

The volume closes with Vitor Gaspar's overview, in which he strongly emphasises the inter-action between the economic and political dimensions of European integration, especially in the case of monetary unification. This had been proved to be possible because of the general consensus embracing the importance of price stability, central-bank independence and transparency and accountability. EMU was accomplished through the transition to a single monetary policy, while a single currency was specifically seen to be the necessary complement to a single market. However, the European Commission was largely concerned during the early 1990s with reducing exchange-rate volatility whereas, a decade later, one academic researcher, Rose, has emphasised the very substantial trade-generating effects enjoyed by a currency union. His results are still debated but have received some confirmation. Although it is still too early to assess the impact of the European Monetary Union, nearly all this volume's contributions refer explicitly, or implicitly, to the relationship between trade and common currencies. Gaspar goes further in his last sentence by maintaining that the impact of integration dynamics on the markets for services and finance will be long lasting.

P. L. Cottrell, G. Notaras and G. Tortella

CHAPTER 1

Common Currency from Antiquity: *Plus ça change, plus c'est la même chose*

Ioannis Touratsoglou

The invention of coin-shaped currency at the end of the seventh century BC in the area of Lydia and Ionia (western Asia Minor) may be regarded as the culmination of a millennium's experience of trade. The use of metal as a means of exchange was known as early as the third millennium BC, attested alongside the employment of agricultural and livestock products. However, the convenience of coin, together with the value of its metal content, guaranteed by the stamp [*σφραγίς*, *χαρακτήρ*] of the issuing authority (also found on metallic objects exchanged during the period before the invention of coins), gave new possibilities for the economy. Coins' attributes enabled the economy to cast off limitations previously imposed by the imponderable factors that had governed agricultural and livestock production.

Views are divided over both the first authority to issue coins and the needs that they were designed to serve. Ionian merchants or bankers, or priests and even the kings of Lydia have all been advanced as the supposed inventors [*heuretai*] of coins. The accumulation of wealth, payment for services and the conduct of trade were all given an impulse by whatever innovator. Nonetheless, coinage, besides its essential function as a means for economic transactions, was always a vehicle for administrative control, political propaganda, religious symbolism, inscribed messages, collective beliefs, ideas and goals, common traditions and customs, major artistic trends and so on.

Although the objects used for exchange in the pre-coinage economy were for the most part capable of responding to the requirements of international trade and exchanges, coins gave an impulse to a development of a different kind. This emerged after the Greek city-states began the minting of coins. The stamp, giving legitimacy and a public character to these metal objects so making them coins [nomisma from nomos – law in ancient Greek], also referred to their various issuing authorities. For their respective coin issues, the Greek city-states and *ethnē* used differing weight standards based upon systems for measuring their agricultural products. Each city-state, as an independent political unit, attempted – especially when it succeeded in acquiring certain power – to impose its own currency policy through seeking, frequently by legislation, to dictate the use of its own coinage for commercial exchanges. 'The national coinage' [*ἡμεδαπόν, πάτριον νόμισμα*], was described as 'having value for ourselves, but unfamiliar to the other people' [*autois men entimon, tois de allois anthrōpois adokimon*]. As a result of this process, zones of currency-economic influence were created, and this development may also be seen in the voluntary fragmenting of these zones. The evidence comes from ancient Greek literature, inscriptions and, of course, the coins themselves, together with the extent of their respective circulations and the production of imitations.

In some cases, political and geographical unions of a federal character decided, in the context of common ties, aspirations and institutions, to conduct joint political affairs and military operations and to issue a common coinage. In a similar fashion, some of the Hellenistic kingdoms (the Ptolemies in Egypt, the Attalids in Asia Minor) pursued a largely introspective economic policy, and imposed on their states the use of their own issues. Either at a peripheral, local level (tribes, federations), or in the wider Mediterranean area (through powerful issuing authorities, such as Aegina, Corinth, or Athens), the Greek mints gradually led to the emergence, initially latent, of the need for the creation and imposition of a coinage that met with general acceptance. The particular reasons behind the predominance of particular coin issues varied, characteristic examples being the electrum staters of Kyzikos, the hectae [sixths] of Phokaea and the gold darics of the Great King of Persia. These series were widely acceptable during the fifth and fourth centuries BC, mainly because the Greek cities no longer issued electrum currencies and did not strike gold coins, except in emergency.

The turtles [*χελῶναι*] of Aegina, found in countless hoards in mainland Greece and the Aegean islands, and also in the East with burial dates in the second half of the sixth and the early decades of the fifth centuries BC, constituted perhaps the first international coinage. The reasons for their predominance can be found in both the context of the very considerable trading activity of the issuing authority, and the ability of this island mint to supply the market with money, having secured control of mines abroad and having exploited the potential afforded by this control and by the carrying trade.

Corinth, whose foals [*πῶλοι*] are found primarily in hoards in west Greece, constitutes a different case. This city on the isthmus, under the aegis of the Kypselid tyrants, sought to secure markets for its own products by founding colonies, mainly along the Ionian and Adriatic shores, that it placed under its own political control. The types and weight standards of these colonies' coinages were, with the exception of Potidaia, aligned with those of the mother city. Hence, the only difference between the coins of the metropolis and those of the colonies was the reference, under the belly of the obverse Pegasus, of the relevant city name through the acrophonic letter of its ethnic: *A* for Anactorion, *Λ* for Leucas, *Δ* for Dyrrhachion, and so on.

On the morrow of the fine victory won by the Athenians and Spartans at Mykale, the city of Athens undertook to protect the interests of the Greek cities against the Persians, aided by silver from Laurion and the fleet victorious at Salamis, to which was now added the fleet of the Delian League. Using the tribute that flowed into the League's treasure chest and exploiting a complex system of political and economic influence, Athens developed to be the leader of an economic empire. The owls [*glaukes*] flooded the markets of the eastern Mediterranean and became the 'coinage common to all' [*to koinon tois pasi nomisma*].

It is indicative that, during the Peloponnesian War when Athens not only had to meet enormous war costs but also fund her ambitious building policy, especially on the Acropolis, the city attempted to exploit the advantages of a common currency, and of common weights and measures standards, by imposing the Attic standard upon her allies. However, this attempt was unsuccessful. Nevertheless, when Athens was facing difficulties during the late fifth century BC, coins influenced by the owls were in circulation in Asia Minor and local requirements were met by this currency. During the fourth century BC, imitations of the – still strong – Athenian currency circulated in Egypt, Palestine and Arabia. In his *Poroi*, Xenophon gave a detailed account of the purchasing value of the Athenian currency on all the Mediterranean markets. In the Platonic dialogues, which outline the currency policy to be followed by the state, the Athenian tetradrachm serves as a model for the 'common Greek currency' [*to koinon hellēnikon nomisma*], in contrast to the 'currency for everyday transactions' [*to nomisma heneka allagēs tēs kath'ēmeran*].

The basis for Macedonian expansion was established by Philip II (361/0–336 BC), who created a powerful kingdom in the Balkans. His gold and silver coins were disseminated – and imitated – mainly in the territories of the Celtic tribes of the Balkans and central Europe. His successor, Alexander the Great (336–323 BC) took the Athenian currency as his model, and began, probably after the victory at Issos (333 BC), to issue silver and gold coins on the Attic weight standard. Throughout Alexander's vast empire the iconography of the young monarch's coinage reflected the pan-Hellenic spirit, which characterized the Asian expedition to the East. His coinage was struck by a series of mints from Aegae to Babylon, and from Amphipolis to Memphis. The Alexandrian tetradrachms [*τετραχμα*], struck during his lifetime by the warrior king and subsequently by Greek cities and 'barbarian' rulers in his name, replaced Attic tetradrachms in hoards dating from the late fourth and third centuries BC, and dominated the markets. Tetradrachms and drachms on the Attic standard became the 'common currency' [*κοινόν νόμισμα*] of the Hellenistic period, flooded markets and spread out to the far reaches of the East – from Phoenicia to present day Afghanistan. A typical example of the popularity enjoyed by Alexander's issues is provided by the large number of imitations struck by various peoples on the fringes of the Greek world: Thracians, Celts of the Balkan peninsula and of central and western Europe, and Arabs of the shores of the Persian Gulf.

Issues by the Diadochi (successors of Alexander) functioned in a comparable manner. From the second century BC and throughout the late Hellenistic period, when coins of Alexander were no longer issued, other coins attempted to fill the huge gap. The Athenian tetradrachms [stephanephora: wreath-bearing] – known as 'New Style' tetradrachms in the modern bibliography – again acted as an international currency, clearly demonstrated by hoard evidence. The roles that had been played during the classical period by Persian darics and the coins of Kyzikos and Lampsakos, brought to the Greek world as payments to mercenaries, were now assumed by the so-called pseudo-Rhodian coins and the tetrobols of Histiaea, found in a large number of hoards dating from the second century BC onwards.

In addition to the decree imposing the Attic weight standard on the members of the First Athenian League, other attempts at the systematic imposition by a state or inter-state organization of a common currency are also known, either with a specific purpose or as a long-term option. Coins with a common reverse, bearing the legend *ΣΥΝ* [*συνμαχικόν*: of the allies], issued towards the end of the fifth or the beginning of the fourth centuries BC by cities in the eastern Aegean and the Propontis, and 'the silver of the allies' [*συμγαχικόν ἀργύριον*] of the Hellenistic period, reflect the issuing of a common currency by alliances – that is, by multistate organizations.

The issue and imposition of a common currency by cities, kings, ethne or koina [confederacies] marks an extension, and is to be seen within the context of a currency policy that first found an expression in Athens with the Law of Nikophon (375/4 BC). Within the borders of the kingdoms of Macedonia, the Ptolemies (Egypt, Coele Syria, Cyprus and Libya), and the Attalids of Pergamon, royal rescripts imposed the exclusive use of coins struck locally and dictated the rates of exchange for foreign coins. These coins' lower weights restrained their export, while their exchange for tetradrachms on the Attic standard brought huge profits to royal treasuries. The same policy was pursued by Rhodes through the import of so-called plinthophoroi (drachms with a square-shaped pattern on their reverse).

The currencies issued by the Koina of ancient times seem invariably either to have been the result of pressing economic need, or to have been part of a general attempt to give expression to shared national and religious features that normally formed the basis of these organizations. These issues reflected an underlying common acceptance of political or military activity, or reveal initiatives almost invariably abortive due to the lack of rich metal reserves and the absence of political success and economic prosperity. Despite the determined efforts of some of the Hellenistic Leagues (Aetolian League, Achaean League), the power and spheres of influence of these federal states and their coinages were ultimately limited. According to hoard evidence, the 'Chalcidians in Thrace' [*apo Thrakēs Khalkideis*], the leagues of the Thessalians, Euboeans and Boeotians, the Delphic Amphictyony, the Achaean League, and the federal states of the Aetolians, the Akarnanians and the Epirotes, all attempted to impose a common coinage policy, mainly on the territories under their control. Foreign coins that entered these zones either were commonly accepted currency, such as the Alexandrian tetradrachms of the Hellenistic period, or their arrival is associated with specific historical events. These trends are reflected and recorded in the passage in Polybios comparing the Peloponnese under the Achaean League with a city (having common laws, institutions, and weight standards), and the fact that in Euboea the artists of Dionysos wished to be paid in coins issued by Demetrios Poliorketes [Demetrieion], struck on the Attic standard.

During the long history of numismatics from antiquity to modern times there were, on certain occasions, several attempts by various cities and states to form federations and alliances – usually of regional character and influence – with common goals, (occasionally) common institutions, common political agendas and common coinage. In an analogous framework, other coinages, mainly issued by cosmopolitan centres or by powerful empires, were imposed by several means (for example trade, colonization, conquest). They became widely accepted in the ancient or the medieval world, playing a significant role as regulators in the economies of various peoples and, thus, expressed a common will of another kind for monetary uniformity. From these sketchy remarks, it is evident that the idea for a sole, common monetary means is in fact an old one. It actually originated from the attempts of various ancient and medieval societies to achieve the aforementioned goal.

During modern times, in the colourful mosaic of economic/political developments, the spotlight was taken by the coinages of powerful or developing countries, which were internationalized mainly through worldwide commercial transactions. These were the Spanish gold escudos and silver reales (produced in both the heartland of the kingdom and the colonies), the Maria Theresa Thaler (of the multinational Austro-Hungarian Empire), the British pound (of the once vigorous colonial power), and recently, the American dollar. Another attempt at economic uniformity was centred (mainly) in Europe, and focused on the French franc: the Latin Monetary Union (1865–1927), which may, to some degree, be considered the forerunner of the European unification under way at the close of the twentieth century.

The transition to the third millennium AD is highlighted by the birth of the euro, the common coinage of the gradually consolidating European Union. Great expectations are reflected in this coin, associated with the establishment of a prosperous federal organization, which aspires to a better, common future for the inhabitants of the Old Continent. Faithful to her rich tradition, Europe moves 'Back to the Future'.[1]

---

1 Select Bibliography: M. Crawford, *La moneta in Grecia e a Roma* (Bari, 1986). C. Kraay, *Archaic and Classical Greek Coins* (London, 1976); G. Le Rider, *La naissance de la monnaie. Pratiques monétaires de l'Orient ancien* (Paris, 2001); O. Morkholm, *Early Hellenistic Coinage. From the Accession of Alexander to the Peace of Apamea, 336–188BC* (Cambridge, 1991); D. Nash, 'The Celts', in M. Price (ed.), *Coins. An Illustrated Survey, 650BC to the Present Day* (London, 1980); J. Williams, J. Cribb and E. Errington (eds), *Money. A History* (London, 1997).

**Figure 1.1a–b. Silver stater of Corinth (ca. 520–510 BC). Obv.: Pegasus l. Rev.: Incuse.
Numismatic Museum, Athens.**

**Figure 1.2a–b. Silver stater of Aegina (ca. 500 BC). Obv.: Turtle. Rev.: Incuse.
Numismatic Museum, Athens**

**Figure 1.3a–b. Silver tetradrachm of Athens (ca. 479–450 BC). Obv.: Head of Athena r. Rev.: Owl r.
Numismatic Museum, Athens**

CHAPTER 2

Monetary Integration in the Roman Empire

Juan Carlos Martinez Oliva[1]

He is said to have shown Alexander an instructive emblem of government, which was this. He threw a dry shrivelled hide upon the ground, and trod upon the edges of it. The skin when it was pressed in one place still rose up in another, wheresoever he trod round about it, till he set his foot in the middle, which made all the parts lie even and quiet. The meaning of this similitude being that he ought to reside most in the middle of his empire, and not spend too much time on the borders of it.

Plutarch, *The Lives of the Noble Grecians and Romans. Alexander*
(translated by John Dryden).

Introduction

During its first two centuries, commencing with Augustus, the Roman Empire reached its apex in terms of extension and power. Its territory stretched from the Iberian peninsula to the Red Sea, from Scotland to northern Africa. Its population amounted to 50 or 60 million, an enormous number by all previous standards, closely unified by a common legal framework, a network of 40,000 miles of paved roads,[2] and a common currency. The common currency played a crucial role, providing a broadly accepted medium across the Empire and beyond for payments, as with payrolls, tax collection, trade and daily transactions.

The process of monetary integration within the Empire began at the end of the second Punic War and took about a further 200 years to be accomplished. Two centuries of stability followed. The Empire's decline, beginning in the third century AD, was characterized by debasement and inflation that called for two rounds of monetary reform, under Aurelian and Diocletian. These efforts failed to restore the stability and confidence of the early Empire. This chapter analyses the process that,

---

1 I am indebted to Emilia Bonaccorsi di Patti, Vítor Gaspar, Yadira González de Lara, Cécile Morrisson and Peter Temin for useful comments on an earlier draft. I also thank the participants at the conference 'From the Athenian Tetradrachm to the Euro' for a stimulating discussion. Irene Paris deserves a special mention for her skillful assistance. The views expressed are those of the author and not necessarily those of the Banca d'Italia.

2 A. Maddison, *The World Economy: A Millennial Perspective* (Paris, 2001), p. 50; K. Hopkins, 'Centro e periferia. L'economia politica dell'impero romano', in V. Castronovo, *Storia dell'economia mondiale, vol. 1: Permanenze e mutamenti dall'antichità al medioevo* (Bari, 1996), p. 213.

first, brought about the monetary unification of the Mediterranean basin under the Roman standard and, eventually, led to the system's disintegration.

Extending modern international monetary analysis to the ancient Roman world is tempting, but in this particular field caution is essential. In the contemporary world international monetary arrangements are the result of cooperation among nations, when each spontaneously gives up portions of its monetary independence in exchange for expected increases in economic efficiency.[3] In the ancient world, by contrast, monetary integration was the consequence of Roman imperial expansion at the expense of other countries. It was imposed unilaterally by conquerors as a part of a wider process of economic exploitation. The evolution of the Roman monetary system can accordingly be regarded as an essential ingredient of an imperial strategy of military conquest, economic exploitation and accumulation of wealth.

This pattern would appear to support the core/periphery view of ancient civilizations, whose advocates have sought to counter the long-dominant visions of the Karl Polanyi school in anthropology and of M.I. Finley and others in ancient history.[4] The core/periphery approach sees past civilizations as parts of a hierarchy of centres of accumulation, dominated by one or more hegemons. The maintenance of the centre's position within an empire, it is argued, depends upon what determines net economic flows within the overall system. It is dynamically unstable, mainly because of emerging failures of the mechanism of exploitation. This occurs primarily 'where the revenue absorbed from the existing accumulation cycles increases more slowly than the accumulation itself'.[5] In such a case, economic decentralization sets in, leading to a weakening of the centre relative to other areas. With regard to the Roman Empire, decentralization resulted in a virtual bankruptcy of the centre, where the costs of imperial maintenance far exceeded the intake of tributes.

Set within a core/periphery mould, this chapter describes how, following its initial expansion, Rome tended to increase its economic potential through plunder, taxes and trade. These allowed for an ever greater accumulation of wealth, the creation of a new monetary system and the distribution of land and economic privileges to a growing mass of beneficiaries. Roman elites stabilized and reinforced the political relationship with the provinces by exacting tribute and creating cities and

---

3 Such gains arise from the elimination of transaction costs associated with currency exchange, and the elimination of exchange-rate risk. P.C. De Grauwe, *The Economics of Monetary Integration* (3. revised ed., Oxford, 1997), p. 53.

4 K. Ekholm and J. Friedman, '"Capital" Imperialism and Exploitation in Ancient World Systems', in A.G. Frank and B.K. Gills (eds), *The World System: Five Hundred Years or Five Thousand?* (London, 1993). The article was first published in 1979. A thorough survey of the main aspects of the core/periphery approach is found in C. Chase-Dunn and D. Hall, 'Conceptualizing Core/Periphery Hierarchies for Comparative Study', in C. Chase-Dunn and D. Hall (eds), *Core/Periphery Relations in Precapitalist Worlds* (Oxford, 1991).

The debate still rages and is lively; see, for example, K. Greene, 'Technological Innovation and Economic Progress in the Ancient World: M.I. Finley Re-Considered', in *Economic History Review*, 53, 1, 2000, pp. 29–59; and P. Temin, 'A Market Economy in the Early Roman Empire', *Discussion Papers in Economic and Social History*, n. 39 (University of Oxford, March 2001).

5 Ekholm et al., '"Capital" Imperialism', p. 70.

infrastructure. The denarius, the cornerstone of the Roman monetary system, visibly marked the Empire's territory. Yet Roman coins also circulated outside its borders, reaching the farthest parts of the known world. From the very inception of the Roman monetary system, rulers paid careful attention to the production, accumulation and supply of coins. This meant guaranteeing their weight, metallic content and availability; in short, the practice, if not the theory, of money management was part of the Roman government's cultural baggage.

When the relationship between the Empire's centre and its periphery weakened, the inevitable consequence was the system's ultimate collapse. The economy's progressive decentralization created the conditions for an irreversible deterioration of the central government's power. Booty, tribute and export proceeds no longer exceeded growing military expenses and the cost of imports.[6] Currency debasement, the traditional means of covering larger expenditure, culminated in the almost complete erosion of the denarius and its total degeneration. Towards the end of third century AD, Diocletian attempted to create a fiduciary currency but it failed to gain the necessary confidence of the public, leading to the most virulent inflation in the Empire's history.[7]

It should be noted that the very concept itself of money and monetary relations has been subject to radical criticism, largely related to the so-called Finley debate. Originated by Finley's famous Sather Classical Lectures at Berkeley in 1972, the debate fed into the long-running dispute over whether ancient economies were primitive or modern; market or non-market; capitalist or pre-capitalist.[8] Finley attached very little importance to the role of money in the Roman economy, on a number of grounds. He considered that the coins in circulation were limited in number and, thus, scarcely relevant as a means of exchange.[9] Furthermore, he maintained that the Roman economy was tied to the soil rather than to manufacturing.[10] Lastly, he put forward that coins were invented primarily for collecting taxes, while their commercial use was rare and archaic.[11] In a similar vein, Michael Crawford claimed that 'the Roman government had no policy concerning supply of coinage and

---

6 This approach is consistent with the analytical views found in Hopkins, 1978, and in Anderson, 1974, quoted in Chase-Dunn et al., 'Conceptualizing', p. 29.

7 This view contrasts with the hypothesis advanced by Duncan-Jones that it was the rising inflation in the course of the third century that subverted the monetary system and the money economy. R. Duncan-Jones, *The Economy of the Roman Empire* (Cambridge, 1974), pp. 12–3.

8 The lectures were the origin of M.I. Finley, *The Ancient Economy* (London, 1973).

9 'Money was coin and nothing else, and shortage of coins was chronic, both in total numbers and in the availability of preferred types or denominations', ibid., p. 166. Harl observes that the references cited in support of Finley's claim date from 66 BC–33 AD, when Roman aristocrats ran short of hard cash in their eagerness to acquire the vast amounts of Italian land available in the wake of civil war. K.W. Harl, *Coinage in the Roman Economy, 300 BC to AD 700* (Baltimore, 1996), p. 3.

10 Finley's claim is that even investment in land was never 'a matter of systematic, calculated policy, of what Weber called economic rationality', Finley, *Economy*, p. 117.

11 Ibid., p. 141. Among other critical remarks, Finley stresses the absence of paper money, bank money and bearer securities.

no monetary policy except in matters which directly affected its own interest'.[12] However, these criticisms have been very largely dispelled by recent research based upon archaeological and numismatic analysis.[13] This has added fresh support to the idea that coined money's role in the ancient economy was far from negligible and so encouraged further efforts to analyse the Roman monetary system.

The article is structured as follows. The first section discusses, in the context of the world-system literature, hegemony and core/periphery relations, which provide the theoretical framework for the subsequent analysis. The second section describes how the rise of Roman monetization between 200 and 30 BC was boosted by conflict with neighbouring societies, most notably Carthage. In this phase a learning-by-doing process helped to advance monetary integration within the Empire, and paved the way for the Augustan monetary reform. This is followed by an analysis of the system's functioning under the Principate, 30 BC–200 AD, and the gradual shift of power from the core to the periphery that occurred with the progressive deterioration of the Empire's balance. The final section illustrates the emerging crisis of the Roman currency over the course of the third century.

Hegemony, core/periphery relations, and Roman monetary dominance

Analysis of past civilizations within a hierarchy of centres of accumulation has recently received special attention.[14] In this framework, countries are viewed as part of a 'world system' characterized by the existence of a communication network. The 'rise' and 'fall' of successive hegemonic powers became popular among historians following the seminal contributions of Toynbee, Eisenstadt and others.[15] A more recent generation of scholars has suggested that the definition of hegemony should focus on economic processes 'while not separating these completely from the

12 M. Crawford, 'Money and Exchange in the Roman World', in *The Journal of Roman Studies*, 60, 1970, pp. 40–8, here p. 48. In a similar vein, see also A.H.M. Jones, *L'economia romana* (Turin, 1984), and M. Crawford, *La moneta in Grecia e a Roma* (Bari, 1986). A thorough critique of the 'primitivist' view, including Crawford's arguments, is found in M. De Cecco, 'Monetary Theory and Roman History', in *Journal of Economic History*, 45, 4, 1985, pp. 809–22.

13 C. Howgego, 'The Supply and Use of Money in the Roman World 200 BC to AD 300', in *The Journal of Roman Studies*, 82, 1992, pp. 1–31; Harl, *Coinage*. It should be noted that, on the contrary, Duncan-Jones has recently tried to demonstrate that the diffusion of coins from the mint was slow, and that their circulation velocity (as measured by loss of coin-weight, or wear) was much less than in comparable modern currencies, implying that there were fewer transactions per coin R. Duncan-Jones, *Money and Government in the Roman Empire* (Cambridge, 1994), p. 106.

14 See for example the contributions included in Chase-Dunn and Hall, 'Conceptualizing', and in A.G. Frank and B.K. Gills (eds), *The World System: Five Hundred Years or Five Thousand?* (London, 1993).

15 A.G. Frank and B.K. Gills (eds), *The World System: Five Hundred Years or Five Thousand?* (London, 1993); A.G. Frank and B.K. Gills (eds), *The World System: Five Hundred Years or Five Thousand?* (London, 1993).

realm of politics and military power'.[16] Other studies have defined hegemony as the achievement of supremacy sequentially in production, trade and finance.[17] Keohane redefined the hegemony using both economic and political criteria. He explains the existence of an international economic regime (such as a monetary arrangement or a trade regime) in terms of a single wealthy, powerful and technologically advanced state that creates and maintains the conditions for the smooth operation of the regime itself.[18] This approach suggests possible explanations for the leading power's eventual demise. The system is supposed to be dynamically unstable because either its intrinsic features lead to a weakening of the hegemon's power, or external forces emerge, directly or indirectly influenced by the hegemon.[19]

A major examination of the economic implications of hegemonic shifts has been made by Gilpin, who takes the rise and decline of empires to be a function of the generation and dissipation of economic surplus.[20] As Gills suggested,[21] Gilpin's analysis also implies that both the domestic character of surplus extraction and the dynamics of international trade are relevant for the pattern of hegemonic transition.

The simultaneous recognition of the importance of the 'balance of empire' and the role of communication networks characterizes the core/periphery approach to ancient civilizations.[22] This school holds that the emergence of a centre of 'high culture' depends upon the accumulation of resources from a wide area. In other words, the economic base of the locally developed society is the result of its central position within a larger system.[23] The existence of core/periphery systems, and the possibility that different hegemonies may be consolidating simultaneously within the same world system, highlights the role of the communication network in the progressive integration of ancient cultures and societies.[24]

---

16 Gills, 'Transitions', p. 116.

17 This definition, due to Wallerstein, first appeared in 1974. Gills, 'Transitions', p. 117.

18 R.O. Keohane, 'The Theory of Hegemonic Stability and Changes in International Economic Regimes', in C. Roe Goddard, J.T. Passe-Smith and J.G. Conklin (eds), *International Political Economy: State-Market Relations in the Changing Global Order* ([1980] London, 1996).

19 This approach has been tested by Barry Eichengreen for the classical gold standard, the interwar gold-exchange standard and the Bretton-Woods system. While noting that hegemonic stability theories are 'helpful' for understanding some features of the regimes considered, Eichengreen observes that much of the evidence 'is difficult to reconcile with the hegemonic stability view'. B.J. Eichengreen, 'Hegemonic Stability Theories of the International Monetary System', in *Can Nations Agree?: Issues in International Economic Cooperation* (Washington, 1989), p. 287.

20 R. Gilpin, *War and Change in World Politics* (Cambridge,1981).

21 Gills, 'Transitions', p. 126.

22 See fn. 4.

23 Ekholm et al., '"Capital"', p. 61.

24 W.H. McNeill, 'Foreword', in A.G. Frank and B.K. Gills (eds), *The World System: Five Hundred Years or Five Thousand?* (London, 1993), p. xi. In this respect various authors have observed that, by the first century AD, the entire world system was organized into an unbroken belt of interlinking hegemonies, stretching from Rome to Parthia in Mesopotamia and Persia, the Kushan in central Asia and the Han in China. For a survey, see B.K. Gills and

Core/periphery relations are, by definition, imperialistic since they involve the core's accumulation of wealth and resources produced in the periphery. The model is said to represent a core/periphery hierarchy in the presence of the political, economic or ideological domination of one society over another and the extraction of resources through raiding, taxation, tribute and unequal economic exchange.[25]

A very interesting feature of this approach is the prediction that core/periphery relations are dynamically unstable because of the vulnerability of centres to outside developments, which are difficult to control. The system breaks down when the balance of the empire – broadly, the difference between revenues from booty, taxes and exports, and expenditures on the overall cost of empire plus imports – turns negative. This leads to what has been termed 'hegemonic shifts' – changes in the hierarchical structures of centres of surplus accumulation according to a continuous 'rise and fall' pattern.[26]

The rise of Roman monetization

The key, seminal event at the origins of the Roman monetary system was protracted conflict between Rome and Carthage. Initially, the Roman Republic had a primitive currency, archaic fiscal institutions and an almost negligible store of precious metals. In contrast, Carthage had attained the status of a monetary economy in the fourth century BC, following contacts with the Greek poleis.[27] War put an enormous strain upon the Republic's finances. Rome's minting effort yielded 6.5 million denarii, while Carthage was able to strike an amount equivalent to about 245 million denarii, which went to pay mercenary troops in Sicily.[28] In spite of this initial disparity, the Roman response was bold and effective. While the citizens fought on the battlefields and offered their personal resources for the war, a radical reorganization of the war economy was undertaken. Given the scarcity of gold and silver, the production of bronze currency reached exceptional levels.

Following the example of the more highly developed Greek monetary system,[29] Rome learnt how to avoid massive defaults in a crisis by devaluing the existing silver coinage and minting emergency gold aurei[30] and quinarii[31] from various sources,

---

A.G. Frank, 'World System Cycles, Crises, and Hegemonic Shifts, 1700 BC to 1700 A.D', in A.G. Frank and B.K. Gills (eds), *The World System: Five Hundred Years or Five Thousand?* (London, 1993).

25 Chase-Dunn et al., 'Conceptualizing', p. 19.

26 Gills et al., *World System*, pp. 143–99.

27 E. Ercolani Cocchi, 'Un'economia monetaria', in V. Castronovo, *Storia dell'economia mondiale, vol. 1: Permanenze e mutamenti dall'antichità' al medioevo* (Bari, 1996), p. 184.

28 Harl, *Coinage*, p. 27.

29 For example, during the Peloponnesian war Athens issued copper tetradrachms when the city was under attack by Sparthan troops, the Laurion mines being unreachable. Ercolani Cocchi, 'economia', p. 183.

30 The aureus was struck at the standard weight of 1/48 pound of gold and used for bulk payments.

31 The quinarius was half a denarius.

including foreign short-term loans, such as the Syracusan staters obtained by Hiero II.[32] During the Second Punic War (218–201 BC), the Republic introduced a new system of silver and bronze coins that, with the help of decentralized minting, soon replaced all earlier coins in the Italian peninsula. The key currency of the system was the new silver denarius, divided into 16 bronze asses.

The crushing victories of Scipio Africanus brought the long war to an end. Scipio negotiated the peace, imposing harsh terms although allowing Carthage some independence.[33] From the defeated enemy, Rome took the vital sources of precious metal – silver and gold – in southern Spain. The exploitation of the silver mines began quickly in south-eastern Spain, to be followed much later by working the silver mines of Sierra Morena.[34] The silver bullion and coin available to the Roman mint between 201 and 151 BC has been estimated at over 600 million denarii (at 84 to the Roman pound).[35] Jones reports that Carthage alone paid 4,400 Attic talents (equivalent to 28.5 million denarii) in reparations after the First Punic War, and 10,000 talents during 50 years after the Second.[36] The booty from the conquest of Spain (206–196 BC), before the introduction of a regular tax system, yielded more than 20 million denarii.

The idea that the acquisition of strategic sources of specie and revenues could pay for war and yield a profit soon became the imperial axiom underlying overseas expansion. A self-feeding process was triggered. The conquest of new populations resulted in the exploitation of local precious metals and slaves that, in turn, enabled Rome to cover the rising military costs of the conquests.

Beginning in 88 BC, Sulla seized the treasures of Delphi, Olympia and Epidaurus, and exacted from the cities of Greece and Asia Minor more than 120 million denarii. As most of the cities that had borrowed money from Roman financiers defaulted, within a few years their debt exploded to over 700 million denarii. Lucullus and Pompey sacked royal treasuries in Anatolia, Armenia and Syria, netting about 350 million denarii in 71–63 BC. Similarly, Pompey, Julius Caesar and Mark Antony each collected amounts of metal estimated at several hundred million denarii, which was promptly turned into Roman coins. Furthermore, in 43–42 BC Cassius and Brutus put together an amount of gold sufficient to strike over 7 million aurei.[37]

While this process unfolded, bringing a flood of resources to the conquerors, a throng of traders and contractors followed the military penetration, helping to replacing local currencies and habits with Roman. The construction of military

32 Harl, *Coinage*, p. 33. Among other measures, in 213 or 212 BC the Roman state devalued the denarius by 50 per cent. During the period following the defeat at Cannae, in 216 BC, the Republic adopted a number of other measures, including foreign borrowing, both in money and in kind, and fiscal measures. Ibid., p. 31.

33 G. Clemente, 'La guerra annibalica', in *Storia di Roma, vol. 2: l'Impero mediterraneo, I: La repubblica imperiale* (Turin, 1990), pp. 85–6.

34 Howgego, *Supply*, p. 7.

35 Figures from Frank, ESAR I, reported in Harl, *Coinage*, p. 42.

36 Jones, *L'economia*, p. 149.

37 Harl, *Coinage*, p. 71.

highways in northern Italy in 150–100 BC and their extension into Narbonese Gaul and Spain helped spread Roman coins to provincial markets in the West.[38]

The transformation of the Mediterranean basin into a Roman monetary area went hand-in-hand with military conquest. From the Roman military camps denarii and asses started to circulate on native markets. The process initially affected the Italian peninsula, then Sicily, Sardinia, Corsica, and Cisalpine Gaul. Only bronze local currencies survived, as in several areas, particularly southern Italy, they were pegged to the denarius as token fractional coins.

The costs of overseas administration made it more urgent to have a currency accepted for transactions on local markets in the Provinces, and this problem was addressed in various ways. In most cases, as in the Celtic world, the denarius simply replaced local coins that were melted down and their metal re-minted. Otherwise, the cities were allowed to mint lesser silver coinage or to use bronze coins for small transactions. In a few instances, as in Asia Minor and Syria, former royal silver money became provincial currencies. Many Greek cities were allowed to mint their own fractional coins, pegged to the cistophorus, the provincial silver coin created by Rome in Asia.[39] The success of the Asian cistophorus initially encouraged Rome to use tetradrachms in other provinces. During the first century BC, most of the oriental silver currencies were subsequently replaced by the denarius. In particular, the Sullan exactions, Pompey's administrative reorganization after the Mithridatic Wars, and the Roman civil wars involved the re-minting of great amounts of cistophorii and tetradrachms into aurei and denarii. This intense minting activity brought about a proliferation of control marks of the issuing moneyers, and also of types of denarii. In the process, the roles of money changers, money assayers and moneylenders became very important.

By about 30 BC the Romanization of the western Mediterranean and north-western Europe was complete, with the denarii and asses used for trade and military expenses having come into general use. Increasingly, Roman coins penetrated the most remote markets of Europe and Asia, marking the new status of Rome as the centre of the network of trade relations in the Mediterranean.

The Augustan monetary system in the early Empire

The enormous scale of minting during the civil wars created a large variety of differently struck denarii and brought about the widespread use of aurei, minted from bullion and local coins exacted from the Eastern provinces. The coins' metallic content varied enormously due to the extensive minting of debased or alloyed denarii by different contenders. Augustus restored confidence in the aurei and denarii by reinstating the standard created by Julius Caesar in 47–46 BC when, using the proceeds from his conquest of Gaul, he had first begun to mint gold coins on a large scale.

38 Ibid., p. 45.
39 Ibid., p. 69.

The new Augustan issues of aurei and denarii were practically pure, struck at a standard of 40 and 84 to the Roman pound (322.5 grams) respectively.[40] They were minted with the same design and inscriptions and, occasionally, from the same dies. Each coin was accompanied by one of half its value, the gold or silver quinarius. Fractional token coins were also provided.[41] Mints were initially located close to the sources of precious metal. During the reign of Augustus minting was concentrated at Lugdunum (Lyons) and Augusta Emerita (Merida), and in Rome.

The success of the Augustan reform was assured by the economic growth stimulated by the Pax Romana. And the new system itself, by facilitating trade and payments, helped stimulate economic activity. New trade relations were opened up with Scandinavia, the southern shores of the Baltic and the area between the Rhine and the Vistula, occupied by free German tribes. Trade apparently peaked in intensity towards the end of the second century, as indicated by the number of shipwrecks found by marine archaeologists.[42]

The discovery of the monsoons by Hipparchus of Alexandria in the late Ptolemaic, or early Roman, period led to the establishment of a direct route by sea between Egypt and India.[43] Trade between Rome and China was a further important source of revenue for Arabian merchants, who acted as the middlemen.[44] Trade does not seem to have represented a major drain of specie for the Empire as a whole, except with regard to some luxury goods drawn mainly from northern Europe, China and India.[45] The regulation of Tiberius, which prohibited the wearing of (imported) silk

40 Ibid., p. 74.

41 These were the sestertius and the dupondius, respectively worth 1/4 and 1/8 of a denarius, and the aes (1/16 of the denarius) and its quarter, the quadrans. Harl reports that Augustus resisted the temptation to overproducing lucrative sestertii and dupondii, and thus won public approval of the new coins, Harls, *Coinage*, p. 77. The issue of how monetary authorities supplied small change in the historical experience is analyzed in T.J. Sargent and F.R. Velde, 'The Big Problem of Small Change', paper prepared for the 4th EHES Conference, Oxford, September 2001. The two authors conclude that the problem led monetary theorizing and experimenting to uncover the two centerpieces of the twentieth century concept of a 'well managed fiat' system: the quantity theory of money and the need to restrain the suppliers of token money from creating inflation.

42 K. Hopkins, 'Taxes and Trade in the Roman Empire', in *The Journal of Roman Studies*, 70, 1980, pp. 101–25, here p. 105; T.M. Lucchelli, *La moneta nei rapporti tra Roma e l'Europa barbarica: aspetti e problemi*, La Nuova Italia (Florence, 1998), p. 205.

43 M.I. Rostovtzeff, *The Social and Economic History of the Roman Empire* (Oxford, 1926), p. 93.

44 Reflecting the fact that the control of the Mesopotamia passage was under the control of Parthians first and of Sassanian Persians later. Gills et al., 'World System', p. 89.

45 Rostovtzeff, *Social and Economic History*, pp. 65–6.

in Rome,[46] in force from 14 until 37, might nonetheless be interpreted as a sign of concern over a potential gold drain.[47]

In the classical analysis of Hopkins, the Empire was broadly divided into three concentric spheres. The centre, comprising Italy and Rome, consumed a large volume of resources. The inner ring of wealthy territories (Spain, southern Gaul, northern Africa, Asia Minor, Syria and Egypt) provided a surplus in taxes and commodities. The presence of defensive armies in the outer ring of frontier provinces, located close to the limes – the border dividing the Empire from the barbaricum – absorbed resources.[48]

Coins constantly circulated between Rome and the provinces through state expenditure, taxes, and trade. Persuasive evidence in this respect is provided by Hopkins's analysis of silver coin hoards from different periods, discovered in many sites across the Empire.[49] A strict correlation holds between finds in many different parts of Europe for the period ranging from 50 to 180. This evidence suggests that, during the first two centuries AD, a flow of taxes and trade redistributed state-issued silver coins throughout the Empire, which 'was integrated into a single monetary economy'.[50]

The production of bullion for minting was crucial for the mechanism's correct functioning. Under Augustus, the exploitation of Spanish silver and gold mines accelerated with the help of new technologies and more efficient use of existing ones. Concurrently, the spectacular inflow of treasure from Egypt contributed mightily to the increase in coinage. Following Augustus's long reign, there were no new sources or discoveries, save perhaps the gold mines of Dacia, following its annexation by Trajan.[51] Most of the main mining areas ceased activity or went into decline during the first two centuries AD.

The symptoms of the centre's decay became evident at the end of the first century, indicated by the incipient depopulation of the Italian peninsula and the concurrent decline of agriculture. Initially, Italy held leadership in trade and industry but the provinces soon began to develop their own agriculture, and productive

---

46 Following Needham, Schneider suggests a link between the regulation and a series of Chinese reforms aimed at calling in gold coins, which, according to Needham, caused a supposed 'drain on world gold circulation'. J. Schneider, 'Was There a Precapitalist World-System?', in C. Chase-Dunn and D. Hall (eds), *Core/Periphery Relations in Precapitalist Worlds* (Oxford, 1991), p. 57.

47 The decline in internal and external trade, followed by the demonetization and final disintegration of the Han empire, eventually interrupted the great 'silk route'. Gills et al., 'World System', p. 168.

48 See M. Corbier, 'Svalutazioni, inflazione e circolazione monetaria nel III secolo', in A. Giardina (ed.), *Società romana e impero tardoantico: istituzioni, ceti, economie* (Rome Bari, 1986), for an interesting discussion of Hopkins's analysis.

49 Hopkins, 'Taxes', p. 113. An exhaustive survey of the literature on the diffusion of Roman coins in the barbaricum is found in Lucchelli, *moneta*, pp. 130–63.

50 Hopkins, 'Taxes', p. 112.

51 Howgego, 'Supply', p. 7.

and commercial activities.[52] Efforts were made to reverse or halt these tendencies. Domitian prohibited the planting of vines in the provinces. Nerva tried to repopulate Italy by redistributing land to poorer citizens and instituting alimenta, a form of public child-support payments.[53] Trajan forbade emigration from Italy and settled Roman veterans in the vicinity of Rome. Furthermore, a policy of cheap credit favouring Italian landowners was instituted; but its benefits were only transitory.[54]

Under the Flavians and the Antonines thousands of Italians, alongside veterans, settled in the ancient cities of Baetica and in parts of Tarraconensis and Lusitania. These areas' huge variety of natural resources led to the growth of prosperous local economies. Many Romans of both the senatorial and equestrian classes invested in Spanish land.[55] Even more than in Baetica, landed property in Gaul was concentrated in the hands of a few Roman private owners. Similar situations were recorded in many other parts of the Empire. This expansion reached its apogee under Hadrian.

Rostovtzeff has reported that, since Roman citizens were offered much better living opportunities in the provinces, Italy was steadily drained of her best men with the gaps filled by slaves. When the supply of slaves became less abundant, Italy began to decay because emigration continued. Meanwhile, the provinces experienced growth and prosperity.[56]

The mismanagement of tax policy interacted with the centre's depopulation, contributing to the core/periphery shift. During the stage of imperialistic expansion, tax collection had been devolved to intermediaries. This had the obvious consequence of reducing state revenue while allowing provincial governors and their delegates to enrich themselves.[57] It weakened the relationship between the centre, i.e. the central government, and the periphery – affluent landowners, who were often former tax-collectors from the Roman élite and had invested their profits in land, together with local town-councillors. Hopkins argues convincingly that the reform of the tax system during the early Principate (which ended the predominant reliance on tax farming) was a negative rather than a positive development for the stability of the imperial finances.[58] This was because it eliminated the only corporations that could offer private wealth to support state finances in an emergency. As a consequence, when the regular income of the state was inadequate for emergency needs, instead of prudently increasing the taxes which they disliked, emperors resorted to compulsory labour, requisitions and supplementary levies – methods that preserved revenue but attacked private capital.[59]

52 M.I. Rostovtzeff, 'Les classes rurales et les classes citadines dans le Haut Empire romain', J. Andreau, 'Mercati e mercato', in *Storia di Roma, vol. 2: l'Impero mediterraneo, II: I principi e il mondo* (Turin, [1926]1991), pp. 369–70.

53 Duncan-Jones, *Economy*, pp. 291ff.

54 Rostovtzeff, *Social and Economic History*, p. 313.

55 Ibid., pp. 198–9.

56 Ibid., p. 328.

57 On the increase of corruption following the growth of Roman imperial power, see E. Gabba, 'L'imperialismo romano', in *Storia di Roma, vol. 2: l'Impero mediterraneo, I: La repubblica imperiale* (Turin, 1990), pp. 189–233.

58 Hopkins, 'Taxes', p. 116.

59 Rostovtzeff, *Social and Economic History*, p. 343.

With this situation in the mid-second century, debasement understandably became an expedient of growing importance. Many years earlier in 64, Nero had undertaken a number of substantial monetary innovations. He had had gold, silver and orichalcum coins reduced in either their prime metallic content or their weight, resulting in the gradual disappearance of all previously struck coins. Silver fineness, which had declined slightly under Vespasian, recovered again under Titus. Domitian, who had attempted to restore the pre-Neronian standard, after three years had to resume Nero's silver fineness while retaining a higher denarius weight. Precious metal content remained high during his reign for both gold and silver coins. But his forced actions again resulted in the almost total disappearance of Domitian's coins. After Nerva's brief reign, Trajan resumed the Neronian weight standard for the aureus and, in 107, further reduced the silver content of the denarius.

The silver fineness of the denarius fell considerably during the reign of Antoninus Pius. The debasement of 148, which lowered the purity of the denarius by five percentage points to 83–4 per cent, probably helped to defray the costs of the emperor's millennial celebrations (see Figure 2.1).

Within months of their accession, Marcus Aurelius and Lucius Verus exhausted reserves and tax revenues on accessional gifts in a costly Parthian war. The only remaining resource was the 4 per cent debasement of 161, which dropped the fineness of the denarius to under 80 per cent, its lowest level ever. The subsequent series of debasements and restorations of the denarius's silver content under Marcus Aurelius were closely correlated with the costs of frontier wars against the Parthians and Germans.[60]

The dynamics of the collapse in the third century

The Parthian and German wars brought the Empire's finances near to collapse, forcing Marcus Aurelius to reduce the silver fineness of the denarius to historic lows.[61] This policy, intended to protect the Empire's integrity, was continued by Commodus in order to finance his extravagant expenditures. Both the weight (down to 1/104 of a Roman pound) and fineness (down to 74.25 per cent) of the denarius were reduced. By the end of his reign, the silver content of the coin had been cut by 20 per cent, the then biggest single change in coinage standards. It has been

60 Harl, *Coinage*, p. 235. Lo Cascio has tried to challenge this view by suggesting that, rather than a revenue-raising measure, debasement was meant to maintain constant the ratio between silver and gold. However, the only episode that seems to support his claim is that of the debasement in 107, which might be interpreted as an attempt to keep the relative price of silver and gold unchanged after the huge amounts of gold from Dacia had lowered the price of the latter. E. Lo Cascio, 'State and Coinage in the Late Republic and Early Empire', in *The Journal of Roman Studies*, 71, 1981, pp. 76–86, here p. 79.

61 In those critical circumstances, the Emperor even disposed of his own valuables by a public sale, which covered the costs of the war for two months Rostovtzeff, *Social and Economic History*, p. 326.

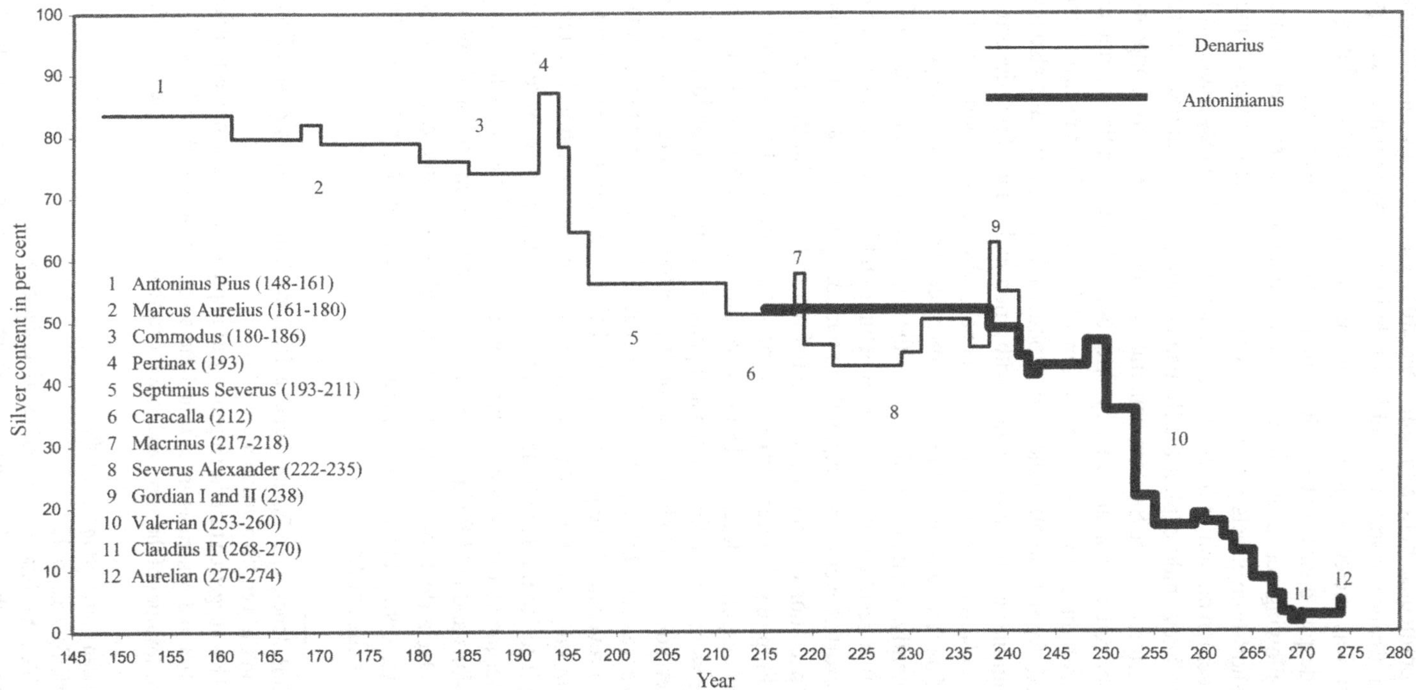

Figure 2.1 Pattern of money debasement under the Roman Principate

suggested that the devaluation may have been partly due to the closing of the Rio Tinto mines, following raids by the Moors.[62]

After Commodus, both Septimius Severus and Caracalla further alloyed the denarius to finance wars and ambitious building programmes. The policy of debasement was meant to provide salary incentives to soldiers during military campaigns despite their negative effects on prices. These were only perceived with a lag, thus allowing net surplus revenues to the imperial government that exceeded inflation's short-term effects.[63] The policy of the Antonine and Severan emperors was far from a demonstration of ineffective, or short sighted, management, as has been suggested.[64] They could exploit the Roman currency's two-centuries old reputation of stability. Moreover, the Severan denarius maintained the external appearance that had characterized the Roman currency since 64.[65] With Caracalla, the fineness of the denarius was reduced to a new historic low of 50, while the standard of the aureus was lowered (from 45 to 50 to the Roman pound). In 215, Caracalla also introduced a new denomination, the antoninianus, with a nominal value of two denarii, but only 80 per cent of the silver content of two denarii. As a result, there was widespread hoarding of denarii, with tangible effects on prices and exchange rates.

Subsequently, particularly following the unsuccessful campaigns of Severus Alexander that resulted in his troops rebelling and his own assassination in 235, emperors resorted ever more frequently to temporary tax increases and debasement, with the expectation of windfalls of specie from victories. But the growing pressure on all the Empire's frontiers turned the previous pattern of victory and conquest into a mere desperate defence. The eastern provinces of Mesopotamia, Syria and Asia Minor were repeatedly invaded and plundered by the Sassanids, while Saxons, Franks, Alemanni and Goths pressed on the northern frontiers. Political instability at the centre was such that during a single year, 238, six different emperors reigned. There was a reversal of the process that had characterized the last two centuries, as the Axumite kings used east African gold for their own fractional staters, instead of sending it to Rome. Hundreds of thousands of antoniniani were re-minted into dirhems after the victory of Shah Shapur over Emperor Valerian, who was captured by the Persians and held for six years until his death. From 250 until 260 the Goths devastated Dacia (lost for ever in 257–8) and also Dalmatia, and the Moors again raided Spain, disrupting mining operations.[66] Furthermore, North African mines began to be exhausted.[67]

62 G.D.B. Jones, 'The Roman Mines at Rio Tinto', in *Journal of Roman Studies*, 1980, pp. 146–65; in Corbier, 'Svalutazioni'.

63 Harl has suggested that the emperors who improved the purity of the denarius, notably Pertinax in 193 and Macrinus in 217, and the senatorial teams of 238 found themselves outbid for the loyalties of the army, and so went down to ignomimous defeats. Harl, *Coinage*, p. 126.

64 Duncan-Jones, *Money*, p. 100.

65 Harl, *Coinage*, p. 127.

66 Corbier, 'Svalutazioni', p. 506; Harl, *Coinage*, p. 129.

67 Cyprian, bishop of Carthage, wrote about 250: 'The diminished quantities of gold and silver suggest the early exhaustion of the metals, and the impoverished veins are straitened and decreased day by day'. H. Michell, 'The Edict of Diocletian: A Study of Price Fixing in

Roman emperors began to purchase peace, paying humiliating tributes that further drained precious metal. The collapse of the monetary system was now so evident that populations quoted prices in a notional currency unit, called the denarius communis and convertible into antoniniani at the current market rate. The latter, which when struck by Caracalla had a silver content of 2.65 grams, fell to a content of only 0.08 grams under Aurelianus in 270, its fineness declining from 52 to 5 per cent. Only one minor improvement was recorded in 50 years, following the decisive victory over the Goths at Naissus, under Claudius II, which brought about the recovery of Spain.

In 64, Nero had moved the mint from Lugdunum to Rome, thus increasing the emperor's control over minting.[68] However, the unprecedented scale of re-coining following the recurrent debasements of the third century forced the re-decentralization of minting. Gordian III established the first imperial mint outside Rome, in Antioch in 240. By 274 there were eight, under Aurelian, totalling 40 officinae.[69] The reorganization of minting activity allowed for a monetary reform based on a new currency, the aurelianianus, a coin of improved manufacture, weight (3.88 grams) and silver content (4.5 to 5 per cent) that, together with its fractions, was minted on a large scale.[70] Nonetheless, the aurelianianus failed to provide adequate liquidity for all parts of the Empire. Particularly in Britain, Gaul and the East, imitations were struck unofficially to meet the local demand for money, unfulfilled by an adequate supply from imperial mints.

Diocletian made a far more ambitious effort at a full-fledged reform of the imperial currency. In 293 he re-established the standard of the aureus at 60 to the Roman pound, tariffed at 600 denarii communes. He also created a new silver coin, the argenteus nummus at 96 to the pound and tariffed at 25 denarii communes, presumably minted from bullion from newly conquered Armenia.[71] Furthermore, he replaced the aurelianiani still in circulation with a silver-wash piece called a nummus, tariffed at 5 denarii communes. Even if the argenteus nummus totally corresponded to the Neronian denarius, the system was mainly based on the aureus – named solidus – and the nummus, with small copper subdivisions for minor transactions.

In spite of the rapid conversion of older coins into nummi, and their appealing look,[72] the new coin was not accepted at its nominal value. Prices rose as confidence

---

the Roman Empire', in H. Rockoff (ed.), *Price Controls*, Elgar Reference Collection [1947], p. 11.

68 Duncan-Jones, *Money*, p. 100. On the relevance of mint centralization, fifteen centuries later, the jurist and philosopher Jean Bodin wrote: 'Et pour oster toute occasion de falsifier, altérer, ny changer la loy reçue des monnoyes d'or et d'argent il sera besoin de forger toutes les monnoyes en une seule ville, où résideront le juges des monnoyes et de supprimir les autres' – *Les sis livres de la République* (Paris, 1577), p. 957, quoted in T. Guggenheim, 'Some Early Views on Monetary Integration', in H.G. Johnson and A.K. Swoboda (eds), *The Economics of Common Currencies* (London, 1973).

69 Harl, *Coinage*, p. 144.

70 As reported by the historian Zosimus, quoted by Harl, *Coinage*, p.146.

71 Michell, 'Edict', pp. 4–5; Corbier, 'Svalutazioni', p. 506.

72 As compared with the aurelianianus, the nummus was better struck, three times heavier and with two and a half times its silver enrichment.

in the nummus eroded. The imperial government's response was to raise its quotation, as well as those of the other coinages, in order to keep them in line with inflation. But the mistrust of the new system was so deeply rooted that both government officials and the public continued to quote prices in ghost currencies, like the denarius communis or other units of account.[73]

As confidence in the Roman monetary system reached its nadir, payments in kind for taxes and troops' salaries became customary. In 301, to stop the inflationary process fed by the revaluation of the nummus, the Tetrarchs[74] promulgated a Price Edict, which established maxima for most prices across the Empire. The Edict is an early example of the ineffectiveness of price regulation as a substitute for a bad currency. It utterly failed in its purpose and induced the total disappearance of traded goods from markets, and had to be withdrawn. On 1 September, the Tetrarchs issued a second monetary Edict, which doubled the value of all denominations above one denarius communis. But the common practice of denominating prices in denarii communes deprived it of all practical relevance.

Diocletian's monetary reform was a bold and innovative attempt to introduce a fiduciary currency, which could have helped to resolve the Empire's monetary troubles. The nummus was nonetheless mistakenly allowed to circulate alongside silver and gold coins, whose nominal values were considerably closer to their intrinsic value.[75] Its unrealistic relationship with the other coins was soon perceived by the public. They preferred the aureliani ani (still circulating) and the silver nummi, determining the convergence of the market value of the nummus with its intrinsic metallic value, while at the same time driving other coins out of circulation. The violent depreciation of money forced the government to institute payments of taxes in kind, the so-called annona. A number of other payments also came to be made in kind, including some public salaries and benefits.[76] This certified the failure of the most ambitious monetary experiment since the birth of the Roman monetary system and contributed to the Empire's demonetization.

Conclusion

One consequence of the disruption of the Roman monetary system during the third century AD was the virtual disappearance of all the professions connected with

73 The relation between real and ghost currency in the historical experience is analysed by L. Einaudi, 'Teoria della moneta immaginaria nel tempo da Carlomagno alla Rivoluzione francese', in L. Giusso, *Teoria delle unioni monetarie e integrazione europea* (Naples, 1974). An English version of the article, which first appeared in 1936, is found in F.C. Lane and J.C. Riemersma (eds), *Enterprise and Secular Change* (London, 1953).

74 As a part of his reform of administration, Diocletian divided the task of ruling into four, by appointing three associate emperors.

75 According to Harl, the 24 argentei exchanged to the aureus contained 40 and 76% more silver than the equivalent of 120 nummi in 293 and 96 nummi in 301 respectively. Similar considerations hold for aureliani ani; see Harl, *Coinage*, p. 155.

76 Corbier, 'Svalutazioni', p. 528.

money and moneylending.[77] Depopulation, which in the early Empire had been confined to Rome and Italy and mainly caused by emigration to the provinces, became the outstanding feature of life in the Empire during the third century.[78] The general insecurity of business life led to a fluctuation in the rate of interest, which in the second century had been as stable as prices.[79] Following the depreciation of currency and overall economic stagnation, there was an almost complete cessation of commercial relations with the other areas. Trade was not resumed until the Byzantine period, when order and a sound gold currency were re-established.[80]

77 J. Andreau, 'Declino e morte dei mestieri bancari nel mediterraneo occidentale (II-IV DC)', in A. Giardina (ed.), *Società romana e impero tardoantico: istituzioni, ceti, economie* (Rome, 1986).

78 Rostovtzeff, *Social and Economic History*, p. 424.

79 Ibid., p. 421.

80 See the chapter by Cécile Morrisson in this volume.

CHAPTER 3

'One Money for an Empire': Achievements and Limitations of Byzantium's Currency from Constantine the Great to the Fall of Constantinople

Cécile Morrisson

Introduction

The Roman model has left such an imprint on European civilization and played such a part in our education (at least until the 1970s) that one tends to imagine empires as most likely having centralized administration and, necessarily, a unique currency. But this is not always the case, not even with regard to the Roman Empire and nor, as will be shown, its successor state, the Eastern (and Christian) Roman Empire, which we call Byzantium. During the centuries before Christ, the Achaemenid dynasty had never tried to impose a unique coinage upon its Persian Empire, nor did its conqueror, Alexander the Great. In both cases, however, successful dominant denominations such as the Achaemenids' gold darics and silver sigloi, or Alexander's renowned tetradrachms, flourished and enjoyed an international reputation and role (Touratsoglou, this volume).[1]

The process of creating a unified currency for the Roman Empire throughout its expanding territory proved to be long, taking several centuries.[2] Its unified monetary system was only systematized under Diocletian and finalized under Constantine during the late third and early fourth centuries. Constantine's reign marks the start of 'Byzantine' history – a modern concept derived from the ancient name (Byzantium) of the city on the Bosporus, which he chose to renovate and recreate as Constantinopolis in 324 and inaugurate in 330. This 'New Rome' evolved from being the capital city of the Eastern Roman Empire into the metropolis of the entire Roman Empire after 476, when the last Western emperor was deposed.[3]

1 See Touratsoglou's chapter in this volume.

2 See A. Burnett, Coinage in the Roman World (London, 1987); see Martinez Oliva's article in this volume.

3 Odoacer, the Barbarian commander ruling Italy, sent back the imperial insignia to the East and was content with the title of *rex*. Like Odoacer, Theodoric and his successors were still requesting from Constantinople imperial confirmation for promotions in the Roman Senate or appointments in the Italian administration. Most Barbarian kings (*reges*) recognised, in principle at least, the supreme authority of the Emperor.

The so-called Byzantines always considered themselves as successors to, and heirs of, the Romans and termed themselves so (Romaioi in Greek), as evidenced by the title Basileus Romaion [emperor of the Romans] often heralded on coins. It is only natural that, albeit under dramatic constraints and changes, they continued the Roman monetary tradition to 1353, a century before the fall of Constantinople in 1453. Their gold coins were accepted not only everywhere within the Empire's large territory but also beyond. They circulated all over the oecumene, the known world of the time, from Britain or Scandinavia to Ceylon, India and occasionally China.[4] In the words of Cosmas Indicopleustes, a sixth-century Egyptian merchant:

> There is another mark of the power of the Romans, which God has given them. It is in their nomisma that every nation conducts its commerce, and it is accepted in every place from one end of the earth to the other. The nomisma is admired by all men and all nations, for in no other nation does such a thing exist.[5]

It achieved a remarkable stability from the fourth to the tenth century, and was an efficient instrument of a powerful state and of active inter-regional exchanges.

Two preliminary observations should be made. First, our documentation is restricted to textual sources that seldom address monetary questions directly. Furthermore, none of the statistical records of late-medieval western Europe have survived, and the documentation must be completed by evidence derived from the coins themselves – the value or composition of their alloy, the possible origin of their metal, and their distribution in time and space. Second, historians concerned with this period (and I am no exception) rarely master the basics of economics sufficiently to set the emerging pattern into a consistent model. With these limitations in mind as a plea for understanding, there follows an outline – necessarily very schematic – of, first, the achievements represented by supplying an immense territory and its sometimes up to 30 million inhabitants with a unified coinage. The second part is concerned with adaptation to the limitations imposed by the successive, nearly constant, invasions and the hostile pressure on all the Empire's borders. Lastly, the chapter addresses how Byzantine gold coinage continued to act as one of the 'dollars of the Middle Ages' from the eleventh to the mid-thirteenth century, and why and how it collapsed in the mid-fourteenth century.

---

4 For the wide distribution of Byzantine coin finds, see C. Morrisson, 'La diffusion de la monnaie de Constantinople: routes commerciales ou routes politiques?', in C. Mango and G. Dagron (eds), *Constantinople and its Hinterland* (Aldershot, 1995).

5 Cosmas Indicopleustes illustrates this statement by reporting an often quoted episode about the king of Ceylon being more impressed by the beauty and purity of the Byzantine gold nomisma as compared to the Persian silver coin, E.O. Winstedt (ed.), *Christian Topography* (Cambridge, 1909), p. 81, 323–4.

Production and distribution of a unified coinage (fourth–fifth centuries)

Its characteristics

Since there was never any private appropriation of monetary rights as in the medieval West, it may be surmised that the Byzantine government could exert some control over the money supply. Although this does not imply that it was in a position to conduct a monetary policy in modern terms, the government could adapt to its immediate financial needs the quantities of coins struck and their metallic content or nominal value.

From antiquity, the striking of coinage was an industrial process, involving the standardized production of a great number of stamped flans with a value recognized and guaranteed by the respective issuing authority. During its most flourishing phase the Byzantine state may have annually struck up to several hundred thousand gold coins and a million or more copper coins that comprised the everyday currency required for a large territory and its population of some 30 million. The hundreds of thousands of surviving specimens testify to the ability of Byzantine coin engravers and mint makers.

Flexibility was provided throughout by a varied multi-denominational structure (see Table 1.1 below), and the existence throughout the Empire's millenary history of a partly token (fiduciary) bronze or copper coinage as opposed to the 'real' value of the gold coinage.[6]

Sophisticated metallurgical know-how enabled Byzantine minters to cope with altering/debasing monetary alloys as precisely as they could with refining it. Byzantine *khymeia*, 'alchemy', entailed the sacred art of the transmutation of metals into gold (or silver), with its development of both a mystical and allegorical nature and recipes of tinctures and colouring for making alloys appearl ike more expensive ones. Furthermore, there was the compilation of alchemists' texts[7] containing information on how to test for falsifications by others, or to check the purity of the material to be used for transmutation.[8] This science was part of the culture of the Byzantine learned man, as shown by a letter 'On how to Make Gold' of c.1045–6, addressed by Michael Psellos to Patriarch Michael Keroularios, in which he gave recipes for the extraction of gold and alloying it with copper.[9] His pupil, the future

6 See C. Morrisson, 'La monnaie fiduciaire à Byzance ou "Vraie monnaie", "monnaie fiduciaire" et "fausse monnaie" à Byzance', in *Bulletin de la Société française de Numismatique*, 34, 1979, pp. 612–6.

7 For a presentation see R. Halleux, Les textes alchimiques grecs (Turnhout, 1979). Publication of the 4th century Leyden and Stockholm papyri by R. Halleux, *Les alchimistes grecs, vol. 1* (Paris, 1981), and of more recent papyri (Zosimus of Panopolis, Blemmydes' Chrysopea etc.) by M. Berthelot and Ch. -E. Ruelle, *Collection des anciens alchimistes grecs*, 3 vols. (Paris, 1888–9, reprint Osnabrück, 1967).

8 R. Halleux, 'Méthodes d'essai et d'affinage des alliages aurifères dans l'Antiquité et au Moyen Age', in C. Morrisson, J.-N. Barrandon et al., *L'or monnayé, vol. 1: Purification et altérations. De Rome à Byzance*, Cahiers Ernest-Babelon 2 (Paris, 1985).

9 Peri tous orôn poiètéon khryson, § 7 ff., § 10, J. Bidez, *Catalogue des manuscrits alchimistes grecs, vol. 6* (Bruxelles, 1988), p. 26–41. Ital. transl. (with a reproduction of the

emperor Michael VII Doukas (1071–78), must have learned from him all these techniques:

> He understood every detail of finance exactly: its organization and management; how much the treasury paid to each person and how much each paid back to the treasury, the production of coins and the equilibrium of a balance; excesses and deficiencies of weight, how the touchstone worked; and how many measures of pure material each of the pieces of stamped gold contained.[10]

This technical capacity allowed for elaborate 'fine-tuning' in the quantity control of coins struck in relation to available metal resources, as will be shown in several examples below.

Proton activation of fourth-century Roman gold coins, undertaken by Barrandon in 1982–5, proved that refined gold solidi [solidi obryziaci][11] issued in accordance with the series of laws dating from 366–369, all contained more than 99 per cent gold, and as much as 99.9 per cent in the case of a coin of Valentinian I in the Bibliothèque Nationale de France. This is a level of purity that modern experts say has only been surpassed in the late twentieth century. It means that, in Roman, or Roman-derived, coinages, even limited variations in fineness, from 1 per cent and higher, should be considered significant, as we shall see below.

Its bases

Political will

> A unified coinage was undoubtedly the expression, and result, of Roman imperialism and its dominance of previously autonomous Greek cities and kingdoms. As Dio Cassius wrote in the third century: 'None of the cities should be allowed to have its own separate coinage or system of weights and measures; they should all be required to use ours.'[12]

In the sixth century, when the uniformity of the coinage was well established and taken for granted, the Latin writer Cassiodorus invested it with three functions: 'embellish the ruler's liberalitas, display his effigy for the present and future centuries and nourish his subjects through commerce'.[13]

---

text publ. by Bidez) by F. Abini, *La Crisopea* (Genua, 1988).

10 M. Psellos, *Chronography*, ed. Leib, B., II, 173, transl. E.R.A. Sewter (London, 1953).

11 Codex Theodosianus XII. 6. 12 (366 AD), and XII. 6.13 (367 AD). In Latin the word *obrussa* appears in Cicero and in Pliny for fire assay. The resulting refined gold is called *ad* or *ex obrussa* and finally *obryza* in Greek. E. Benveniste has shown the origin to lie with the Hurrian (Hittite) word *hubrushi* (crucible). See Halleux, 'Méthodes', pp. 48, 74.

12 Dio Cassius LII, 30, 9 cited by C. Howgego, *Ancient History from Coins* (London, 1995), p. 56.

13 Cassiodorus, Variae 6.7, commenting on the attributions of the Count of Sacred Largesses, the financial high official responsible for imperial expenses and imperial manufactures, including mints.

The monetary system's pivotal unit – a coin of pure gold, weighing 1/72 of a pound (c. 4.55 g)[14] – was to be the accepted currency all over the Empire 'provided the pieces are of the prescribed weight and fineness' [*modo ut debiti ponderis sint et speciei probae*]. And Byzantine legislation continued to repeat the fourth-century provisions preserved in the Justinian Code. In the early tenth century, Leo VI prescribed that 'every sort of coin should keep its value and rate, provided it be of authentic die, of unalterered content and exact weight'.[15] By then, the solidus/nomisma had preserved its original standard for some 600 years.

During all of Byzantine history, coins were a powerful means of conveying to the public not only the real or, later, stereotyped figure of the emperor but also the ideals of the government. They offer well-dated evidence on the very gradual Christianization of official ideology.

Economic basis The early Byzantine (or late Roman) empire relied on substantial economic resources and trade – substantial, of course, in relation to the conditions of the time – which both supported, and were supported by, the coinage. Its territory extended from the straits of Gibraltar to the Euphrates and from Egypt and North Africa to Hadrian's wall and the Rhine *limes*.[16] The Mediterranean, Black Sea and great rivers like the Nile or the Danube were favourable assets for transportation and exchanges between fertile and diversely endowed regions with different climatic conditions. The population of the Western part of the empire in the fourth century numbered less than 20 million inhabitants, while the Eastern part alone may have counted some 24 million in 350 and 30 million under Justinian before the outbreak of the Great Plague in 542.[17] Its great cities counted hundreds of thousands of inhabitants (Rome possibly 700,000; Constantinople attaining 500,000 in the fifth century, Alexandria 500,000, Antioch 200,000 etc.).

Economic production and active interregional exchange are documented by texts, inscriptions and papyri together with archaeological finds of kilns, wine or oil presses, tanning and dyeing installations, irrigation devices, pottery sherds, glass, coins and shipwrecks. Large-scale trade involved a wide range of commodities from luxury items like silk, silver plate and spices to more common ones, like copperware, nails, vegetables or fish and, of course, the huge quantities of wheat, oil and wine for provisioning the metropolis.[18]

---

14 I.e. 24 carats, a Roman weight of ± 0.18 g. The present reckoning of fineness in carats (24 = 100%; 18 = 75% etc.) go back to the weight and purity of the Late Roman solidus.

15 Leo VI, Novel 52: *parapoiēton tēn morphēn ekhon kai tēn hylēn akibdēlon kai tēn holkēn teleion.*

16 M.F. Hendy, *Studies in the Byzantine Monetary Economy, c. 300–c.1450* (Cambridge, 1985), p. 382.

17 According to J. Russell, 'Late Ancient and Medieval Population', *Transactions of the American Philosophical Society*, n. s., 48, 3, 1958, pp. 1–152. Such estimates, proposed on a comparative basis, are of course very uncertain but provide an order of magnitude.

18 For a synthetic update see J.-P. Sodini and C. Morrisson, 'The Sixth Century', in A. Laiou (ed.), *Economic History of Byzantium* (Washington, 2002), and the stimulating S. Kingsley and M. Decker (eds), *Economy and Exchange in the East Mediterranean during*

Though too little is known about mining, a few texts and some archaeological finds show that gold was available in Thrace and Macedonia, the Egyptian desert[19] and the Caucasus, while silver and copper were exploited in several areas in Asia Minor (Bithynia, Pontus, the Taurus mountains and Cyprus).[20] Trace-element analysis has revealed a spectacular rise in coins' platinum content around 346 from some 30–40 ppm to nearly 900 ppm in the late fourth century.[21] This shows that a new source of gold, probably in the Balkans, with a higher platinum content was being used in sufficient proportion to modify the metallic composition of the whole coin stock and increase it significantly.[22] Gold resources were not always in great abundance, but must have been sufficient to compensate, at least in the long run, for the various forms of metal losses: wear, wastage and hoarding in or beyond Byzantine territory.

Elaborate fiscal resources and administration

Relying on these natural resources, Diocletian soundly reorganized an elaborate administrative and fiscal system that remained relatively unchanged until the late sixth century, and was probably less oppressive than usually assumed in textbooks.[23] The budget in the sixth century was of the order of some 6 million solidi (27 tons of gold). In Constantine's time it was certainly larger. The pay-roll included some 600,000 military in the fourth century and still 300,000 to 380,000 in the sixth century, against some 10,000 civilian officials. Monetary demand was thus increased not only by active inter-regional exchanges but also by the state's financial and fiscal needs, since public expenditure and taxation made in cash were predominant. The state, in turn, ensured an adequate money supply that provided for all levels of exchanges and for all classes in the population. It had a multiple-denomination system, ranging in value from 1 to several thousand (compare with the present range – from the 500-euro banknote to the one-cent coin), see Tables 3.1–3.2 below. There was a continuous circulation of money and a high level of monetization, comparable to that for the early Roman Empire, which R.W. Goldsmith estimated – probably

---

Late Antiquity. Proceedings of the conference held at Somerville College, Oxford, 29 May 1999 (Oxford, 2001).

19 Excavations undertaken by the University of Chicago at Bir Umm Fawakhir, C.E. Meyer, in *Journal of Roman Archaeology*, 2000.

20 B. Pitarakis, 'Mines anatoliennes exploitées par les Byzantins : recherches récentes', in *Revue Numismatique*, 1998, pp. 141–185.

21 C. Morrisson et al., *Museum Notes, American Numismatic Society*, 32, 1987, p. 205, fig. 12.

22 C. Morrisson, J.-N. Barrandon et al., *L'or monnayé, vol. 1: Purification et altérations. De Rome à Byzance*, Cahiers Ernest-Babelon 2 (Paris, 1985).

23 See the recent discussion by J.-M. Carrié and A. Rousselle, *L'empire romain en mutation des Sévères à Constantin* (Paris, 1999), pp. 607–9, relying on Carrié's previous work and referring notably to R. Bagnall, 'Agricultural productivity and taxation in Later Roman Egypt', in *Transactions of the American Philological Association*, 115, 1985, pp. 289–308.

overestimated – at a maximum of 50 per cent in the first century AD.[24] Whatever the exact figure, it was undoubtedly much higher in the fourth to eleventh centuries in the East than in the West and, *a fortiori*, in the *Barbaricum* beyond the Rhine and Danubian frontiers. There it was almost non-existent, except for trading posts on the limes or within the area restricted to a one-day walking distance from the frontier.

Adapting to changes and crises: the age of regionalization (sixth-ninth centuries)

Invasions and the creation of barbarian coinages in the West

In the fifth century, the Western Roman Empire fell prey to various Germanic peoples. They founded several states [regni] practically independent but still respectful of imperial authority's pre-eminence. One measure of this recognition was that most, for decades, issued only 'imitative' coinages in the name of reigning (or sometimes deceased) Roman emperors. These coinages also respected the Byzantine standard at first but were gradually debased.[25] Several factors interplayed in this development: increased insecurity, a negative commercial balance with the East, a difference in the gold:silver ratio and the decline of the fiscal system.

Following Justinian's costly campaigns of reconquest, the Byzantine Empire during the sixth century recovered part of Roman Africa (an area corresponding roughly to present Tunisia and eastern Algeria) from the Vandals, Italy from the Ostrogoths, and southern Spain from the Visigoths, thus encompassing the whole Mediterranean basin. But the barbarians still held Gaul and most of the Iberian peninsula, as well as Noricum and Pannonia, controlled respectively by the Franks and the Suevi, and the Visigoths and the Lombards. The Danubian limes, after continuous breaches by Huns and Goths in the fourth century, ceased to offer any protection to Dacia and Thrace from the 540s. During the 570s, episodic raids gave way to a more concentrated and permanent occupation of central Greece and some coastal regions by the Slavs. In the seventh century, Avars and Bulgars settled in areas north of the Danube, while Lombards extended their control of northern and central Italy. Growing insecurity combined with the demographic consequences of the plague weakened the economy as a whole and, thereby, imperial finances. Money evolved within this context.

In the reconquered provinces, the Byzantines adapted themselves to supersede existing 'barbarian' systems, striking, for example, abundant silver issues, otherwise very rare in the East, which compensated for the absence of fractions of the solidus. These specificities were paralleled by a marked regional character in the circulation of lesser coins, given that each province was for the most part, although not exclusively,

24 R.W. Goldsmith, 'An estimate of the size and structure of the National Product of the early Roman Empire', *Review of Income and Wealth*, 1984, pp. 263–88; C. Morrisson, *Monnaie et finances à Byzance: analyses, techniques* (Aldershot, 1994), art. III, pp. 294–5.

25 Updated and masterly reference book on this complex subject: P. Grierson and M. Blackburn, *Medieval European Coinage, vol. 1: The Early Middle Ages* (Cambridge, 1986).

Table 3.1 The Byzantine Monetary System

a) Late Fourth and Fifth Century*

	GOLD	(± 98% Au)	SILVER (± 98% Ag)	COPPER
Solidus Nomisma (4.53g)	*Semissis*	*Tremissis*	*Heavy and light miliarensia, siliquae* (±5.43, 4.53, 2.26g)	*Maiorina (decargyrus), Centenonialis, Half-centenonialis* (±5.4, 2.26, 1.1g)
1	2	3		1500? , 3000?, 6000?

* The situation is very complex and changing and the uncertain relations between the gold and the subsidiary denominations are given here as rough indications.

b) Sixth–Seventh Century (from 498)

GOLD	(± 98% Au)		SILVER	COPPER				
Solidus Nomisma	*Semissis*	*Tremissis*	*Hexagram (from 615)*	*Follis*	*Half-follis*	*Dekanoum-mion*	*Pentanoum-mion*	*Nummus*
1	2	3	12	288	576	1152	2304	11520

c) Eighth–Eleventh Century

GOLD (± 97%) (debased from ±90% to 10% in the 11th c.)*	SILVER**	COPPER
Solidus Nomisma	*Miliaresion*	*Follis*
1	12	288

* From the late 10th century light nomismata of 22 carats (*tetartera*) (4.13g) were also struck. The full-weight nomismata were called *histamena*

** In the eleventh century, fractions of 2/3 and 1/3 miliaresion were also struck.

d) The Period of the Gold Hyperpyron (1092–1353)

GOLD *Hyperpyron nomisma*	ELECTRUM *Nomisma trachy aspron*	BILLON *Aspron trachy (stamenon)*	COPPER *Tetarteron*	*Half-tetarteron*
1 (progressively debased from 90% to 45% Au)	3 (eventually 10 or 12 when issued in silver)	48 (eventually 288-384)	864	1728 ?
	1304–ca 1353 AD SILVER *Basilikon*	1304–ca 1353 AD BILLON (± 23% Ag) *Tournesion*	1304–a 1353 AD COPPER *Assarion*	
	12	96	768?	

e) The Period of the Silver Hyperpyron/Stavraton (1367–1453)

(Money of account) *Notional gold hyperpyron*	SILVER	(±95% Ag)		COPPER	
	Stavraton	*Half-Stavraton*	*Doukato-poulon (aspron)*	*Tornese*	*Folaro*
1	2	4	16	192	576 ?

supplied by its local mint.[26] Integration and the mixing of the coinage still persisted, but to a lesser degree than during the fourth century.

The gold coin retained its ubiquity and uniform value, now symbolized by the 'CONOB' mark used by all mints from Constantinople to Carthage or Ravenna. Prices expressed in gold remained stable, and analyses of metallic content show that the provincial mints followed the Constantinople standard down to the late seventh century. Thus, they were still following the Pragmatic Constitution of 554 for Italy, where Justinian stated that 'solidi struck with the Roman Emperors' die must be accepted in all provinces free of any exchange fee'.[27]

However, budgetary difficulties were reflected in the East by the decline in weight and value of the bronze coin [follis], which led to the progressive disappearance of smaller denominations. The increase in the supply of bronze (semi-fiduciary) money entailed a rise in prices – as expressed in these units – contrasted with unchanged prices in gold. At the same time, the series of light-weight solidi (of 23, 22 or 20 keratia/carats instead of the original 24 carats) issued from 537 to 687, may represent a currency of forced exchange used by the state for expenditures during various periods of crisis.

Surviving in a contracting context after the Persian wars and the Arab conquest

From the early seventh century the Empire wielded all its forces in a long, renewed war against the Persian Empire. Heraclius's victory at Ctesiphon, the Persian capital, in 626 proved to be a short respite. In 636 the Arabs' victory on the Yarmuk gave them control of Syria, Palestine and Egypt. Six decades later they had gained the whole of North Africa and were soon to enter Spain.[28] This was a major catastrophe for Byzantium since the Empire had lost several of its richest and fiscally most productive provinces. They could no longer play their previous role of provisioning the cities and stimulating economic transactions. Many cities were abandoned while most were reduced to small, fortified areas. Trade diminished and was, more and more, regionalized, and bullion stocks, coin production and monetary transactions all declined. This is clearly shown by the decrease in the number of coins preserved in museum collections or of those found on excavated sites (sometimes completely absent) as well as by a tenfold drop in the number of hoards.

The elaborate hierarchy of the earlier monetary system with its eight or more denominations was dramatically transformed in the East. It was replaced by a much simpler structure of three denominations, one for each metal: gold, silver and copper, with a much-restricted range of values (see Table 3.1). In the late seventh century,

26 'Coin and its use in Byzantium', online exhibit displaying 118 Byzantine coins described, commented and accompanied by explanatory texts on the history of the coinage, its mints and system, its political and economic function and its iconography, http://www.doaks.org/CoinExhibition/First/First1Main3.html

27 Corpus Iuris Civilis, Nov., App. VII, '... sancimus solidos Romanorum principum forma signatos sine permutationis dispendio per omnes provincias ambulare et per eos celebrari contractus ...'.

28 'Coin and its use'. For maps, see under 'Mints', or Laiou, *Economic History*, ch. 42.

the gold solidus underwent a progressive but very limited debasement in weight and fineness, which must have been deliberate. From 721 the replacement of a full-bodied silver coin [hexagram] by a token fiduciary one [miliaresion] on the model of the Arab dirhem also aimed at conserving metal. Meanwhile, provincial coin production evolved on lines greatly divergent from the standard of Constantinople, the Sicilian solidus for example falling to 80 per cent, then 50 per cent of the norm. A more regionalized circulation is another sign of the fragmentation of the once unified monetary zone.

However defensive and reduced its situation, the Empire retained important assets, of which the most important was a powerful navy that the Arabs could never entirely defeat. This sustained control of the main routes linking the remaining littoral territories and islands, some like Sicily still relatively prosperous.[29] Although greatly reduced, long-distance trade and monetary transactions did not disappear entirely. Nor did the taxation in cash that Emperor Constantine V demanded more systematically in order to finance, amongst other things, the tagmata, an élite force of imperial guards more efficient than the land-settled troops of the themes. Monetary fragmentation was never complete, and gold from Constantinople still reached the provinces on a limited scale.

Byzantine finances, though they had fallen to a third of their former extent under Justinian, were only surpassed by those of the Caliphate in Baghdad. In no way could the Carolingian West, which had turned entirely to silver (striking only the denier and occasionally its half, the obol), compete. As a high Byzantine official bluntly put it to the Lombard bishop Liudprand, ambassador of the Western Emperor Otto II to Constantinople in 968: 'As we surpass all other nations in wealth and wisdom ... With our money, which gives us power, we will rouse the whole world against him [your emperor] and we will break him in pieces like a potter's vessel.'[30]

Money for an expanding Empire: the golden age of the bezant (tenth-twelth centuries)

The Byzantine's proud and prejudiced affirmation dates to 960, when Byzantium was, or would soon be, regaining part of its lost ground (southern Italy, Crete, Cyprus, eastern Anatolia, inland regions of the Balkans and Bulgaria). This recovery was no doubt rooted in the Empire's finances, which gave it a clear advantage over its less monetized enemies.[31] Instead of the loosened and often isolated, mainly littoral, strongholds of the 'Dark Centuries' (c. 650–830), it controlled an ever more continuous and enlarged territory. Increasing security favoured a demographic and

29 Laiou, *Economic History*, ch. 42, pp. 954–8.

30 Liudprand of Cremona, *The Embassy to Constantinople*, trans. J.J. Norwich (London, 1993), pp. 202–3.

31 As pointed out later by R. Cantillon, *Essai sur la nature du commerce en général* (London, 1755 [repr. Paris: INED]): 'Les revenus de l'Etat où l'argent abonde se lèvent avec bien plus de facilité et en plus grande somme comparativement, ce qui donne à l'Etat, en cas de guerre ou de contestation, de gagner toutes sortes d'avantages sur ses adversaires chez qui l'argent est plus rare', ch. 8, p. 105.

economic revival which archaeological surveys and archive documents from Italy, Mount Athos and elsewhere have highlighted.

Moderate debasement for an expanding state and economy

This period's monetary history has been debated since the 1950s, when Grierson first measured by specific gravity the fineness of eleventh century gold nomismata and attributed their alteration to the profligacy of Constantine IX (1042–55). Subsequent analyses of the coinage during the 1970s and 1980s by neutron and, eventually, proton activation gave a deeper, precise knowledge of the coins' metal composition, measuring not only the three major elements – gold, silver and copper – of the alloy but also its trace elements, revealing processes of debasement.

Since, as commented above, the Byzantine minters must have been quite aware of any departure from the 99 per cent theoretical norm, every deviation from it, however slight, can be considered as a symptom of 'creeping debasement' or at least a slackening of the standard. Such a deviation is to be observed as early as the late tenth and early eleventh century, when the gold content drifts from an average 95 per cent under Constantine VII Porphyrogenitus (914–59) to 90 per cent under Michael IV (1034–41). This first moderate phase of alteration, at an average annual pace of c. 0.04 per cent, which may have entailed a maximum increase of the circulating medium by 0.2 per cent, is followed by a second (1042–c.1069), when debasement's pace quickened at an average annual rhythm of 0.4 per cent, possibly increasing at overall annual rate of 1 per cent.[32]

The activation analyses help to understand how the first debasement was carried out. This was not, as one might think, by adding baser metals (silver and copper) to the alloy, but simply by not refining the newly mined or natural gold ore, which may contain as much as 30 or 34 per cent silver.[33]

The phenomenon can be put in an economic perspective by applying Fisher's equation of exchange.[34] In order to account for the increase in the number of coins struck (the material consequence and aim of debasement), if a deficit was the main explanation, then since there is no reason to expect an increase in V (velocity of circulation) nor a significant change in the volume of the available metal, the only way would be to postulate a corresponding increase in P (the price level). As no signs of a price increase are observed before the 1070s, we have to postulate, on the

32 Laiou, *Economic History*, ch. 42, fig. 2.

33 This is demonstrated by plotting the lead content of coins against silver, see Morrison, *Museum Notes*, p. 201, fig. 9. Even refined silver retains some 0.6 to 0.7 per cent lead, a residue of the original argentiferous lead ore. Therefore when silver enters the alloy separately, for example when it is deliberately added to gold, the lead content rises along a correlated line whose slope corresponds to the lead amount in the added silver. But when silver enters the alloy together with gold, the percentage of lead remains constant whatever the amount of silver. The lead curve for Byzantine eleventh century debasement clearly distinguishes the first two phases carried out by merely adding non-refined gold from the later phase when only silver was added, Hendy, *Studies*, p. 382.

34 Morrisson, *Monnaie*, art. IX, for this economic interpretation. For the metallurgical processes and context, see Morrisson-Barrandon, *L'or*.

contrary, a correlated increase in T (the monetized part of transactions), induced by the increase in the empire's territory and in monetary needs for taxes paid in cash and monetary circulation in towns. This interpretation could well be taken as highly speculative and has been much criticized as being inspired by 'parachronistical' views. Nonetheless, it has been largely confirmed by further historical and archaeological research. Apparently, the peace and relative security established during the 1020s by Basil II's victories and the extension of Byzantine territory created conditions for an increase in state expenditures and needs that, in turn, stimulated trade and monetization. Increased and increasingly monetized production and trade were made possible by the injection of new liquidities, and at this time debasement did not entail inflation, as it so often had in Roman times and was to do in the following phase.

Accelerated debasement in times of crisis (late eleventh century)

From c.1069 the military disasters and the dramatic consequences on finances of the Turkish advance in Asia Minor led to an accelerated alteration of coins' metal. Given the rather restricted use of transfers, exchange contracts or credit, 'coinage' in Byzantium coincided virtually with 'money'. Consequently, tampering with precious metal ('bullion' money) was, as in Roman times, almost the only way of dealing with a growing deficit. Within two decades the nomisma's gold content fell from some 70 per cent to 10 per cent. The process implied now adding silver – not non-refined gold as before – to the alloy, simply taken from the available silver currency. The manipulation was a vicious circle. The gold coinage debased with silver implied debasing silver coins with copper. In turn, using debased silver issues to debase gold further meant introducing more and more copper into the nomisma (up to some 14 to 18 per cent in Alexius I's early coinage). This process was much less efficient in increasing the number of coins struck than that of debasing with non-purified gold. The consequent drop in gold content needed to ensure the necessary money supply was much sharper. Contemporary historians, who had not mentioned the earlier creeping and 'painless' debasement,[35] tell of the dire straits in finances – how salaries had to be paid in silk and not in cash – of the state's default on payment of rents attached to offices, of the 'borrowing' of ecclesiastical silver plate and the melting of the imperial family's reserves. As well, they comment on the dramatic rise in the price of wheat, which increased tenfold and more in the winter of 1077–8, when Constantinople was full of refugees and the Seljuqs and Petchenegs were not far off.[36]

Restoring a sound international currency: the hyperpyron (twelfth – mid-thirteenth century)

It was Alexius I Comnenus (1081–1118) who, after fighting on all fronts – against Turks in the East, Petchenegs to the North and Normans from Sicily invading Greece

35 Also not perceptible to the eye since there is no change in colour before the silver content reaches 30 per cent.

36 For reference to some contemporary texts see Morrisson, *Monnaie*, art. IV, p. 305.

– achieved some degree of military and monetary restoration. A new monetary system was established in 1092 which took into account the paucity of new metal available and the metallurgical constraints arising from previous debasement. The restored gold coin at 20½ carats (86 per cent) was called the hyperpyron (not 'hyper-pure', but 'fire refined'!). It was not on the Roman standard of 24–23.5 carats, which had been more or less respected between the fourth and the ninth century, or even on the tenth-century one of 22.5 carats. Rather, it corresponded to the average fineness of the early debased coins, owing to the 10 per cent silver of the alloy which the refining process, the techniques of the time, were not able to extract. It was accompanied by a gold/silver-alloy ('electrum') coin, originally valued at a third of a hyperpyron, called the nomisma trachy aspron or tricephalon,[37] whose metal content, at 30 per cent gold, 60 per cent silver and 10 per cent copper, represented the average composition of the debased 'gold' coins of the third phase and probably resulted from their re-minting.[38] Apparently, the hyperpyron was struck in lesser quantities than its fraction of a third that was more frequent in local or regional transactions. But it dominated Byzantium's outward payments, and played an important part in international trade where it was still known as bisantius, a term which became a general one for gold coin.[39]

The 'pure gold' standard going back to the model offered by the Roman and Byzantine solidus/nomisma was now embodied only in the Fatimid dinars before it was taken up once more by the newly created Western gold coins in the late thirteenth century. The Comnenian hyperpyron enjoyed a wide circulation in Mediterranean trade as evidenced, for example, in Venetian documents of the period.[40] This may explain why it also set the standard for several gold issues by neighbouring states: the bezant struck in the Crusader kingdom of Jerusalem in the mid-twelfth century or the augustale of Frederick II Hohenstaufen.

The end of unity and its causes (mid-thirteenth – fifteenth centuries)

In the first half of the thirteenth century, despite the fatal blow caused by the fall of Constantinople to the Latin armies of the fourth crusade in 1204 and the partition of the empire, the hyperpyron, issued mainly from the 1220s by the Greek Empire of Nicaea on a reduced standard of 18 carats, still acted as a 'dollar' in Mediterranean trade alongside Islamic dinars. It was eventually superseded in this role by the Venetian ducat and the florin of Florence, both first issued in 1284, which came to dominate international circulation in the East and in Western Europe respectively.

---

37 By playing ambiguously on its three figures' iconography (the Virgin on the obverse and the emperor and another religious figure on the reverse) and on its value.

38 Laiou, *Economic History*, ch. 42, fig. 2.

39 Hence the origin of *bezant* in heraldry.

40 A. Laiou, 'Byzantine Trade with Christians and Muslims and the Crusades', in A. Laiou and R.P. Mottahedeh (eds), *The Crusades from the Perspective of Byzantium and the Muslim World* (Washington, 2001), pp. 156–96.

The military and financial collapse of the Byzantine state

The thirteenth century proved to be the last flourishing episode of Byzantine coinage. In spite of the recapture of Constantinople from the Latins in 1261, the new Palaeologan dynasty progressively lost ground in both Asia Minor and Europe to the Turks (Smyrna, 1344; Gallipoli 1354; Adrianople 1362; Thessalonica 1387). Public income from land taxation was reduced accordingly by territorial losses and growing insecurity within the Empire's remaining areas. Meanwhile, income from commercial and customs duties was greatly impaired by the exemptions or reduced rates conceded to Italian mercantile cities in reward or hope for their military help, or simply under the pressure wielded by their powerful naval forces.

The various phases of the final debasement of Byzantine gold coinage are clearly related to known episodes of financial difficulties for the Palaeologi, as the contemporary Greek writer George Pachymeres (1242–c.1310) precisely stated:

> And he [Andronicus II, 1282–1328] debased the nomisma according to need. For at first under John [III] Ducas [1221–1254] the refined gold of nomismata amounted to two-thirds of their weight [i.e. to 16 carats] and this situation continued for some time. Then, under Michael [VIII Paleologus, 1259–1282], after the recovery of the City, because of the expenses then necessary, not least with regard to the Italians, he [Michael] altered the reverse of the old design by means of a representation of the City, and reduced the measure of gold by a carat, so that it became 15 [carats] compared with [a total] of 24. Later, when he was succeeded, it amounted to fourteen [of] gold, compared with ten [of alloy], and now [ca. 1308] the purity [of the gold coin] is said to be mixed by half [i.e. 12 of gold compared with 12 of alloy] ...[41]

Italian merchants were as well informed through their own assays of this decline and by the respective metal value of the various issues which Francesco Balduccio Pegolotti, a Florentine trader, labelled according to their iconography (inginocchiati referring for example to the kneeling-emperor coins of Andronicus II, tre santi to the two figures of Andronicus II and his son Michael IX crowned by Christ, and so on).[42] The markets lost confidence in an overly manipulated currency, as the Venetians complained in 1303 to Andronicus II concerning 'a defect found in the emperor's yperperi delivered by messer Ugolino Giustiniani'.[43]

The commercial revolution and the return to gold in the West

The cessation of issues of any sort of hyperpyron (by now reduced to less than half of its original fineness at some 45 per cent fine gold) was also linked to the

41 G. Pachymérès, Relations historiques, in A. Failler (ed.), *Corpus Fontium Historiae Byzantinae XXIV/1–4*, 4 vols. (Paris, 1984–1999), p. 540 (= Bonn II, pp. 493-4). See also Laiou, *Econmic History*, ch. 42, fig. 4.

42 Laiou, *Economic History*, ch. 42, fig. 4.

43 R. Cessi and P. Sambin, *Le deliberazioni del Consiglio di Rogati (Senato)*, Serie 'Mixtorum', vol. I, p. 105, n. 24, cited by T. Bertelè, 'Moneta veneziana e moneta bizantina (secoli XII–XV)', in A. Pertusi (ed.), *Venezia e il Levante fino al secolo XVI, vol. 1: Storia-Diritto-Economia* (1960, Venice, 1983), p. 20.

period's international monetary context. From the twelfth century, in the wake of the Crusades, the 'commercial revolution' had brought more and more Western merchants to the East, so intensifying the relations and interdependence of the various Mediterranean countries' economies. As is well known, the widely diverging silver: gold ratio between Byzantium and the Islamic world, on the one hand, and Western Europe on the other induced large-scale exports of bullion between these zones, well documented by commercial archives of the period.[44] It led to a double and converse shift of monetary systems. There was the return to gold in the West, first in Italy, then in other areas (England, France and Germany),[45] while from 1367, Byzantium shifted to the issue of a coinage almost entirely composed of silver denominations marked by a high level of purity even down to the siege of 1453.

In this last period (late thirteenth–mid-fifteenth centuries), the circulating medium in the shrinking Byzantine Empire, now reduced to Constantinople, Thessalonica and the Morea, and the neighbouring Balkan states (which had progressively set up their own national coinages), became an extremely complex mix of various currencies in, and with, which the local and, above all, the Italian merchant-bankers traded competently. As early as the 1290s, the hyperpyron's declining fineness undermined the public's confidence and it was often specified that transactions in hyperpyra were to be carried out in 'good Venetian [silver] ducats at the rate of 12 for each hyperpyron'. Of a high and stable fineness, the Venetian silver ducat or gros, issued as a multiple of the debased denier in 1199, penetrated the Aegean from the 1260s, where it enjoyed a wide circulation and was imitated by Serbians and Byzantines alike (for the basilikon, issued by Andronicus II from 1304, see Table 3.1).

In the *Libro dei Conti*, the ledger kept in Constantinople by the Venetian merchant Giacomo Badoer from 1436 to 1439, the hyperpyron (perpero) survives as a money of account. Going back to Constantine the Great's solidus, it was divided into 24 carats and was represented by two big silver coins of c. 7.2g, called stavrati. But its role as the period's 'dollar' had been taken over in eastern Mediterranean by the Venetian gold ducat, now the object of many imitations or forgeries of inferior quality by the Turks or the Genoese.

44 P. Spufford, *Money and its use in Medieval Europe* (Cambridge, 1988), pp. 132–86, 267–288, with more references, including A. Watson, 'Back to Gold – and Silver', in *Economic History Review*, 20, 1, 1967, pp. 1–34; J. Day (ed.), *Études d'histoire monétaire* (Lille, 1984); J. Day, *Monnaies et marchés au Moyen Âge* (Paris, 1994); F.C. Lane and R.C. Mueller, *Money and Banking in Medieval and Renaissance Venice* (Baltimore, 1985).

45 The Iberian peninsula had first and precociously issued gold on the Islamic standard, even copying its Arabic inscriptions like Barcelona's *mancusi* imitating Omeyyad dinars of Cordoba in the 11th century or Castile's *anfusini* (or *maravedis*) based in the twelfth century on the neighbouring Almoravid dinar. Catalonia and Aragon shifted to the Italian standard in the fourteenth century, but Castile and Leon, which depended more on their relations with Andalusia than on Mediterranean commerce, kept the Islamic standard up to 1497.

Conclusion

The survival throughout an entire millennium of a unified currency dominated by a precious-metal, high-value strong denomination circulating inside a vast Empire's territory and beyond is a unique phenomenon in monetary history. The nomisma or 'bezant' (symbol of Byzantium's riches and power) was characterized by the relative stability of its gold standard. This may have been protected by the total money supply's flexibility, ensured by the existence at all times of a partly token (fiduciary) silver – or alloyed gold – and bronze or copper coinage.[46]

The factors underlying this long history may be considered as follows: political will and 'universal' ideology,[47] an elaborate permanent tax system and an administration focused on wielding military power and ensuring the greatest possible security – an essential for a flourishing economy – and, finally, a sophisticated monetary policy based on refined techniques and metallurgical knowledge. The order of these factors does not imply any ranking. All contributed to shaping the empire-unifying and 'international' status of Byzantine (gold) coinage. When one or two of these factors withered, as happened during the fourteenth century, the coinage collapsed. As a French scholar of the 1930s quipped: 'L'empire byzantin disparut lorsqu'il eut dépensé son dernier sou [The Byzantine Empire disappeared once it had spent its last penny]'.

46 The situation was very different in Western Europe where no copper or bronze coinage was struck (except in Byzantine Italy, or in Italian states with a Byzantine heritage) from the mid sixth century (by the Merovingians in Marseilles) or early seventh century (by the Visigoths in Southern Spain) up to the late fifteenth or mid sixteenth century. This does not imply, on the contrary, that Western medieval currencies were never overvalued.

47 'Byzantium as Oecumene' was the subject of an international colloquium organized by the Institute for Byzantine Research (National Hellenic Research Foundation) in Athens, 29 Nov.–2 Dec. 2001, proceedings forthcoming. See also 'To Byzantio os oikoumene', catalogue of the exhibition, Byzantine and Christian Museum, Oct. 2001–Jan. 2002 (Athens: Hypourgeio Politismo, 2001).

CHAPTER 4

On the History of German Monetary Union

Richard H. Tilly

Introduction

The history of nineteenth-century German unification has long served as a beacon for subsequent discussions of European integration.[1] This probably has to do with the successful fusion of economic and political integration that this historical episode seems to embody. Most recently, attention has focused on monetary union – admittedly an important element of Germany's earlier unification. A vast literature has accumulated on this particular question.[2] The following consideration builds on that historiography but it does so in – it is to be hoped – a critical vein, with the intent of revising some of its arguments. The first section attempts a brief characterization of the historiography. The chapter then proceeds to describe the several stages of nineteenth-century German monetary unification. The third section offers some revisionist comments, while the last attempts a critical interpretation of the 'lessons of history' that the German example has been alleged to contain.

Historiography

The older, long standing, historiography had the founding of the German Reich in 1871 at the centre of the historical stage. On the heels of the victorious war over France came the introduction of the new gold-standard currency, the mark and, almost simultaneously, a new national bank of issue, the Reichsbank. An essential part of this view was the interpretation of pre-1871 monetary history. This emphasized the heterogeneity, even chaos, of monetary conditions before 1871 and

1 An early brilliant, but polemical, contribution was J.M. Keynes' *The Economic Consequences of the Peace* (1920). Interest in the topic was rekindled in the 1950s. See J. Viner, *The Customs Union Issue* (New York, 1950); also W. Fischer, 'Der Deutsche Zollverein, die Europäische Wirtschaftsgemeinschaft und die Freihandelszone', Europa Archiv, 5, 1961.

2 C.L. Holtfrerich, 'The Monetary Unification Process in Nineteenth-Century Germany: relevance and lessons for Europe today', in M. de Cecco and A. Giovannini (eds), *A European Central Bank? Perspectives on Monetary Unification after Ten Years of the EMS* (Cambridge, 1989); T. Theurl, *Eine gemeinsame Währung für Europa. 12 Lehren aus der* Geschichte (Innsbruck, 1992); W. Vantour, *European monetary union since 1848. A political and historical analysis* (Cheltenham, 1996).

the improvements, especially the homogenization of the coinage, which followed. Karl Helfferich in 1903 lent his authority to this line of argument, among other things, by depicting German conditions during the 1850s and 1860s as backward, especially in comparison with France or Britain.[3]

The 1870s were doubtlessly important, and their significance will be considered in the next section. However, a generation of economic historians has been busy revising the interpretation that takes the 1870s as the virtual beginning of German monetary unification. These scholars have emphasized the important steps toward integration undertaken in connection with the development of the German customs union, the Zollverein, founded in 1834.[4] In particular, they have drawn attention to the fact that by the end of the 1860s integration had already gone so far as to reduce the number of separate currency areas, for all practical purposes, to just two: the north German taler area, and the south German gulden area. Moreover, the taler, as will be shown, was already the dominant money standard (and means of payment).

This welcome revision, however, would be misleading if it left the impression that the crucial steps toward monetary integration came first with the Zollverein. In fact, two further historical factors critically conditioned the process – and thus deserve attention. First, the Kingdom of Prussia, Germany's largest state, itself achieved monetary union during the two decades following the Napoleonic Wars (c.1815–1830s), and this generated a 'cost-benefit' model for subsequent integration. Second, concurrently, the world's economically most important countries, Great Britain and France, demonstrated a strong commitment to monetary stability and, in particular, to the maintenance of currency convertibility with fixed exchange rates based on commodity money.[5] This naturally encouraged the German states to adhere to such a system, but it left monetary policymakers with less autonomy than a system of paper (or 'fiat') money would have provided, i.e., it limited the impact of monetary union.

---

3 K.T. Helfferich, *Das Geld* (1903, Leipzig, 5th ed. 1921), pp. 153–9; K. Borchardt, 'Währung und Wirtschaft', in Deutsche Bundesbank (ed.), *Währung und Wirtschaft in Deutschland 1876–1975* (Frankfurt, 1976).

4 Holtfrerich, 'Monetary Unification'; B. Sprenger, 'Harmonisierungsbestrebungen im Geldwesen der deutschen Staaten zwischen Wiener Kongress und Reichsgründung', in E. Schremmer (ed.), *Geld und Währung vom 16. Jahrhundert bis zur Gegenwart*, supplement, Vierteljahrschrift für Sozial- und Wirtschaftsgeschichte, 106 (Stuttgart, 1993); H. Rittmann, *Deutsche Geldgeschichte 1484–1914* (Munich, 1975).

5 From the perspective of the current fiat money standard this is a striking feature. To be sure, adherence to a commodity-money standard was as old as the history of money itself. Nevertheless, the British return to gold in 1821 (after nearly 12 years of the 'paper pound') was a significant departure, as was the post-1815 French resolve to restrain paper-money circulation and maintain convertibility. See Helfferich, *Geld*, pp. 129–31; also C. Kindleberger, *A Financial History of Western Europe* (London, 1984); A. Feaveryear, *The Pound Sterling. A History of English Money* (Oxford, 2nd ed. 1963), esp. chs. 8–10; and A. Milward, 'The Origins of the Gold Standard', in J. Braga de Macedo, B. Eichengreen and J. Reis (eds), *Currency Convertibility. The Gold Standard and beyond* (London/New York, 1996).

Stages of Germany's monetary unification

Prussia's currency reforms

The peace that concluded the Napoleonic Wars brought Prussia large territorial gains, above all the western provinces of Rhineland and Westphalia. The kingdom's rulers assigned high priority to the economic integration of its western and eastern parts, in which financial and currency reforms played an essential role. The customs union of 1818 eliminated internal trade barriers and represented a very significant step toward the harmonization of indirect taxes. Reaping the benefits of financial integration, however, called for transparent monetary conditions – that is, the replacement of regional currency diversity by a national standard. Under prevailing circumstances, this meant reform of the coinage since metallic coins were the principal means of payment and store of value for most of the population. The most important step forward came with the Coinage Law of 30 September 1821, which unified the coinage on the basis of the so-called 'Fourteen-Taler Standard' [Vierzehntalerfuss], with 1 taler equivalent comprising 30 silver groschen and 360 pfennige.[6] Short-run problems abounded, especially within border regions where coins of neighbouring states circulated along with Prussian ones. Nevertheless, in the long run, the reforms proved successful, furthered by, among other things, the Prussian government's readiness to assume the costs of re-coinage and adhere to low seignorage charges. By the 1830s, the Prussian taler had established itself as a stable currency enjoying a high degree of acceptance. Contemporary complaints concerning a perceived lag in the supply of metallic money behind demand probably reflected the rapid monetization of economic transactions more than anything else.[7]

Coinage policy and the Zollverein

The founding of the Zollverein in 1834 soon called attention to the question of currency diversity amongst the German member states. Several different standards

---

6 Fourteen-Taler corresponded to a contemporary measure – the 'Cologne Standard ['Kölner Maß'] – representing 233.85 grams of fine silver; see Rittmann, Geldgeschichte.

7 A relative shortage of metallic money may have been a global problem in the post-Napoleonic era. According to A. Soetbeer, *Materialien zur Erläuterung und Beurteilung der wirtschaftlichen Edelmetallverhältnisse und der Währungsfrage* (1879, Berlin, 2nd edn. 1886) world production of the precious metals probably declined between c. 1800 and the 1840s. Nevertheless, the rate of growth of metal money in Prussia was much lower than that in France or Great Britain during this period (1815–35): ca. 1.8 per cent per annum, compared with 2.1–2.2 per cent per annum for France and nearly 5 per cent for Great Britain. This probably reflected Prussia's parsimonious financial policies. See R. Tilly, *Geld und Kredit in der Wirtschaftsgeschichte* (Stuttgart, 2003), pp. 48f. For the cited estimates see R. Cameron, 'England', in R. Cameron et al. (eds), *Banking in the Early Stages of Industrialization* (New York, 1967a); R. Cameron, 'Scotland', in R. Cameron et al. (eds), *Banking in the Early Stages of Industrialization* (New York, 1967b); R. Cameron, 'France', in R. Cameron et al. (eds), *Banking in the Early Stages of Industrialization* (New York, 1967c); and R. Tilly, 'Germany', in R. Cameron et al. (eds), *Banking in the Early Stages of Industrialization* (New York, 1967).

prevailed, of which the two most important were the taler and gulden, mentioned above. The main problem, however, concerned the varying metallic content and market value of coins having nominally identical value. This discrepancy arose from differences in age and quality of coins in circulation and also from interstate differences in rates of seignorage, i.e. the difference between the amount of silver paid into a government mint and the amount of silver received in coins in exchange. The problem was complicated by each currency system comprising a whole hierarchy of coins, ranging from heavy gold coins of relatively high value to low-value copper coins. Transactions involving the exchange of such coins naturally required mutual trust and/or translation costs. Motivation to overcome this problem of currency diversity derived from interest amongst Zollverein member states in a 'fair' distribution of the customs revenues collected at the custom union's borders. Apportionment among the states depended on reaching an agreement on the 'exchange rates' between the different monies.

The required agreements came about in two treaties negotiated and signed in 1837 (Munich Coinage Treaty) and 1838 (Dresden Coinage Treaty). In the former, the states of southern Germany agreed on a standard seignorage charge of 10 per cent of the nominal value of their silver coins – which were to be mutually recognized as legal tender in all states. At the same time, these states accepted the taler area's 'Cologne Standard', which equated 14 talers with 233.85 grams of fine silver. This represented a step toward recognition of the taler standard.[8] The Dresden Treaty generalized the Munich agreement, fixed the taler:gulden exchange rate at 1 taler:1.75 gulden and approved the minting of a common Zollverein coin having a value of 2 taler (and 3.5 gulden), which was to be legal tender in all member states. This coin proved to be impractical (too heavy for wholesale business, too valuable for most retail transactions), but its introduction nevertheless marked the recognition of the taler's leading role in the Zollverein.[9] The same treaty also obligated government mints to exchange small-denomination coins (whose mint value exceeded their value in metal) for gold or silver coins at no cost to the party presenting them in lots of 100 taler or more. This shut the door on the possibility of seignorage profits from small-coin production, and thus represented a further strengthening of the monetary union.

The next step forward in the German monetary union came around 20 years later, in the form of the Treaty of Vienna of 1857, an agreement that underscored Austria's intention to join the Zollverein. The treaty's importance, however, lay more in what it revealed than in what it proscribed. First, it documented the taler's central position in the union. A slight change in metallic content led to parities favouring the taler, one taler being equivalent to 1.5 Austrian gulden and 1.75 south-German gulden. Moreover, the Zollverein-wide legal tender status of the two-taler coins

---

8 A concession that downgraded the Gulden somewhat; see Holtfrerich, 'Monetary Unification'.

9 The 2-Taler Zollverein coin ['Vereinsmünze'] became notorious as the 'Champagne Taler', a title which reflected the standard price of a bottle of champagne – a luxury good with a price far above that of most retail commodities. See once again Holtfrerich, 'Monetary Unification'.

was extended to one-taler coins. Second, the treaty included statements explicitly endorsing adherence to the silver standard and weakening the status of gold coins, this in response to an Austrian initiative.[10] Third, it explicitly forbade the recognition of non-convertible paper money by member states as legal tender. This was, once again, aimed at Austria, a state with a long history of inconvertible paper money.[11] Indeed, within a year, Austria had made paper money convertible. One year later, however, the war in Italy put such pressure on Austrian finances that its brief phase of convertibility had to end. Nevertheless, the Zollverein position on paper money was important not only as a pawn in the Austro-Prussian rivalry but also – and especially – as a sign of the strength of its commitment to a sound currency.

Founding the German Empire and currency reform: the advent of the Goldmark

The final stage of German monetary unification actually began with the Austro-Prussian War of 1866. One obvious consequence was the end to Austrian Zollverein aspirations. From the perspective of monetary union, however, even more important was the formal transfer of power over monetary policy from individual German states to a new central authority, the North German Confederation, founded in 1867. In 1870 supplementary laws formalized the Confederation's control over banknote and government paper-money circulation. With the outbreak of the Franco-Prussian war, this centralization was extended to the member states of southern Germany. Thus, even before the Empire had been founded, a German monetary union was in place. Nevertheless, momentous changes followed the war and foundation of Empire. Following the literature, we see them as three related, but distinct developments: first, the introduction of a new national currency, the mark, in place of the taler and gulden (with 1 mark equivalent to 1/3 taler and 7/12 gulden); second, the transition to the gold standard (with 1,395 marks equivalent to 1 pound of fine gold and 15.5 pounds of fine silver); and, third, the establishment of a national, central bank of issue, the Reichsbank.

The first two of these developments began chronologically with what was initially an emergency measure, the cessation of silver purchases in July 1871, which, in retrospect, marked the end of the silver standard. The new Reich government's first step was the Coin Act of 4 December 1871, which introduced the mark, authorized ten- and 20-mark gold coins, forbade the minting of silver coins by the individual states and provided for the retirement of silver coin from circulation at the expense of the new Reich government. This law was supplemented by a further Act of 9 July 1873, which authorized the minting of five-mark gold coins, and free gold coinage for private account, as well as invalidating silver coins – with the exception of the silver taler and small coins with some silver content. With these measures, Germany

10 Rittmann, *Geldgeschichte*, pp. 728–9.

11 Interestingly, this came one year after Prussia had retired most of its paper money from circulation by a measure that made the bank of issue, the Prussian Bank, absorb these treasury notes as a *quid pro quo* for the extension of its banknote circulation. See Tilly, 'Germany'.

moved to the gold standard.[12] However, one further point remains to be stressed. It concerns the obvious fact that, without the five billion gold francs indemnity imposed upon France, the reforms would have caused tremendous domestic political and financial tensions in Germany. As it was, no interest group had to bear the initial costs.[13]

The Coinage Act of 9 July 1873 also affected banknote and paper-money circulation by, for example, setting the lowest banknote denomination at 100 marks and making provision for the retirement of government paper money. Banknote circulation was, however, regulated mainly by the Bank Act of 14 March 1875. This subjected the circulation of the (33) still existing banks of issue to quantitative limits as well as to stringent gold-reserve requirements. The thrust of the legislation was to induce these banks to surrender their note-issuing privileges. Its positive aspect was the establishment of the organizational basis for the new central bank of issue, the Reichsbank. To a large extent, it was constructed on the model of the largest German bank of issue, the Prussian Bank, whose network and note circulation it absorbed.[14] By 1870 the Prussian Bank's note circulation had already represented about two-thirds of the German total. Over the following years, the Reichsbank's share grew steadily further, and the bank itself augmented its monetary leverage by the building of a dense network of branches and a system of giro payments that spanned the entire country. This was a time, we recall, when banknotes began to rival metal coins as the principal form of money used by the German population.[15] The Reichsbank was no doubt one of the most important institutions, if not the most important, promoting the monetary integration of Germany in the 1876–1914 period.

A slight digression on the nineteenth-century commodity-money standard

In order to appreciate the achievement of German monetary union, it is useful to consider the international monetary context within which it developed, in particular, to comment briefly on the question of the international commodity money standard. Highly significant was Great Britain's role as the world's leading economic and political power. Britain's official adoption of the gold standard in 1816, related to its

---

12 The exceptions mentioned, which remained in force until 1907, have caused some observers to describe the German currency status as based on a 'limping' gold standard. See Rittmann, *Geldgeschichte*, p. 777; Borchardt, 'Währung', pp. 8–9; and Holtfrerich, 'Monetary Unification', pp. 230–1.

13 See M. Flandreau, 'The French Crime of 1873: an essay on the emergence of the international gold standard, 1870–1880', in *Journal of Economic History*, 56, 1996. As Flandreau points out, the French move toward the gold standard was also powerfully affected by the Franco-Prussian war, for it was French unwillingness to buy Germany's discarded silver which led her to suspend free silver coinage.

14 For a while the Prussian state was one of the strongest opponents of the Reichsbank, mainly because of the importance of the Prussian Bank. On this, see Holtfrerich, 'Monetary Unification', pp. 233–4; Rittmann, Geldgeschichte, pp. 797–8; and Borchardt, 'Währung', pp. 10–11.

15 B. Sprenger, *Geldmengenänderungen in Deutschland im Zeitalter der Industrialisierung* (Cologne, 1982), pp. 162–3.

greater need for high-value coins, strengthened the international demand for gold. This followed not only directly from Britain's needs but also from those of its trading partners to make payments there. One might say – and quite a few historians have done so – that therewith an important step toward international adoption of the gold standard had already been taken.[16]

It would be wrong, however, to view the gold standard as an irresistible nineteenth-century force since that would overlook the important international role played by French bimetallism and the silver standard in the 1815–71 period. According to recent research by Flandreau and Oppers, French bimetallism worked fairly well, serving as a buffer between silver-standard countries (like the German states) and gold-standard ones (like Great Britain), probably with stabilizing effects.[17] In a short-run perspective, to be sure, shifts in the gold:silver parity, a reflection of wars, discoveries and other special factors, could create difficulties. In France, the mint price was fixed at the gold:silver parity of 15.5, with the result that shifts in their market prices led to gold and silver movements, at times substantial. During the 1840s, these led to gold movements out of France, but during the 1850s, owing to gold discoveries in California and Australia and to special demand in Asia, silver flowed away. During the 1860s, it was the American Civil War that diverted world demand for cotton to silver-standard countries and that lay behind the outflow of silver. Figure 4.1 shows these short-run effects in relation to the French mint price. Even so, the latter set limits to market-price movements in the abundant metal, and the conclusion that bimetallism did possess a workable price stabilizer holds.[18]

Figure 4.2 adds to the bimetallic story by showing the long-run picture of stability – until the 1870s. It also shows the long-lasting rise in the gold price (or fall in the silver price), which came thereafter, as country after country went over to gold.

It is doubtful, though, whether contemporaries were capable of foreseeing this long-run price development. The tenuous character of monetary arrangements during the period is reflected in the running debate on the gold and silver standards and on bimetallism that especially marked the 1860s. Due to the great economic and political weight of France in Europe, it is not surprising that that country became the centre of the debate. France was already linked to Belgium and Switzerland in a quasi-coinage union and also had close monetary relations with Italy. As the shortage of silver looked like becoming acute (due to the discrepancy between market and mint prices noted in Figure 4.1), these countries revalued their silver coins such that their nominal value exceeded their market value as bullion. A further step was to coordinate these efforts and provide for a common silver coin. That came with the formation of the Latin Monetary Union in 1865 (LMU), a partial monetary union

16 G. Hardach and S. Hartig, 'Der Goldstandard als Argument in der internationalen Währungsdiskussion', *Jahrbuch für Wirtschaftsgeschichte*, 1998; Milward, 'Origins'.

17 Flandreau, 'French Crime'; M. Flandreau and B. Eichengreen, 'The geography of the gold standard', in J. Braga de Macedo, B. Eichengreen and J. Reis (eds), *Currency convertibility. The gold standard and beyond* (London/New York, 1996).

18 For a sophisticated discussion of this stabilizing effect in bimetallism despite the virtual absence of the coins minted from the scarce metal, see S. Oppers, 'Recent Developments in Bimetallic Theory', in J. Reis (ed.), *International Monetary Systems in Historical Perspective* (Houndsmill/London, 1995).

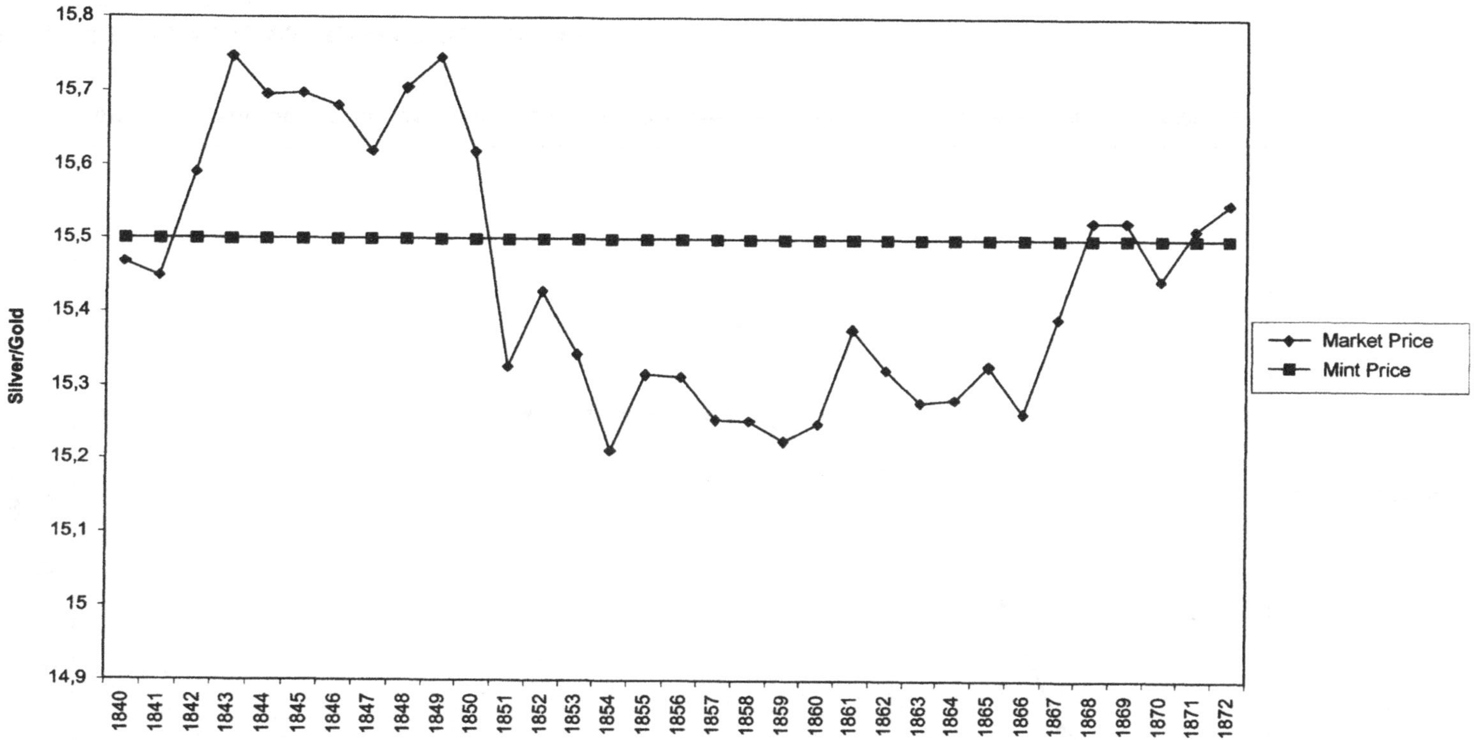

Figure 4.1 Silver–Gold Mint and Market Price in France, 1840–72

Source: J. Schneider and O. Schwarzer (eds.), Statistik der Geld- und Wechselkurse in Deutschland, 1815-1913 (St. Katharinen, 1990) and author's calculations.

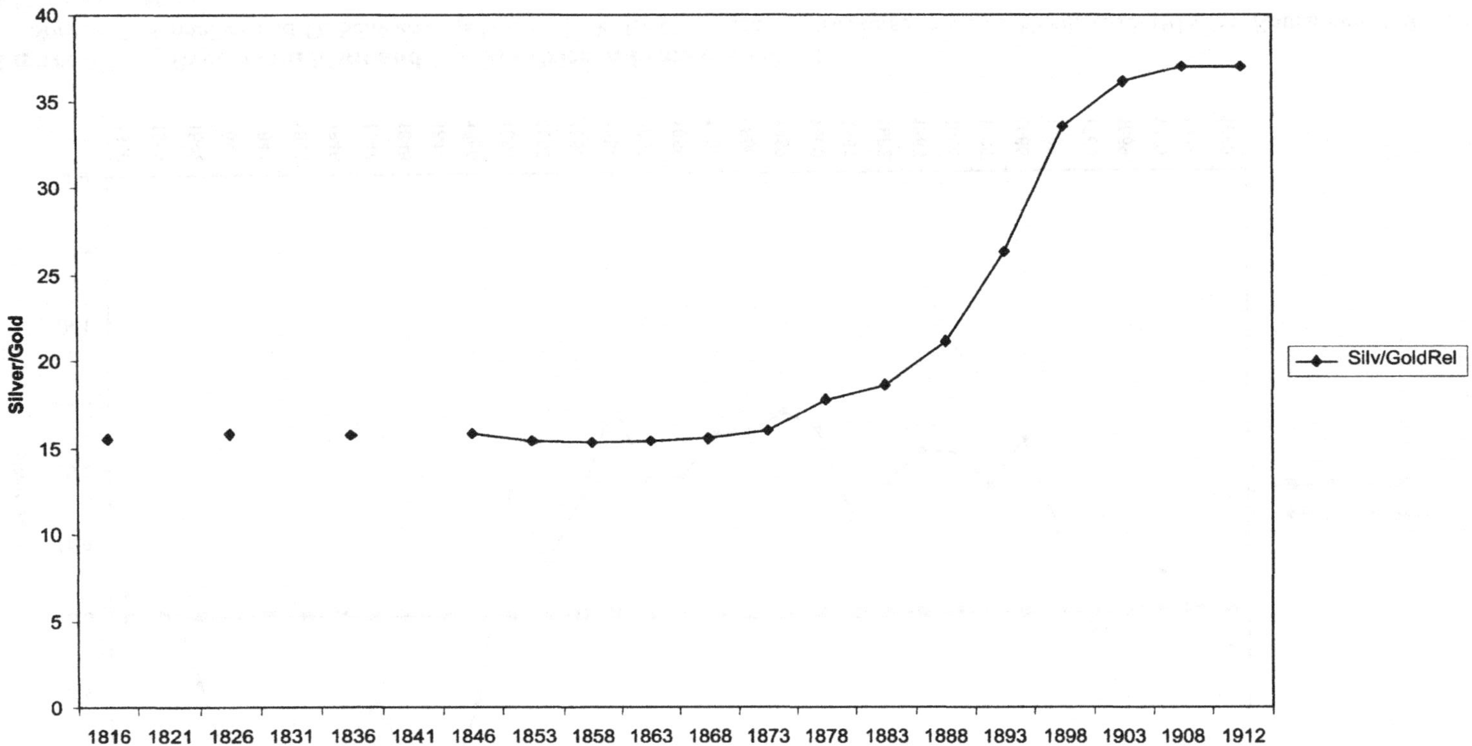

Figure 4.2 Silver–Gold Market Price, 1816–1912
Source: Helfferich, Geld.

(which encouraged the virtually free interchange of silver coins among the member countries). French leaders apparently saw LMU as a step toward a more universal, worldwide union in which one single monetary standard would prevail (preferably, as they thought, based on French bimetallism). In 1867, at an international conference in Paris, this possibility was discussed, but the majority of those present, particularly representatives from Great Britain and the United States, showed a preference for the gold standard. A widening of LMU thus became improbable. Nevertheless, it would be wrong to see LMU *ex ante* as a monetary dead-end. During the 1860s, for example, German interest in joining such a union was strong. It was Franco-Prussian rivalry and the war of 1870–1 that definitively closed the door on French bimetallism and silver as an international monetary standard.

To sum up: the purpose of this 'digression' is to suggest that the degree of instability of those international monetary arrangements which governed the relations between national standards of account was not so great, even at their weakest part – the bimetallic exchange – that huge gains in transaction efficiency necessarily had to follow on from national monetary unions of the nineteenth-century type. The next section pursues this hypothesis further.

Structural change in the money supply and the institutional foundations of monetary unification

So far, the discussion has focused mainly upon the regulation of the coinage. The importance of metal money during the early nineteenth century justifies that emphasis. But it has a price. It neglects structural change in the money supply away from metal money toward bank notes and bank deposit liabilities that also marked the period. Figure 4.3 shows the shift we have in mind.

Oversimplifying somewhat, the discussion of German monetary union has concerned what was rapidly becoming the economy's 'small change'. That is important, not only as an empirical addition to our story but also because it offers a wider interpretative perspective. It is one that has actions of private economic agents as driving forces of structural change – which force governments to adaptive political measures. Considering such structural change helps to appreciate the almost spontaneous, autonomous emergence of an international commodity-money system, driven by market forces that marked the period and which restricted the autonomy of individual states' monetary policies. More specifically, intra-German government competition before 1870 can be seen as not only a disintegrative element but also an opportunity for private economic agents to realize institutional innovations.

Take the development of note-issuing banks as one example. During the second third of the nineteenth century they became objects of public debate in Germany, especially in Prussia. Mercantile interests called for the establishment of a 'modern' system of banks of issue on the English or Scottish model. The official answer in Prussia came in 1846 with the founding of the Bank of Prussia, which was given

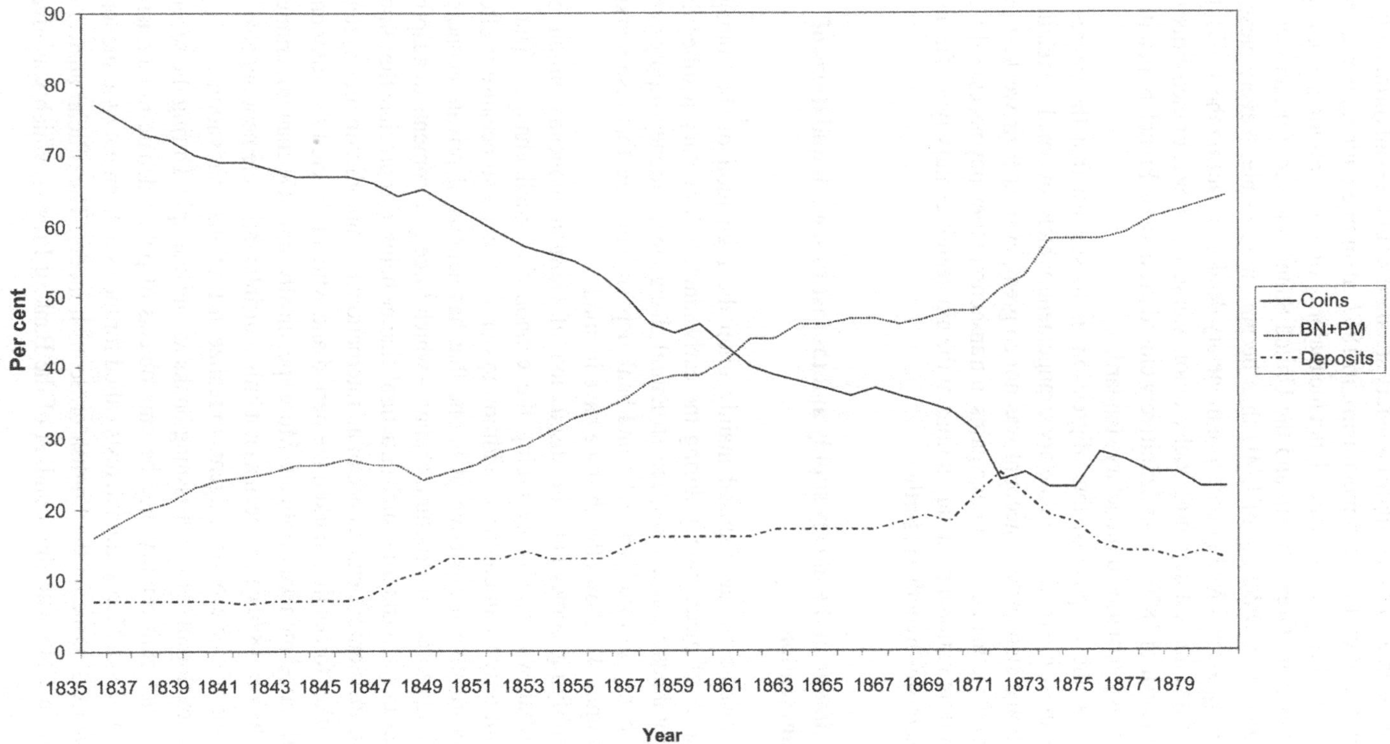

Figure 4.3 Structural Change in the German Money Supply, 1835–1880 (% of estimated total)

Source: Sprenger, Geldmengenänderungen.

a virtual monopoly of note issue.[19] This institution proved inadequate for growing needs, however, and one response was the creation of note-issuing banks in neighbouring states that circulated their notes in Prussia. By the mid-1850s, indeed, their note circulation was equivalent to that of the Prussian Bank.[20] A ban on their circulation in Prussia, enacted in 1856, seemed ineffective and, in that same year, a more appropriate answer was found: the statutory limitation on the Prussian Bank's total note circulation was lifted. Thereafter, the note circulation 'took off'. Indeed, Prussian Bank notes soon became an integral part of the money supply in other German states, as an accompaniment to the spreading use of Prussia's silver taler currency. This development thus represented a step toward unification. Nonetheless, it is important to remember that the initiative behind it came from private mercantile and financial interests, while the role of the state was to react, albeit in a positive manner.[21] It is also important to see this episode as an example in which private, commercial and financial interests could profitably exploit intra-German state competition.

From a purely quantitative view, the greatest shift in the structure of the German money supply derived from the spreading use of bank deposits as money. This was related to the employment of bills of exchange as a means of payment and short-term credit. Recipients of goods and services paid for them with bills, which were essentially orders to pay at some specified future date. Endorsement by the payees of such bills could turn them into means of payment for additional transactions. Merchants with strong credit standings found ready takers for bills bearing their particular endorsement – which amounted to assuming liability for the bills when they fell due – and such bills began to circulate as a kind of money. Over the second third of the nineteenth century a significant number of these merchants thus became 'bankers', whose liabilities had 'money character'. Contemporaries, to be sure, regarded their liabilities as credit instruments that could be temporarily substituted for 'real money', as 'money substitutes' convertible into true money – a status attributable only to coins – quickly and at little cost. Nevertheless, though not money, they were close substitutes for it, and many contemporaries also acknowledged that such instruments in part represented a private economic response to a restrictive government policy with respect to the growth of bank notes and paper money.[22]

19 For the semi-public debate and response in Prussia see R. Tilly, *Financial institutions and industrialization in the Rhineland, 1815–1870* (Madison, 1966), ch. 3; also D. Ziegler, 'Der "latecomer" lernt. Der Peel's Act und die preußische Währungsgesetzgebung im Zeitalter der Industrialisierung', in H. Berghoff und D. Ziegler (eds), *Pionier und Nachzügler. Vergleichende Studien zur Geschichte Großbritanniens und Deutschlands im Zeitalter der Industrialisierung* (Bochum, 1995).

20 Tilly, *Financial institutions*, ch. 3; Sprenger, *Geldmengenänderungen*.

21 Readers are reminded that Prussian entrepreneurs, e.g. Gustav Mevissen and the Oppenheims of Cologne, were involved in this undercutting of official Prussian state policy. See on this J. Hansen, *Gustav von Mevissen. Ein rheinisches Lebensbild*, 2 vols. (Berlin, 1906), vol. 1, pp. 658–9; Tilly, *Financial institutions*, pp. 42–3.

22 Two points are worth remembering: (1) not even banknotes were legal tender in Germany before the twentieth century; and (2) contemporaries speculated about the relationship between the supply of metal money and government-controlled paper money and

The use of bills drawn on banks as money naturally reflected the needs of trade. With each widening of the sphere of commerce, the circle of users and producers of such 'money' also widened. This was true of both interregional German and international trade. It is not unlikely, therefore, that agreements, such as that at Leipzig in 1847, which provided for common German-wide practices regarding bills of exchange, were just as important for German monetary integration as the coinage treaties already discussed.[23] Or just as unimportant, as it needs to be borne in mind that, for the larger transactions, virtually the same rules applied to interregional trade as to international trade. This once again raises the question of the extent to which inter-German agreements could create improvements in monetary integration that the needs of international trade would not have generated anyway. This question deserves a closer look.

The idea we have in mind can be quantified, if only crudely and incompletely. Figure 4.4 depicts two of Germany's important (bill) exchange rates – the taler: sterling (in Berlin) – and the key interregional taler:gulden rate (in Frankfurt-am-Main). Using rates of change of the annual averages, we note at once the greater instability of international exchange rates. This is particularly true at the beginning of the period, marked by the transition from wartime conditions to peacetime ones, while improvement (in the sense of declining rates of change) characterized both internal and international rates. This does not suggest the uniquely positive role of Germany's internal monetary unification.

One way to pursue this question somewhat further is to compare explicitly the movements of the rates in the periods preceding, and following, the coinage treaties of the late 1830s. Table 4.1 offers such a comparison, based on the coefficient of variation for yearly changes in the 1815–40 and 1842–60 periods (and using the same data as in Figure 4.2).

banknotes, on the one hand, and the circulation of these 'money substitutes', on the other. See Tilly, *Financial institutions*, chs. 3 and 4.

23 See the article 'Wechsel' in Handwörterbuch der Staatswissenschaften (Jena, 3d ed., 1911), p. 655.

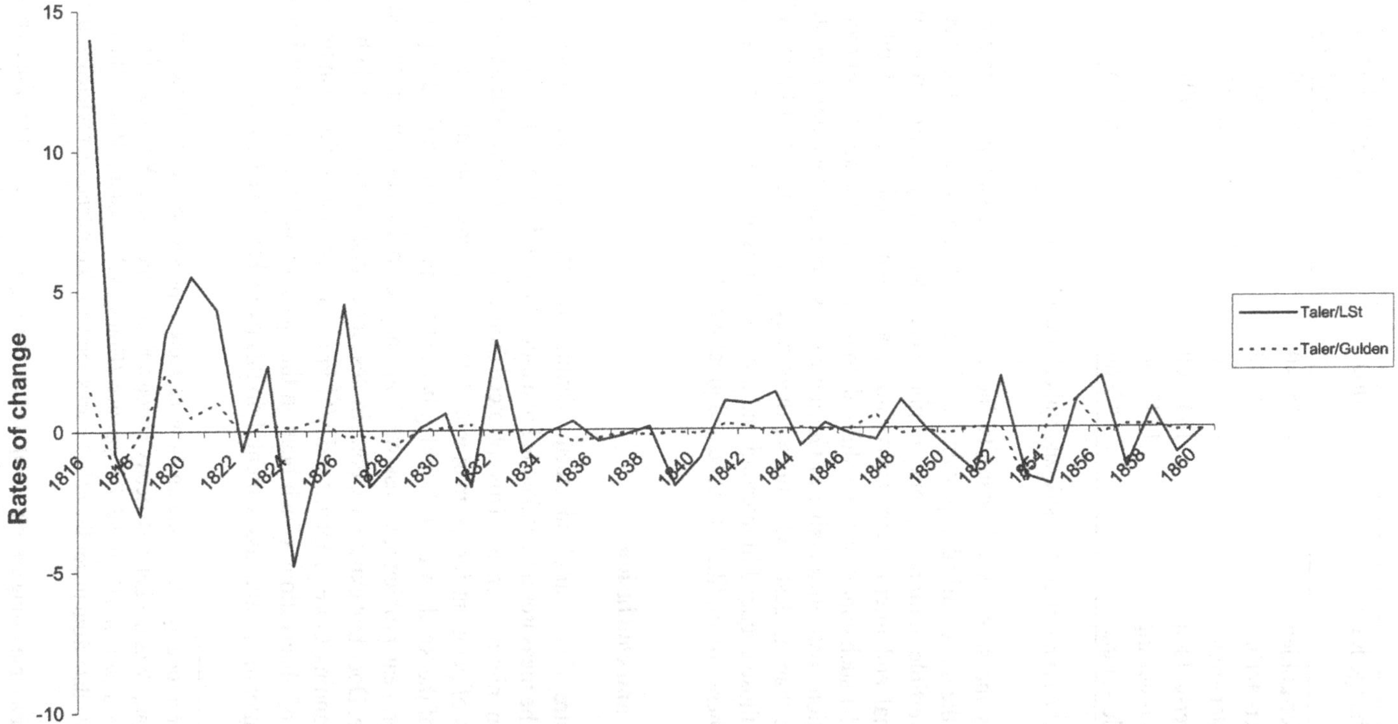

Figure 4.4 German Interregional and International Exchange Rates, 1815–1860 (Annual Rates of Change)

Source: Schneider et al., Statistik, and author's calculations.

Table 4.1 German Interregional and International Exchange Rates, 1815–60 (Coefficient of Variation on Annual Changes in Two Periods)

Exchange Rate	Period	Coefficient of Variation (σ/μ)
taler-gulden	1815–40	0.010
taler-sterling	1815–40	0.046
taler-franc	1815–40	0.017
taler-gulden	1842–60	0.004
taler-sterling	1842–60	0.017
taler-Franc	1842–60	0.005

Source: Schneider et al., Statistik, and author's calculations.

On this measure, overall stability increased but international exchange rates registered the most marked improvement. The collective and cumulative experience with convertible currencies, one might conclude, strengthened trust in both interregional and international transactions, and generated greater stability as a result. Under such conditions, it is difficult to imagine that the additional reductions in transaction costs attributable to Germany's nascent monetary union could have been more than modest.[24] Of course, there may have been redistribution effects, favouring those engaged in interregional trade and most dependent on payments in coin, but these are not likely to have had great weight.

Summary and conclusions

At the centre of Germany's nineteenth-century monetary unification stood coinage reforms. The measures undertaken led to a much higher degree of standardization of the metal monies most in use. This enhanced their roles as a general standard of value and means of payment for German interstate transactions – all this well before the founding of the Reich in 1871. Looking back at this process from the perspective of current European problems, we ask what one may learn from that nineteenth-century experience. Does that experience contain 'lessons of history' which might be helpful in understanding those problems today?[25] Previous sections of this chapter contain a number of observations which bear on this question but it may, nevertheless, be useful to attempt a direct assessment. I do this by making five points.

24 For a roughly similar argument using more sophisticated econometric methods see M. Flandreau, 'Was the Latin Monetary Union a Franc zone?', in J. Reis (ed.), *International Monetary Systems in Historical Perspective* (Houndsmill/London, 1995). He draws on discount-rate data from major financial centres showing dependence not related to monetary union.

25 For an interesting assessment almost ten years ago, on the eve of the Euro's birth, see Theurl, Währung; T. Theurl, 'Erfolgsbedingungen für monetäre Union souverän bleibender Staaten: die Beispiele des 19. Jahrhunderts', in A. Mosser (ed.), *Österreichs Weg zum Euro. Aspekte-Perspektiven-Handlungsspielräume* (Vienna, 1998).

First, in the 1815–71 period, we can observe a remarkably comprehensive unification of the German coinage systems, a result that reflected the willingness of the individual German states to surrender an important part of their monetary sovereignty. The incentive to do so lay largely in the financial gains those states derived from membership of the German customs union, the Zollverein. These were substantial, far more important than the net revenues of seignorage that they sacrificed.[26] For current euro members and potential members, in contrast, expected fiscal gains do not seem to play an analogous role.

Second, the degree of monetary integration attained before 1871 depended strongly on the political and economic preponderance of the Kingdom of Prussia. With around 60 per cent of the total German population and national income, Prussia's relative weight in the Zollverein was incomparably greater than that of the EU's largest current member, Germany. Such a preponderance was doubtless a factor which eased monetary union during the nineteenth century because there will have existed economies of scale in the use of a common money, and because a hegemonic power, like Prussia, will have more readily assumed the start-up costs of unification than would have any of the other, smaller German states. Europe at the beginning of the twenty-first century apparently possesses considerable adhesive force but it is far from clear on what this is based. Perhaps it has to do with the high perceived costs of exiting from EU agreements. In any case, it more than compensates for the missing hegemonic power.[27]

Third, however, Prussia's subsequent hegemony in Germany was not predictable as of 1815, at the period's opening. Austria will have appeared to most contemporaries as a greater power than Prussia. And in this period, indeed, many of Prussia's commercial and monetary policy initiatives can be seen as reactions to Austrian preponderance, that is, as a reflection of the missing hegemony. The incentive for Prussia to bear the costs of commercial and monetary unification, mentioned above, doubtless lay in a hoped-for increase in political power. Eventually, as is well known, Austria made several concerted efforts to join the Zollverein but they failed, mainly because of Austria's unwillingness (or inability) to meet the 'stability criteria' of the German union, above all to restore the convertibility of its paper money.[28] That the German states chose to adhere to those 'stability criteria', however, had less to do with German politics than with the wider, international historical context. In any case, no analogous rivalry seems to have been at work in recent and current EU experience.

---

26 There may have been economies of scale realizable through coinage reforms that covered a larger territory than most of the individual German states represented, similar to those related to the collection of customs revenues. On this, see Holtfrerich, 'Monetary Unification', pp. 221–2; Rittmann, *Geldgeschichte*, p. 547.

27 Recent European monetary history is full of references to the hegemony of the German Bundesbank in the field of monetary policy; but that is far from equivalent to Prussia's nineteenth-century political weight in Germany.

28 It may be added here that the Zollverein maintained relatively low tariffs, much lower than those protecting Austrian industry, so Austrian failure to meet Zollverein standards went beyond monetary rules.

Fourth, for two reasons, German monetary unification in the nineteenth century did not represent a significant loss of policy autonomy for individual member states. One reason is that monetary policy in the Germany of the Zollverein era did not have anywhere near the weight that it has had in twentieth-century Europe, partly owing to the incomplete monetization of economic relationships in the earlier period. The other reason is that the nearly universal acceptance of a commodity-money standard in the nineteenth-century world strongly curtailed the potential autonomy of national monetary policies. To put it differently: even without joining the monetary union, individual German states would doubtless have adhered to the system of currency convertibility and fixed exchange rates which prevailed. This seems to be a sharp contrast to the situation at the beginning of twenty-first century, in which national states, bent on joining a larger monetary union, have to pay the price of sacrificing flexible exchange rates as an instrument of economic policy. This difference may be related to the weakness of nineteenth-century German democracy and the, then low, political weight of protectionist domestic economic interests. Nevertheless, a weak analogy is identifiable, namely in the sense that small states at the beginning of the twenty-first century, which stay outside of monetary unions, still face international pressures in the form of capital flows (and economic globalization) which sharply limit their policy autonomy.

Fifth, and last, it must be remembered that Germany's nineteenth-century monetary unification only entered its final stage after two wars had ensured the country's political unification. This experience naturally fits poorly into the European context of the twenty-first century, focused as it is on a monetary union of states whose willingness to surrender individual political sovereignty is still quite limited.

CHAPTER 5

The Latin Monetary Union Revisited Once Again

Marcello de Cecco

Introduction: the *ancien-régime* monetary system

Scholars in the past were persuaded that money was one, perhaps the most important, of the instruments of distributive justice, designed and used by the state to achieve and maintain political equilibrium. Distributive justice, according to Aristotle, was inherently geometrical through being concerned with the relative positions of men in society. It followed that monetary theory, and policy, should be directed to maintaining these relative positions in a state of long-term socio-political equilibrium.

Most of these developments, of course, took place outside the space of the market. The invention of money was consequently due to the need to have a stable unit of account, to reckon what peoples' respective relative places in society were – what was due to each according to relative justice. But money was also an instrument of exchange between people belonging to different *gentes* and, therefore, to different political societies. Exchange between people of different *gentes*, strangers to one another, would often take place in the market space. Here, money would be used not at its face value, as it would be in dealings between citizens of the same state, but rather at its intrinsic value, according to the weight and fineness of the metals contained in the coins. In this way, money ceased to be an expression of sovereignty – a creature of the law – since it was used to regulate exchange between people subject to different units of sovereignty. No longer *pretium*, it would become *merx*. It was thus an instrument of simple commutative justice, in which calculations could be made arithmetically without having to consider the relative position in any society of the individuals taking part in exchange, because they did not belong to the same societal equilibrium but to different societies and states.

The same line of reasoning accounted for merchants being subject to the *lex mercatoria* and citizens to the *jus civile*. The *lex mercatoria* was established by merchants themselves and dealt with transactions between merchants. They were supposed to follow the principles of mercantile behaviour, concerned with profit maximization and devoid of any respect for the position of men in society. Market prices were considered, by definition, to be the only ones relevant in transactions, and the money so employed in their transactions was not the expression of sovereignty but solely measured by its weight and fineness, thus respecting the principles of metallism.

The formation of an international agricultural raw-materials market in Europe between the eighteenth and the nineteenth centuries dramatically reduced the interest of the landed classes. They had been the traditional wielders of power in European societies since the decline of the Italian and Hanse mercantile city-states. Money had functioned according to the principles of distributive justice, that is, was capable of maintaining domestic relative prices, denominated in imaginary money, at levels such as to assure the permanence of *ancien-régime* societies based on status. When the landed classes became exporters of agricultural products they lost interest in the *ancien-régime* monetary system in which relative prices had been expressed and fixed in imaginary money (units of account). Rents were paid in gold coin that was never debased by the sovereign, whereas wages were expressed in silver or copper coins, or in divisionary coins of even lesser intrinsic value, which could be tampered with by the sovereign for fiscal purposes (and frequently were). The distributive justice inherent in such a regime came through appropriate domestic policies that had no reliance upon market prices to assure society's different orders the income by which each could maintain their relative status.

Agricultural exports sold at prices established on the international market resulted in the great nobles losing their vested interest in maintaining the *ancien-régime* monetary system. If they had revenues in gold (other than their tithes), they acquired an interest in the price of gold rising in terms of silver, copper, and other token money. They were won over to the market system and to a monetary system where the relative prices of coins were fixed by the markets. While the aristocracy's social status depended upon the operation of distributive justice (through the stability of a monetary system based on imaginary money, because all costs and revenues had domestic origins), they adhered to the traditional monetary system based on imaginary money. But when nobles began to receive gold for their exports, they began to have an interest in the devaluation of all coins except gold ones and in prices fixed in actual markets.

The *ancien-régime* monetary system can be considered as one in which money was more important as a unit of account than as a performer of the other functions that monetary theory traditionally attributes to it. What was called the imaginary-money system was actually a system of long-term price fixing, in which spot markets had only a residual importance for pricing goods and services. Long-term prices were used to maintain the different orders of society in their traditional relative places. But such a long-term equilibrium of relative prices had not come about automatically. *Ancien-régime* monetary policy had at its core the need to raise, or lower, the value of actual coins relative to those of the unit of account (imaginary money), with the purpose of maintaining unchanging social relativities. Individuals or institutions, depending on their positions in society, had a wage or tithes or taxes (if the government) fixed in the unit of account – the imaginary money – but these incomes and revenues were actually paid in something else – real coin. The 'good sovereign' organized variations in actual coinage which followed movements in exogenous variables but which, nonetheless, disturbed the relative values expressed in imaginary money as little as possible or at least as gradually as possible. Thus, the sovereign made himself the operator of a distributive justice among his subjects. This could meet even the harsher realities of changes brought about by pure commutative justice operating outside his state's borders, and which also applied in transactions between the state's subjects and foreigners.

Of course, this difference, between a monetary system and a monetary policy moved by the need to administer distributive justice on the one hand and the outside realities represented by the values expressed by the metallic content of coins in foreign trade on the other, could only be sustained while the world of commutative justice remained beyond that where distributive justice was administered. This was possible when a country's economic relations with the wider world were minimal. As market relations applied to economic transactions with the outside world, the *ancien-régime* monetary system was disrupted when foreign trade had an increasing effect upon the course of domestic trade – with spot prices obtaining in real markets and paid in coins valued by their metallic content.

The ascent of metallism

It is not without reason that the *ancien-régime* monetary system remained in force while there was a general dearth of monetary metals. As long as this persisted, a monetary system divorced from the metallic content of coins had a reason to exist and remain in existence. After the deluge of specie from America, it became increasingly harder to maintain a system based upon relativities that were far removed from those established between metals in actual markets. Conventionally fixed values respecting relative social status had to yield to those established by the market. Imaginary money lost its rationale when there was an abundance of metallic money. Money's unit-of-account function could now be performed in real markets by real coins, valued at their intrinsic value. It is no accident that a silver standard, as a metallic standard, came first, followed by the gold standard, which continued as long as the South African gold bonanza lasted. Obviously, with the supply from America, there was sufficient silver to make it cheap enough to be used as real currency. There was, later and for a shorter time, enough gold for it to be cheap enough to serve as the basis of real monetary systems in several countries.

The interesting period to examine is that which lies between the gold discoveries of California and those of South Africa. This was the age of the 'Great Boom', which coincided in Europe with the building of railways, first in Britain and then on the continent. It was also the period when the doctrine of free trade spread from Britain to France, and when a surge of trade accompanied the philosophy of internationalization and universalism. An age of depression followed this growth phase in the 1870s, 1880s and early 1890s. It has been maintained that there was a depression of prices, not of output, during the late nineteenth century, and a depression of gold prices in gold-standard countries. Silver-using countries experienced much less steeply falling prices. However, as long as there was sufficient silver to go around and the banking system had not reached the level of development it was to attain by the eve of First World War, the problem of the unit of account did not seem to reappear, since the printing press had not come into fashion again as a quick system to create enough actual means of exchange. This is the period when the Latin Monetary Union (LMU) was created, operated and then went into long-term hibernation (although it was not officially abandoned until 1927).

In the light of the previous discussion, this period can be seen as a bridge between two ages. Great Britain, because of the early prevalence of her mercantile spirit, was won over to metallism as early as the eighteenth century. The gold standard was introduced into Britain in 1717, absentmindedly and almost by default, with the fixing of sterling's parity in terms of gold by Isaac Newton, Master of the Mint. Subsequent economic and political events unfolded in ways that allowed Britain to retain the monetary system which was to be called the gold standard uninterruptedly until 1914, and then from 1925 to 1931 – making it an example that the whole developed world would follow during the two decades between 1895 and 1914. However, it can be put forward that in the rest of Europe, and in the United States, the *ancien-régime* monetary system, whose main features have been sketched above, was not completely repealed until the 1890s.

LMU was an attempt to execute an internationally agreed solution for the monetary problems created by the general transformation of the system of distributive justice into one of commutative justice. It tried to combine the virtues of the *ancien-régime* system with those of metallism by devising what was called international bimetallism. This was a system whereby a group of countries agreed to maintain a fixed parity between gold and silver, while Great Britain had, during the nineteenth century, resolutely moved to depose silver as one of the metals upon which its monetary system was based.

Before proceeding to narrating LMU's mostly unfortunate vicissitudes, some attention must be paid to some other important features of the monetary systems that prevailed in continental Europe until 1914. Nineteenth-century money supplies, although experiencing the gradual encroachment of bank notes and bank deposits, continued to be dominated by metallic currency. The latter consisted essentially of coins, composed of gold, or silver or copper, though not in pure form but rather alloys of various purities, introduced to reduce the wear and tear of handling. The introduction of base metals into the alloy not only increased coins' durability but also came about as a result of the state's desire to exercise its fiscal powers over the currency through a variable seignorage.

In Europe, the precious metals used for minting were obtained from the public, who brought metal bars to be coined according to their own needs and convenience. The mint par – the number of coins of a certain value that the mint would give when it received a certain weight of metal – was thus an essential part, an instrument, of the state's control of the money supply. Its ratio to the market prices of the precious metals was the critical variable that determined a country's money supply at any point of time, because it induced the public to retain these metals as minted coins, or else discouraged them from doing so.

The other critical variable in this decision-making process (in which the public was the ultimate holder of monetary sovereignty because it decided how much pure metal to bring to the mint for coinage) was the free-market price of gold in terms of silver. If, for instance, a new silver mine, or a more efficient method of refining silver, were discovered, then the market price of silver in terms of gold would fall. If, in these circumstances, a country kept a fixed gold:silver mint parity, it would experience a decline in its gold coinage through people selling its gold coins abroad for the higher price they could fetch in silver compared to the country's fixed gold:silver mint parity. If gold coins and silver coins were perfect substitutes for one another, this would have meant little. But they were not. There were two not particularly mutually permeable payments systems in each country: one where silver, the other where gold, coins predominated, to which a third was usually added – where divisionary coins were used. Wages, for instance, were generally paid out in silver and divisionary coins, and these were generally also used for purchasing food and other retail transactions. High-value goods, like houses and land, were bought in gold, also used for obtaining most foreign-trade goods when direct barter was not employed. The overall monetary system was thus similar to that of contemporary weak-currency countries, where 'strong' foreign currencies are used in large transactions, while wage payments and retail purchases take place in the local currency.

By the mid nineteenth century, most European countries had left the *ancien-régime* monetary system and joined the metallist one, where imaginary money no longer played a role. However, in many continental countries the state played a residual role in the administration of distributive justice through maintaining a fixed mint price between gold and silver. It was a way of controlling relative prices, because different goods and services were bought by offering different metal – silver or gold – coins in payment. However, in Britain, the state had declined to have anything more to do with distributive justice from as early as the early eighteenth century. Rather, it had decided merely to fix the mint price of gold while leaving the price of silver to market forces. Other countries in Europe, like Austria-Hungary and the Kingdom of the Two Sicilies, also abandoned involvement in distributive justice, but decided to fix the mint price of silver rather than of gold.

The second half of the nineteenth century, the period when the LMU was born, briefly flowered and then went into early hibernation, was also marked by another important phenomenon: the rise and rapid growth of fractional-reserve banking in two forms, deposit banking and note-issuing banking. The new credit institutions spread to the rest of Europe from Great Britain, where modern banking had begun to flourish during the early years of the nineteenth century. In some cases, banks in continental Europe underwent an important transformation. They started forming organic links with large-scale industry, and thus began to be able to create money in the form of deposits or bank-notes. In this new transformation, Great Britain was not in the lead; rather Belgium, France and Germany were in the van. As a result, the phenomenon of money creation through fractional-reserve banking was studied earlier in these countries than in Britain (if we overlook McLeod's isolated and frowned-upon studies).

The French Alternative

Until late in the nineteenth century, the British model was not the only one available to be imitated in the monetary organization of states. At least as popular were French monetary institutions. The French monetary system was the product of the French Revolution and Napoleon's Empire.

France had had a bimetallic system during the eighteenth century, but the gold: silver mint par was frequently changed. It was only fixed at 1:15.5 in 1785 by Calonne, the Finance Minister. With the revolutionary law of Germinal XI (1803), France chose silver as the standard for its currency but also confirmed Calonne's decision about the gold:silver mint par. Nonetheless, the *Comité de Monnoies* had acknowledged in 1790 that the mint par should be occasionally changed. It recognized John Locke's early and well known strictures about the impossibility of effectively maintaining a bimetallic currency system if the mint par differed from market prices for any appreciable length of time. In this situation, the system would soon become monometallic because of speculation. The French government, when maintaining the mint par at 1:15.5 in 1790, tried to induce the population to return silver and gold coins to effective use. This would place France, so to say, midway between the countries that had a mainly gold circulation, like Britain and Holland, and those that pre-eminently had silver, like Spain and Portugal, in order to prevent the migration of full-weight coins to neighbouring countries.

Napoleonic Europe followed France in the choice of monetary system, with its states adopting many of the institutions created by the French Revolution. The metric system is a case in point, because its monetary interface was the decimal system, a truly revolutionary innovation that Britain did not introduce until the 1970s. In the case of Italy, after the unravelling of Napoleon's empire, it is interesting to note that Piedmont retained its monetary system, while the Kingdom of the Two Sicilies, which had also been swamped by French troops and whose dynasty had been temporarily replaced by Joachim Murat, decided to go on to a silver standard. Other Italian states either kept the French system or adopted silver as their standard.

On either side of the English Channel, differing solutions were found to the problems posed by the aftermath of the Napoleonic Wars. Britain definitely decided to cut itself loose from tradition, and after a brief experience with paper money, in 1819 went back without hesitation to gold at the old parity. What superficially looks like a solution in favour of fixed exchange rates at the time really, as commented above, meant the free floating of silver. The English Mint freely coined gold sovereigns at a fixed mint par, giving anyone bringing a given weight of fine gold a fixed number of gold coins. The French state decided, on the contrary, to flout Locke's law, and managed, with the help of a large number of *ad hoc* measures, to do so until 1914. Although it is dangerous to give too much weight to the influence of theory upon practical policies, the French monetary stance was undoubtedly based on what came later to be known as the 'Staatliche Theorie des Geldes' from the title of G.F. Knapp's famous book. Throughout the nineteenth century the French authorities were able to maintain that the value of money was determined by the laws of the state rather than those of the market.

Bimetallists also had in mind the practical monetary experience of their century, which witnessed two great gold discoveries – California in 1849–51 and South Africa in 1888, two parts of the world where British influence was large – and one large silver discovery in the United States, its particular effects augmented by a dramatic innovation in silver production. As a result of these supply shocks, the market prices of the two metals gyrated wildly for a substantial part of the nineteenth century. Defenders of bimetallism maintained that a country which sustained a fixed mint par would be insulated from the inflationary and deflationary waves generated by the violent changes in the gold:silver market parity ensuing on each of the new metal discoveries, which never coincided for both metals.

As will be shown, the management, and often the mismanagement, of the Italian currency system was among LMU's central problems. Therefore, it is important to comment, at least in outline, on the monetary system that unified Italy chose in 1862. The law of monetary unification extended the Piedmontese system, basically the French one, to the whole kingdom. However, the Report of the Monetary Commission, which introduced the law, stated that it would have been preferable to adopt gold monometallism, following Britain and because the Commission thought that this was the 'system of the future'. The commissioners also showed their awareness of Locke's Law. However, Italy had close commercial links with France and other bimetallic countries. Furthermore, the main monetary problem during the 1850s and at Italian unification was an excess supply of gold, which resulted in the Italian states losing their silver coins to other countries. To overcome this problem, the Commission suggested the minting of divisionary coins with a low silver content, in the hope that speculators might not be interested in exporting them. This would prove, in the context of LMU, an extremely important decision, as will be shown below. In any case, an existing law (Legge Cordova) had imposed a gold circulation (in addition to silver) upon the new kingdom's southern provinces. There a silver standard had been re-established at the end of the Napoleonic hegemony, in order to decrease the demand for scarce silver, and to support the penetration of the new provinces by the Piedmontese Banca Nazionale nel Regno, which thereby became the main bank of issue for the new kingdom.

The division of the international monetary system into two main areas – one where gold monometallism ruled, the other where bimetallism prevailed – persisted until the whole developed world briefly converged towards gold monometallism as a result of the momentous gold discoveries in the Transvaal. It is possible to maintain, as many contemporary observers did and has recently become fashionable again to do (witness a very powerful essay by Milton Friedman), that this global division was while it lasted a source of stability for the whole international monetary system. Furthermore, the whole system's adoption of the gold standard introduced marked instability, which became more and more apparent during the first 15 years of the twentieth century.

The Latin Monetary Union

It is of some interest to note that the Paris Conference, which assembled in November 1865 to discuss the possibility of European monetary union and concluded with the treaty establishing LMU, was called at the insistence of Belgium. The Brussels government sought to remedy the problems posed by the rise in the (gold) price of silver for silver-using countries. During the first half of the nineteenth century, as a result of the expansion of French influence within Europe, first by Napoleon's conquests and thereafter through commercial and institutional links, most of the currency systems of continental Europe reached a high degree of homogeneity. This produced a substantial inter-circulation of coins. However, during the 20 years following the gold discoveries in California this *de facto* monetary integration underwent a substantial crisis. All the countries that had adopted French-style bimetallism experienced an outflow of silver coins, which were replaced by cheaper gold coins. These processes disturbed such countries' socio-economic forces, although silver's replacement by gold was, in fact, a very imperfect sort of substitution. Most everyday transactions were conducted in silver and divisionary coins, because the use of cheques was virtually unknown amongst the largest parts of their populations, who were, equally, not involved in foreign-trade transactions.

The countries represented at the November 1865 conference tried to find a common solution to these problems. Each had previously attempted national solutions by (except in the case of Belgium) reducing the intrinsic content of their silver coins, moving away from the 900/1000 fineness. However, these had not been homogeneous. The various titres chosen by each for their respective silver coins favoured speculation, and reduced the possibility that national coins would legitimately circulate in the rest of continental Europe. The *de facto* commercial and financial integration that the continent had enjoyed since Napoleon seemed to be in danger. An obvious solution would have been to adopt the gold standard, as Britain and Portugal had done.

A recent book by Luca Einaudi,[1] which will remain the modern reference work on LMU for some time, elegantly resolves the role played by de Parieu, a French lawyer, parliamentarian and high functionary.[2] During the debate that took place before, and after, LMU's inauguration, he was the main apostle for European monetary integration based on the gold standard. In his approach, the silver franc was to be reduced to the status of a divisionary coin – to be minted in coins of low silver percentage, according to contingent inter-European agreements. De Parieu was a very influential member of the French ruling élite. However, he seemed ready to forget that France, over the previous half century, had minted silver coins to a value almost three times higher than that for gold coins. He also seemed prepared to ignore the point that, since its creation by Napoleon, the Banque de France had enjoyed the privilege, when redeeming its liabilities, of choosing freely between gold and silver to honour their convertibility. This meant that the Banque had frequently elected to convert its notes to silver, which was heavy and, consequently, difficult to handle and transport. Silver constituted a very imperfect substitute for high-denomination banknotes, still the majority among those issued by the Banque de France, while gold, with its much higher value, was a much better substitute for notes. Thus, the Banque enjoyed a substantial reduction of its convertibility obligations. Its statutes gave it the chance of running a veiled form of *cours forcé* for its banknotes.

---

1 L. Einaudi, *Money and Politics: European Monetary Union and the Gold Standard, 1865–73* (Oxford, 2001).

2 F.E. De Parieu, 'De l'uniformité monétaire', *Journal des économistes*, 3rd ser., 6 (June 1867), pp. 321–56.

It is fascinating to read in Einaudi's book – which deals extensively with British attitudes towards, and reactions to, continental proposals of monetary unification and, later, the LMU – the responses made by British opponents of bimetallism to the claims advanced by its defenders. All point in the direction of the much higher stage of modernization reached by the British financial and monetary system. Clearly, there seemed to be no need to retain silver in circulation in Britain. The Bank of England was certainly not blind to the advantages enjoyed by the Banque de France as far as convertibility of its notes was concerned, hence the soft spot for bimetallism shown by some of its directors at times of distress. But few believed that parliament would replicate those privileges, especially in view of the rising power of other joint-stock banks. And, in any case, many observers were eager to point out that an inter-circulation agreement – the essence of the LMU – meant little to a country like Britain, whose foreign trade had already passed the stage of settlement made in coins, either gold or silver. British trade was worked through bills of exchange since the country was an island, and thus practically closed to the small trade of the 'frontalier' sort popular in continental Europe and the equivalent to 'small-time arbitrage' between national coins.

The 1865 conference, as Einaudi has skilfully reconstructed, commenced with a strong inclination amongst its delegates towards gold monometallism as the basis for European monetary integration. Yet, it ended with a formal agreement maintaining bimetallism at the 1:15.5 mint par. On 23 December 1865, four of the countries that had taken part – France, Italy, Belgium and Switzerland – signed an international treaty, a monetary convention, establishing a monetary union among themselves. Another Napoleon was Emperor of France, and he was intent upon another phase of French expansion within Europe. Whatever the theoretical and ideological considerations we may be inclined to put forward, there is no possibility of avoiding the feeling that LMU was a creature of French hegemony.

Italy had just been united by the crucial intervention of French troops in the war against Austria to liberate Lombardy and the Veneto from Habsburg domination and annex it to Piedmont. A very large part of Italian trade was conducted with France. Furthermore, French banks, of the new type invented in Belgium by Société Générale during the 1830s and copied by the Pereire brothers in France in the 1850s, were founding their subsidiaries in Italy. Their managements were helping to finance the development of badly needed modern infrastructures, especially railways. More generally, French capital was aiding the country's modernization.

In the cases of Belgium and Switzerland, their monetary problems, as small countries with large neighbours, were, as already noted for Belgium, the pervasive difficulties of retaining their respective national coins within their own borders, especially at times of gold or silver supply shocks. A homogeneous standard for divisionary coins with neighbouring countries was thus their main preoccupation in joining a monetary union. And the treaty's main outcome amounted to a homogeneous standard for divisionary coins.

The signatory states agreed to limit the maximum issues of divisionary currency to a total of six francs per inhabitant as far as silver coins were concerned, and to fix the titre of coined silver at 835. Divisionary currency could only be coined by the member states, while free coinage by the public at the mints remained for full-bodied gold and silver coins. Gold and silver full-bodied coins struck by the four states' mints, which had, as far as silver was concerned, a fineness of 900/1000, were to be freely accepted at the member states' respective public treasuries without any limit. Divisionary coins issued by any of the signatories were to be freely accepted by all member states as payment for obligations incurred by citizens of any of the other states up to a maximum of 100 francs per transaction. Private citizens were obliged to accept divisionary coins in payment for obligations incurred by citizens of other member states up to a maximum of 50 francs per transaction. Each state was required to exchange its own divisionary coins, presented by other member states, into gold and silver full-bodied currency. This particular obligation was to continue two years beyond the convention's expiration.

The convention initially had a life of 15 years, renewable thereafter every 15 years. As it happened, it was periodically renewed until 1927. It was open to any other state prepared to accept its rules. Greece joined in 1868, while Spain accepted the LMU monetary system but not the inter-circulation of divisionary coins. The convention was also adopted by Romania in 1867 and, subsequently, by Venezuela, Colombia and Chile, equally without agreeing to the inter-circulation rules. Austria-Hungary had displayed a strong interest in joining, but the arising negotiations were interrupted by the Franco-Prussian war of 1870–1 and never resumed. For the first six years of its life, LMU could be said to have had a measure of success even though its two largest member countries, Italy and France, declared *cours forcés* in 1866 and 1870 respectively, after wars against Austria and Prussia.

The LMU and its problems

Italian fiscal imbalance

Italian inconvertibility in 1866 and its aftermath did, in fact, give rise to one of the main problems in the path of LMU. The new Italian state was born without a solid fiscal base, and government expenditures during the 1860s were almost twice as much as fiscal revenues.

It is not an exaggeration to say that the ambitious kingdom was almost bankrupt when its efforts were rewarded through its sovereignty being extended to the whole of Italy. Piedmontese citizens had become accustomed to relatively high taxation to finance modern infrastructures and equip a large army. Furthermore, Piedmont had incurred a high public debt in furthering its expansionary policies. However, other Italian states had been controlled by extremely conservative dynasties that spent little and taxed even less. The Habsburg Empire had taxed its Italian provinces a little more but it had also built a much better infrastructure on its territory.

The Kingdom of the South had been the most careful of the states that formed united Italy. When Garibaldi conquered it for the King of Savoy it had a full treasury, a small and internationally rated foreign debt and a lax taxation system. No wonder insurrection exploded in the new kingdom's southern provinces when they were subjected to general conscription and heavy taxation. Furthermore, the Catholic Church's enormous landed patrimony, which had been leniently managed with a charitable eye for its peasant lessees, was suddenly sold at high prices to private landowners, who subjected the peasantry to much harsher treatment in order to recover the monies they had paid to obtain the land. While the South was in revolt, the new Italian state decided to join Prussia in its war against Austria. This added the costs of a war for gaining Venice and the Veneto to the huge expenses of a counter-insurgency military occupation of the South. As a result, the finances of the new Italy worsened even further, with expenditures soaring and revenues stagnating because of the fiscal revolt in the South and other new provinces.

In the conditions of monetary integration achieved by LMU, it was inevitable that Italian fiscal problems spilt over national frontiers and affected other members. The inconvertibility declaration of 1866 allowed the Italian National Bank to issue paper money, even in very small denominations. These new notes found little favour with the Italian public and, true to Gresham's law, soon displaced coins, even the divisionary ones which had only a limited silver content. Thus, coins were used to buy goods in other LMU member countries, while the Italian divisionary currency became virtually all paper. Retrospectively, the limit on new divisionary coinage established by the LMU treaty seems to have been an extremely inefficient form of 'stability pact'. The monetary effects, rather than the causes, of fiscal profligacy were addressed. However, a more stringent measure would have induced a feeling of loss of sovereignty sufficiently grave to have aborted LMU.

For the first three decades of its existence LMU was plagued by Italian fiscal inadequacy. Furthermore, the Papal States and Greece soon followed Italian policies. In the case of the Papal States, which joined LMU under French auspices, Luca Einaudi, using material from French archives, has admirably recounted the consequent nightmarish experience for France. While the authorities of Italy and the Papal States knew full well that they could stretch their lack of fiscal discipline to quite a remarkable extent, the French government and the Parisian *haute banque* considered LMU a considerable achievement for French foreign policy and French finance. Consequently, they were resigned to accepting considerable transgressions in order to sustain the LMU convention as an alternative to British and, after the defeat of 1870, German hegemony in Europe.

The tales of diplomatic squabbles within LMU, caused by the monetary effects of Italian and Pontifical fiscal laxity, make for droll reading, especially with regard to the continuing exasperation of Belgium and Switzerland. Nonetheless, Italian and Pontifical coins came to rest in the coffers of the Banque de France, and never constituted a serious problem for its balance sheet, much less for the convertibility of the franc, re-established in 1878. In fact, LMU served to keep a large part of Europe on a bimetallic standard. This was extremely convenient for the Banque de France, and for the members of the Rothschild family, who were always the most eminent among its directors.

This is another convincing explanation for LMU's popularity within France. As Agostino Magliani, Minister of Finance during the eventful years of the early 1880s when Italy returned to convertibility, wrote in a brilliant essay as early as 1874, bimetallism was the monetary system most favoured by international speculators. Precious-metal traders, in particular, loved it. Magliani pointed out that they could use all relative price changes in the two metals to move from coins to metal bars and vice versa, knowing that they were engaging in a one-way speculation since the central banks of bimetallist countries were bound to defend the existing mint par. We can thus see that criticism of the 'peg', as it was later to be known with reference to fixed exchange rates, was fully developed with reference to bimetallism a century earlier. It is little wonder that the house of Rothschild, especially its most forceful representative, James de Rothschild, remained a staunch supporter of international bimetallism until the last, even trying to induce Britain to adopt the system and fostering its adoption and continuation in France and the LMU. In a fascinating book, the result of extensive research in the archives of the Parisian Rothschild bank, Marc Flandreau has described with great clarity how the greatest European financial dynasty organized and controlled the gold and silver markets. It exploited to the full the possibilities offered to clever arbitrageurs by Europe's division into monometallist and bimetallist monetary areas.

Thus, a very important vested interest contributed to maintaining France at the helm of the bimetallist LMU despite Italian and Pontifical fiscal and monetary malfeasance. Magliani's remarks have thus been proved absolutely correct by Flandreau's careful research. His findings have been confirmed by Niall Ferguson, in his monumental history of the Rothschilds, based on the archives of the English branch of the family. However, not being an economist, he did not spend much time on this particular subject.

The fall in the price of silver

Far more serious problems were soon laid on LMU's doorstep, which determined its early hibernation as a functioning monetary union. Constituting a lake of monetary stability within an ocean of continuous monetary perturbations, LMU was able, much like its later equivalent, EMS, to withstand even large shocks in the relative supplies of the main monetary metals, gold and silver. However, when these oscillations reached a magnitude beyond that which had sparked even the wildest fears, the monetary convention had to be practically mothballed – somewhat comparable to what was to happen to EMS in 1992. In the case of EMS, some countries temporarily left the mechanism, while those remaining were permitted to allow their currencies to fluctuate within a larger band – a maximum of 15 per cent each way. In the case of LMU, the wild gyrations that the price of silver experienced from the mid-1870s led its members to decide to suspend the free coinage of silver, while maintaining the fixed mint par between the two metals. As is known, there were political, economic and technological reasons that contributed to the silver price's wild spins both up and down against gold but, in the long term, disastrously down.

At the beginning of the nineteenth century, Augustin Cournot had shown how the relations between a very large stock and a relatively much smaller flow explain the relative stability of the rate of exchange between the two metals that had persisted for a very long time. First of all, the two metals were virtually indestructible. Furthermore, whenever there was a tendency for current demand to rise, or current supply flows to decrease, stocks would be liquidated and so stabilize prices. The same mechanism was activated when demand flagged or current production increased. Cournot's demonstration remained valid until the 1870s. Then, however, many important things began to happen concurrently, and resulted in the long-run fall of the price of silver relative to gold. In a few words, while the production process improved dramatically, so much so that more silver could be extracted from a given quantity of ore, two large and rapidly developing countries, Germany and the United States, decided to go on the gold standard.

After its unification (brought about by the victorious war against France in 1870–1, which also destroyed the French Second Empire), Germany used the huge ransom obtained from the vanquished to move onto a monetary system akin to that to which Great Britain had adhered to for almost two centuries. G.F. Knapp, writing during the early years of the twentieth century, attributed the Reich's monetary choice to a desire to facilitate capital imports from Britain, then the largest world capital market. With the experience of another century, we can agree with the author of *Staatliche Theorie des Geldes*. Time and again rapidly developing countries wanting to rely on capital imports to finance further growth have placed themselves on an exchange rate pegged to the currency of the main capital-exporting country, often also the principal market for their exports and main provider of their imports. This exchange-rate policy may turn out to be extremely felicitous, or extremely unfortunate, for the countries that adopt it. It all depends on what happens to the exchange rate of the country to which the would-be capital importer decides to peg its currency.

In the case of Germany, the Rothschilds, who controlled the gold and silver markets, first amassed huge profits organizing French indemnity payments, as Jean Bouvier aptly proved several years ago. Later, they made it very expensive for Germany to sell its silver and purchase gold. The price of silver providentially collapsed and the Rothschilds again made a killing. The cost of introducing a gold currency became extremely high for Germany, and Bismarck soon decided to stop the operation. He was supposed to have remarked that, had he known the consequences, he would have paid the indemnity to France! However, the collapse in the (gold) price of silver, if it can be considered a French revenge on Germany, was a peculiar sort of revenge. It also made it very difficult for the bimetallist monetary area run by France – LMU – to survive, if the provisions of its founding treaty were to be kept intact.

Attempted solutions

Limping bimetallism

A nineteenth-century opinion, widespread among observers of LMU, was that it could be interpreted, from its beginnings, as a clever attempt by its other three founding countries to proceed gradually to a gold standard without causing too much affront to France, where bimetallism had extremely well-placed supporters. For instance, Charles Conant, and Stanley Jevons before him, noticed that the 1865 treaty's silver-convertibility provisions were really rather limited, while the mint par selected by its signatories was not particularly favourable to silver. Whether or not this is a correct interpretation of reality, it is certainly true that, in the face of the continuous collapse of the (gold) price of silver from the mid-1870s, LMU members could not just stand back. In 1878, when France returned to convertibility and the (gold) price of silver took another plunge, LMU members were compelled to convene another conference. There it was decided to suspend the free coinage of silver.

The Italian authorities were impelled by French resumption of cash payments to prepare for re-establishing the lira's convertibility (suspended in 1866). Almost immediately after the decision to close LMU mints to silver, the Italian authorities asked other LMU members in 1878 to repatriate Italian subsidiary coins and suspend the 1865 convention's provisions for inter-circulation. The requested suspension was to involve only Italy, and to continue only while Italy re-established convertibility. However, Italian coin within the LMU zone could not be returned to Italy in a single operation. To resolve the arising impasse, France undertook the centralization of the retrieval of Italian coins. The French authorities would pay full-bodied cash against Italian divisionary coins that were presented by other LMU states within a year. These coins were then to be returned to Italy within four years. Italy, in turn, undertook to replace its paper circulation with coins repatriated by France, while pledging not to issue paper money again. Yet, following the signing of this agreement, the Italian government was unable to obtain its ratification by parliament, and consequently resigned. After the formation of a new Italian cabinet, LMU negotiations were resumed and, in due course, a new agreement was reached that was less demanding upon Italy. In particular, the clause whereby Italy undertook not to resume the issue of paper money was deleted, it being considered that it violated Italian monetary sovereignty. Instead, Italy and France agreed that Italian coins were to be retained in the vaults until the equivalent amount of paper money had been withdrawn from domestic circulation by Italy. Other minor improvements were also obtained by Italy, and the Italian parliament finally approved the agreement.

The Italian convertibility experiment lasted about ten years, collapsing in the colossal 1893 financial crisis. When Italian convertibility was resumed once more, a large part of the Italian silver currency again migrated to France and other LMU members. Italy was then compelled to repatriate all its silver coins, even subsidiary coinage which had been allowed to circulate freely within the LMU ultimately ending up in the coffers of the Banque de France. With the disastrous fall in the (gold) price of silver, it was only the French central bank that had continued to purchase them at their face value.

The closure of LMU mints to silver coinage in 1878 inaugurated the age of 'limping bimetallism' that lasted until 1914. However, the (gold) price of silver continued to fall. This was one more problem for Italy, whose government decided in 1878, as discussed above, that it could not continue with an inconvertible lira when France was resuming cash payments. However, the lira's convertibility could only be restored with the help of a very large foreign loan to reconstitute reserves and replace the paper circulation. Furthermore, ways had to be found to prevent the proceeds of the Ff640 million loan migrating out of Italy. Everybody in Europe was trying to get out of silver, and there was a very real possibility that, as a result, the Italian money supply would be flooded with silver coins. The Banque de France held a huge, involuntary, reserve of Ff1200 million in silver. France had only managed to stem the plunge in the (gold) price of silver through massive silver purchases.

Consequently, it could be expected that, if the Banque de France experienced a serious gold outflow because of a loan to Italy, it would choose to redeem its notes, as the law permitted, in five-franc silver coins. Yet, this would only further increase silver's devaluation. Therefore, the Italian government decided to borrow Ff400 million in gold and another Ff240 million in silver, in the knowledge that most of it would be disbursed in paying for the repatriation of Italian subsidiary coinage from France.

The 'gold clause' of the Italian loan agreement practically excluded France from the affair. The Banque de France's gold reserve stood at only Ff600m., as against a silver reserve of Ff1,200m. Asked by the loan's 'lead bank' to effect the transfer to Italy, the Banque de France would have been compelled to undertake it in silver. Thus, the Italian government chose to borrow in London, where it was sure it would receive the loan proceeds in gold. As it happened, Ff488m. of the loan were paid in gold, and Ff156m. in silver, of which only Ff38m. entered Italy, the rest being used to pay for the repatriation of Italian subsidiary coin from France. The Italian government also ruled that customs duties were to be paid in gold but this constituted a grave violation of the LMU convention, and the Italian parliament refused its approval. However, the convertibility bill did contain a clause allowing Italy to retain its five- and ten-lira paper notes in circulation up to a total exactly matching the 300m. of Italian full-bodied silver coins still in other LMU countries' monetary circulations.

The liquidation clause

After the Italian government's successful and elaborate attempt to avoid all possibilities that Italy would become the final holder of silver, the French resolved to enter the LMU renewal negotiations with one strategy. This had the objective of inserting a liquidation clause into the treaty that would oblige LMU members to repatriate, at LMU's termination, all their own coins circulating in other LMU countries in exchange for either gold or bills of exchange. It should be noted that this development occurred when diplomatic relations between Italy and France were reaching a nadir.

France had suddenly occupied Tunis, over which Italy had expressed a strong interest and to where many southern Italians, especially from Sicily, had emigrated. In 1882, the so-called reversal of alliances also took place. Italy joined the Triple Alliance as a founding member, along with Austria and Germany, inaugurating a new age of German influence in Italian economic affairs. France and Germany exchanged the foreign loans they had made, France to Italy, Germany to Russia. The LMU liquidation clause was thus aimed directly at Italy by the French government. Furthermore, France was also embarking on a commercial war against Italy. This was to have extremely serious effects upon Italian trade and finance, and continued until the 1893 Italian financial crisis.

But the LMU liquidation clause was also meant to affect Belgium, which had, proportionately to its internal circulation, issued more silver coins than any other LMU member country. After very complex negotiations, in the course of which Belgium withdrew its delegation, the other three LMU members signed an agreement on the liquidation clause accepting the French view. All agreed, in the event of LMU's liquidation, to take back at their face value their coins circulating in other member countries. This renewal agreement also extended LMU's life for a further 25 years.

The continuing fall in the (gold) price of silver reinforced LMU. The chances that one of its member countries would ask for liquidation were substantially decreased because the three main countries had persistently issued silver coins at 1:15.5 whereas this mint par had become completely divorced from the market prices of gold and silver. LMU's members could not be expected to ask for its liquidation, which would have involved repatriating their coins at their face value.

Conclusion

Was the LMU a success? This is a difficult question to answer. The problems arising from Italian fiscal profligacy and monetary and banking disorders have to be considered. There were also other huge exogenous shocks on the (gold) price of silver exerted from the other side of the Atlantic that need to be considered. The United States was becoming an economic giant during the second half of the nineteenth century, but it was still an unruly child in monetary and banking terms. The United States was the largest world producer of silver by far, but it also wanted to have a gold-based currency. It went back to convertibility, after the suspension necessitated by the Civil War, and as a gold-standard country as it relied, like Germany in the same period, upon voluminous capital exports from Great Britain. Early in the nineteenth century it founded the first modern central bank, but it also proceeded to scrap it when the western part of the country felt that the bank was trying to impose some rules on free-wheeling banks. American farmers were net borrowers and large exporters, and thus wanted a strong currency for paying their foreign debts and a weak currency with which to compete on foreign markets. Furthermore, in the silver-producing states a strong silver lobby arose, and managed to have its own men elected to Congress. There they pushed strongly for, and often obtained, huge public purchases of silver to try to support its price. This, of course, played havoc with monetary equilibrium in the rest of the world, particularly LMU.

In view of all these difficulties, and of the additional ones created by the rapidly changing monetary landscape where banks, as time progressed, became more and more important, the experience of LMU can, perhaps, be seen in a more favourable light. It lasted longer than the international gold standard, its arch-competitor. By maintaining a considerable area of bimetallism in Europe, it probably managed to reduce the severity of the 'Great Depression', which raged from the mid-1870s to the mid-1890s and hit the gold-standard countries especially hard. In its midst, a poll taken amongst British economists showed that the most eminent, like Marshall, Edgeworth, Sidgwick and Nicholson, were in favour of introducing bimetallism even into their own country. Stanley Jevons validated the theory according to which bimetallism would stabilize prices but thought that the gold standard was the way of the future for all developed countries, while the huge masses of the impoverished would stick to silver. And he was a good prophet. Leon Walras proved, and subsequently Milton Friedman not so long ago agreed with him, that it was not necessary for Locke's law to apply inevitably. At least at a theoretical level, a bimetallic system could survive without turning into a monometallic one every time the market prices of the two metals substantially changed.

In conclusion, however, it must also be pointed out that LMU lasted as long as it did because France wanted it to. France was prepared to absorb Belgian and Italian silver coin and Italian divisionary coin at par. The French government was prepared to allow the Banque de France to operate as a lender of last resort for other LMU member countries' central banks. The Banque also contributed to smoothing the gold:silver parity by amassing an enormous stock of silver – its regents knew very well they could not sell to anyone without a huge capital loss, and also acted as a buffer between the gold-standard and bimetallic halves of the international financial system.

We may quote Michael Bordo, writing the entry 'Bimetallism' for the *New Palgrave Dictionary of Finance*:

> Bimetallism did ensure greater price stability in the period when it was in force compared to the succeeding period of gold monometallism and, for the United States at least, had it remained in effect from 1873 to 1914, it would have induced a more stable price level than was actually observed.

The LMU's sacrifices, in trying to maintain an area of bimetallism in Europe, can thus be seen to have been not without results.[3]

3 This chapter is based, apart from the aforementioned books by Einaudi and De Parieu, on: M. De Cecco, *Money and Empire* (Oxford, 1974); M. De Cecco, 'European Monetary and Financial Cooperation before the First World War', in *Rivista di Storia Economica*, 3rd ser., 9, 2, 1992, pp. 55–76; R. De Mattia, *L'unificazione monetaria italiana* (Torino, 1959); F. Droulers (ed.), Histoire de l'écu européen du moyen-âge à nos jours et des précédentes unions monétaires (Lagny sur Marne, 1990); M. Flandreau, *L'or du monde, la France et la stabilité du système monétaire international, 1848–73* (Paris, 1995); F. Garelli, *La coopération monétaire internationale depuis un siècle* (Geneva, 1946); W. Vanthoor, *European Monetary Union since 1848, a Political and Historical Analysis* (Cheltenham, 1996); H.P. Willis, *A History of the Latin Monetary Union*, Economic Studies Series no. 5 (Chicago,1901).

CHAPTER 6

The Scandinavian Monetary Union 1873–1924

Lars Jonung[1]

Introduction

At the close of the twentieth century, three Scandinavian countries – Sweden, Norway and Denmark – chose to tread different monetary paths. Sweden adopted a floating exchange rate cum inflation targeting in 1992. Norway maintained a pegged exchange rate during the 1990s, eventually moving to explicit inflation targeting in 2001, while Denmark has for all practical matters been a member of the euro area since its inception. This picture of monetary diversification stands in striking contrast to the monetary unity that once marked Scandinavia. The three countries were united in the Scandinavian Monetary or Currency Union (SMU) from the early 1870s until shortly after the First World War.

SMU is commonly regarded as successful for several reasons. It worked smoothly, with a minimum of tension among its members. It accomplished a high degree of monetary integration, most likely higher than any other monetary union involving sovereign states during the nineteenth century. The monetary marriage survived the political divorce of Norway from Sweden in 1905 that threatened to cause a military conflict. Contemporary commentators, like Knut Wicksell, wished the union to be maintained when it was put under stress.

The purpose of this chapter is to give an account of SMU, describing its origins, its evolution, its impact and its collapse. A number of questions are addressed: Why was the union founded? What effects did it have on nominal and real developments in Scandinavian countries, and what forces caused its break-up? Scant attention has hitherto been paid to SMU in economic research. Thus, the answers given here should be viewed as preliminary, since much work, in particular with a comparative perspective, remains to be undertaken on Scandinavia's gold-standard experience.[2]

---

1 I have received valuable comments from Michael Bergman, Michael D. Bordo, Thomas Hagberg, Cecilia Hermansson and Krim Talia. This article builds upon my joint work with Michael Bergman. Carl-Göran Lemne most kindly gave me access to material from the archives of the Riksbank on the Scandinavian monetary union. Göran B. Nilsson commented on my earlier work in a most constructive way, emphasizing the political forces contributing to the formation of the union. Karel Havik skillfully prepared the figures.

2 Research on the Scandinavian monetary union is concentrated in two periods: a first phase occurred around 1920, see for example E. Heckscher, 'Penningväsendet och penningpolitik', in E. Heckscher (ed.), *Bidrag till Sveriges ekonomiska och sociala historia*

The creation of the Economic and Monetary Union (EMU) in Europe has aroused an interest in the record of past monetary unions. There is now a considerable literature addressing the experience of monetary unification, often trying to draw lessons for the future of EMU from history.[3] The present study is inspired by this literature.

SMU's origins

During the 1860s there was a major effort for cooperation across Europe in the sphere of currency matters.[4] France was the driving force behind the establishment in 1865 of the Latin Monetary Union (LMU) based on gold and silver. Its members comprised Belgium, France, Italy and Switzerland, with Greece joining in 1868. The German states and Austria were united in the German monetary union, based on silver. Furthermore, in Scandinavia there was a lively debate over the proper choice of monetary arrangements. The issues were dealt with explicitly at three meetings of Scandinavian economists: in Gothenburg in 1863, in Stockholm in 1865 and in Copenhagen in 1872. Bankers and politicians were also involved.[5]

Several alternatives were brought out in the public debate, which generally emphasized that any future monetary system should be based upon the decimal system, common to all the Scandinavian countries, and should be international, that

(Stockholm, 1926), and a second in the 1990s. This chapter is based primarily on recent work by M. Bergman, S. Gerlach and L. Jonung, 'The rise and fall of the Scandinavian currency union 1873-1920', in *European Economic Review*, 37, 1993, pp. 507–17; M. Bergman, 'Do monetary unions make economic sense? Evidence from the Scandinavian monetary union 1873-1913', in *Scandinavian Journal of Economics*, 1999; I. Henriksen and N. Kaergård, 'The Scandinavian currency union 1875–1914', in J. Reis (ed.), *International monetary systems in historical perspective* (London, 1995); L. Jonung, 'Swedish experience under the classical gold standard 1873-1913', in M. Bordo and A. Schwartz (eds), *The Classical Gold Standard in Retrospective* (Chicago, 1984); and K. Talia, 'Monetary integration and disintegration. Studies in the Scandinavian Currency Union', *licentiat* thesis (Stockholm School of Economics, 2001). Most work on the union has been carried out from a Swedish perspective. Henriksen and Kaergård, 'Scandinavian currency union', look at the union from a Danish position. There is no recent Norwegian study of the union, to my knowledge.

3 See for example M. Bordo and L. Jonung, 'Lessons for EMU from the History of Monetary Unions?', IEA, Readings 50, London, June 2000; B. Eichengreen, 'One money for Europe? Lessons from the US Currency Union', in B. Eichengreen (ed.), *European monetary unification* (Cambridge, 1997); and L. Jonung, 'EMU – the first 10 years. Challenges to the sustainability and price stability of the Euro-area – What does history tell us?', in M. Buti (ed.), *The functioning of EMU. Challenges of the early years* (London, 2002), for monetary-union lesson-drawing.

4 For a thorough review of the European monetary unification process of this period, see L. Einaudi, *Money and politics. European monetary unification and the international gold standard, 1865–1873* (Oxford, 2001).

5 In Sweden the banker A. O. Wallenberg, founder of the Stockholms Enskilda Bank and of the Wallenberg dynasty, was deeply involved in the debate on the choice of monetary standard for Sweden. See G.B. Nilsson, 'Drömmen om universalmyntet', in *Pecunia*, 1, 1990, pp. 59–74; and Talia, 'Monetary integration'.

is based on gold. The three small Scandinavian countries at the periphery of the European continent had the options of adopting the monetary system of one of the then major financial powers of Europe: Great Britain, or France or Germany. The British option was ruled out since it was not based upon the decimal system. The French alternative, namely to join LMU, had many proponents. Indeed, Sweden and Denmark seriously considered membership; but the Franco-Prussian war put an abrupt end to these plans. France lost its monetary initiative with its defeat in the war, while the German Reich adopted the gold standard, partly financed by the war indemnity from France. Anti-German sentiments in Denmark, following war with Prussia in 1864, blocked an approach to the monetary system of the German Reich. Thus, the Scandinavian countries were induced by outside circumstances to consider a 'domestic' solution. At this juncture thoughts turned to a SMU that had no explicit ties to any of the major monetary powers in Europe.

SMU was established over the period 1872–5.[6] Its members were Denmark, Norway and Sweden, with Denmark and Sweden pushing for its establishment.[7] An intergovernmental monetary commission met in Copenhagen in August 1872, and an agreement to establish a common monetary system was signed in Stockholm on 18 December by the three future members. Surprisingly, the Norwegian parliament refused to ratify the treaty, but Denmark and Sweden went ahead, forming a monetary union on 23 May 1873. Norway finally joined two years later by treaty on 16 October 1875.

Several factors contributed to SMU's formation. First, it provided a method for standardizing the coinage of the three countries. Each had a long tradition of similar currency units that had assisted in generating an extensive exchange of notes and coins between them. Norway had been part of Denmark until 1816, when it was forced into political union with Sweden. Their currencies were all based on silver. Prior to 1873, the three countries used the riksdaler as their currency unit. One Norwegian speciedaler was approximately equivalent to two Danish rigsdaler, in turn more or less equivalent to four Swedish riksdaler. As a result, part of the volume of money circulating in each country comprised notes and coins issued by the two other countries. The divergence between the silver values of the Danish and Norwegian currencies was sufficiently small to make any arbitrage profits from foreign-exchange dealings negligible. However, this was not the case for Swedish silver coins, whose value exceeded 0.5 Danish rigsdaler or 0.25 Norwegian speciedaler to an extent that it gave rise to an inflow of Danish and Norwegian coins into Sweden – an influx that was regarded as an inconvenience by the Swedes, as their currency had a higher silver weight.[8]

6 The official term was den skandinaviska myntunionen – translated here as the 'Scandinavian monetary union'.

7 Finland was at that time a Russian Grand Duchy. Iceland was governed by Denmark. Norway was formally in a political union with Sweden but enjoyed far-reaching political independence.

8 In the bill in the Swedish Parliament in 1873, the argument that the influx of Danish and Norwegian silver currency created permanent costs for Sweden was explicitly used.

The intra-Scandinavian flow of currencies was one motive behind the creation of a common monetary system. But there were others. In all three countries, the debate over the choice of a monetary standard had created support for moving the Scandinavian silver currencies onto a common gold standard, based upon the decimal system. This was recommended for reasons of expediency and rationality. Only the Swedish coinage was based on the decimal system. Other European countries were concurrently adopting the gold standard, most prominently Germany. This put pressure on the Scandinavian countries also to go onto gold. There was a fear that the price of silver would become less favourable if the decision to adopt gold were postponed. The gold standard was regarded as suitable since Scandinavia's leading trade partners, namely Britain and Germany, were also on gold. The adoption of gold was also viewed by some as the first step towards a universal monetary system.

Political factors were at work as well. These prevented an approach to either LMU or the German monetary union. Nationalistic currents, which permeated Europe during the nineteenth century, were expressed within Scandinavia as 'Scandinavianism', an endeavour to bring Denmark, Sweden and Norway closer to each other. A common currency system and a common currency unit were viewed as important symbols of Scandinavian unity and cooperation.

All these factors – a desire to standardize the coinage, imbalances in cross-country flows of currencies, the perceived superiority of the gold standard and the decimal system, the international movement towards gold and the political climate – contributed towards Sweden, Norway and Denmark entering into an agreement to create a common currency union in 1872.

SMU was based on a common view regarding the conduct of monetary policy. Its aim was straightforward: a fixed rate of exchange between the common domestic currency and gold should be maintained. There were then no other conceptions of alternative stabilization-policy arrangements: fiscal policies, labour-market policies and regional policies being constructions of more recent times. Monetary policy was 'denationalized' or 'depoliticized', which made international arrangements easy to accomplish.

The legal framework of the union

SMU's rules were set out in a currency agreement (myntkonvention) reached in December 1872 and given legal force in May 1873. The following should be noted. A common currency unit – the Scandinavian krona – was introduced, equivalent to the old Swedish riksdaler in all three countries. One krona was made up of 100 öre, while the krona's value was expressed in terms of gold, equal to 1/2480 kilo of gold. The basis of SMU was thus the gold standard, putting an end to the silver standard in Scandinavia.

New gold coins were minted in 20 and 10 kronor denominations. Subsidiary coins, coins of lower denominations, were minted in silver (with a silver content of 90 per cent), and copper. All subsidiary coins were legal tender in the three Scandinavian countries. No restrictions applied to the amount of silver and copper coins that could be minted and put into circulation by each member. Initially, such limitations had been considered but found difficult to construct. Each national treasury accepted unlimited quantities of such coins regardless of their country of origin. The only limitation imposed in relation to the validity of the currency was a maximum level in respect of the payment of private debts.[9]

SMU had also an explicit escape clause. Any member state wanting to leave the union had to give other members notice of withdrawal at least one year in advance. This clause was never invoked.

There was no rule concerning any central coordination of monetary policies – or any other policies – within the union agreement. SMU was a truly decentralized union with its three member central banks, the Bank of Denmark, the Bank of Norway and the Bank of Sweden, being independent of each other, only united by the agreements of 1873–5.[10] Actually, much suggests that there was, initially, surprisingly little communication between the three central banks.

SMU meant that the three Scandinavian countries formed a common monetary area – the krona area – within the domains of the gold standard that was then increasingly covering most of Europe. The union represented a tighter form of monetary cooperation than the gold standard, as Scandinavian subsidiary coins, and later Scandinavian notes, circulated freely and extensively within the three countries, especially in border areas.

The evolution of the union

During its 40 years' existence SMU evolved, as any institution does. (For a chronology of the major events see Table 6.1). Although the union was based on gold, the gold standard in Scandinavia did not become a 'pure' one, since gold coins did not circulate in general business. Actually, they were quite rare. They were minted in higher denominations than banknotes, and the use of notes was popular and extensive, particularly in Sweden.[11] Consequently, the holding of gold was concentrated in private note-issuing banks and the central banks, serving as legal reserves backing the volume of notes in circulation. The public trusted the note-issuing banks. Bank runs and financial panics were not common features of the Scandinavian experience during the gold standard, although the international crises of 1877–8 and 1907 did influence the three countries.

---

9 Henriksen et al., 'Scandinavian currency union', p. 94, conclude that no 'free-riding' occurred concerning the issue of subsidiary coins during the reign of the union.

10 The distinction between centralized and decentralized monetary unions is a crucial one when analysing the sustainability of monetary unions. History suggests that monetary unions with a centralized control of the money supply, and thus of the setting of interest rates, tend to be lasting ones, while decentralized unions like the SMU have a significantly higher risk of breaking up when put under stress. See Bordo et al., 'Lessons', and Jonung, 'EMU'.

11 Jonung, 'Swedish experience'.

Table 6.1 A chronology of the Scandinavian monetary union (*Skandinaviska myntunionen*), 1873–1924

Date	Monetary Arrangements
1873	The Scandinavian monetary union is established. Sweden and Denmark accept each other's gold coins as well as subsidiary coins as legal tender. A common denomination is introduced: one Scandinavian krona is equal to one hundred öre. One Swedish krona equals one Danish krona.
1875	Norway joins the Scandinavian monetary union. One Norwegian krona equals one Scandinavian krona.
Late 1870s	Bank of Sweden informally accepts Danish and Norwegian notes at par.
1901	Bank of Norway and Bank of Denmark formally agree to accept each other's notes at par.
August 1914	Sweden, Denmark and Norway leave the gold standard, while no changes are made in the treaty of the union.
February 1916	Sweden introduces a gold embargo.
1916–24	The Swedish krona is traded at a premium to the Danish krona and Norwegian krona.
April 1916	Denmark and Norway establish a gold embargo
June–July 1917	Denmark and Norway prohibit the export of Scandinavian gold coins at the request of Sweden. Scandinavian subsidiary coins still legal tender at pre-war parity in all three countries.
1923–4	Large inflows of Danish and Norwegian coins into Sweden.
October 1924	Danish and Norwegian silver and copper coins lose legal tender status at pre-war parity in Sweden. End of the Scandinavian monetary union.

Comments: The table exhibits major changes in the Scandinavian monetary union. A restoration of the union was discussed on a few occasions after 1924, but to no avail.

Source: Heckscher, 'Penningväsendet', E. Wilhelmsson, 'Den skandinaviska myntunionen', in Bancoposten (utgiven av Riksbankstjänstemännens förening), 8, 6, 15 Dec. 1923, pp. 155–61; and Talia, 'Monetary integration'.

SMU's first developmental modification came about in 1885, when the three central banks introduced a system of mutual drawing rights, facilitating financial transactions across the union, primarily for big business since a minimum payment of 10,000 kronor was required. Transactions between the central banks were to take place without interest or other charges. The central banks would not have concluded this agreement if their managements had expected that subsequent flows of notes and coins within the union might create a permanent disadvantage for any member. The 1885 agreement thus indicated that no country sought to obtain seigniorage profits at the cost of the others.

The flow of money among the Scandinavian countries consisted of notes. In fact, they did not always circulate at the same rates, which caused dissatisfaction since the union agreement did not contain provisions governing notes. The Bank of Sweden accepted Danish and Norwegian notes at par in the 1870s. Sweden and Norway further consolidated the union in 1894 by accepting each other's notes at par without any limitations, but the Danish central bank did not subscribe to this agreement until 1901.[12] By then, SMU was at its most developed stage: notes, gold coins and subsidiary coins of each member were in circulation at par in other member countries.

The dissolution of the political union between Norway and Sweden in 1905 probably induced the Bank of Sweden to withdraw from the clearing agreement of 1885 on 30 September 1905. However, a revised agreement immediately followed, allowing each central bank to charge the other banks fees when using the clearing facility. This option was not used for five years, when it was taken up by Norway and Denmark. This suggests that the Swedish decision of 1905 was motivated by a desire to make a mark in relation to Norway, which was then pushing for full independence from Sweden. For all practical purposes the union continued to function smoothly until the outbreak of the First World War.[13]

SMU does not appear to have been the subject of any notable political or financial tensions before 1914, with the exception of the independence of Norway in 1905. The gold standard ensured stability in monetary policy through its requirement of convertibility into gold, while its three member countries avoided issuing large quantities of silver and copper coins.

---

12 The relatively small quantities of notes in circulation in Denmark may have caused the Danish central bank to regard the matter as less pressing. In 1885, notes represented 26 per cent of the total quantity of money in circulation in Denmark, 41 per cent in Norway and 57 per cent in Sweden, according to Henriksen et al., 'Scandinavian currency union'.

13 The survival of the monetary union in the face of the break-up of the political union between Norway and Sweden is remarkable. There is hardly a case of this nature in history where two countries of roughly equal size have continued a monetary cooperation after political separation. The recent political disintegration of Czechoslovakia and Yugoslavia has been followed by monetary disintegration as well. The case of Ireland in 1922, where the Irish maintained the British pound, is an example of continued monetary cooperation in spite of political independence. However, the Irish in 1922 had far fewer options than the Norwegians in 1905.

Macroeconomic developments within the union

The union operated within a favourable macroeconomic environment. The Scandinavian countries underwent rapid and sweeping change from the mid nineteenth century until the First World War. Economic growth was high and stable, higher than in the United Kingdom, a country that can be taken as a benchmark for comparisons (see Table 6.2). The flow of capital into the area was considerable. The three Scandinavian countries were able to finance their industrializations by importing capital from London, Paris and Berlin. The mobility of labour was considerable, mainly in the form of emigration to the United States. The world economy was not exposed to any major macroeconomic disturbances during the classical gold standard.

Table 6.2 Real per-capita income growth in Denmark, Norway, Sweden and the United Kingdom, 1881–1913, Annual data

Country	Average growth rate
Denmark	1.8
Norway	1.5
Sweden	2.2
United Kingdom	0.9

Source: Bordo and Jonung, 'return', Table 10.

The question that arises is: to what extent did SMU influence macroeconomic developments within Scandinavia? Let us first consider nominal variables, and then real factors.

Nominal effects

Standard economic theory of fixed-exchange-rate arrangements predicts close uniformity in the behaviour of nominal variables within a monetary union. This is also the picture that emerges when comparing the behaviour of the money supplies, the price levels, and the short-term and long-term interest rates across the union (see Figures 6.1–6.5). At this stage, however, no study is available separating the effects of the gold standard at large from the effects of SMU *per se*. Research into this area is lacking.

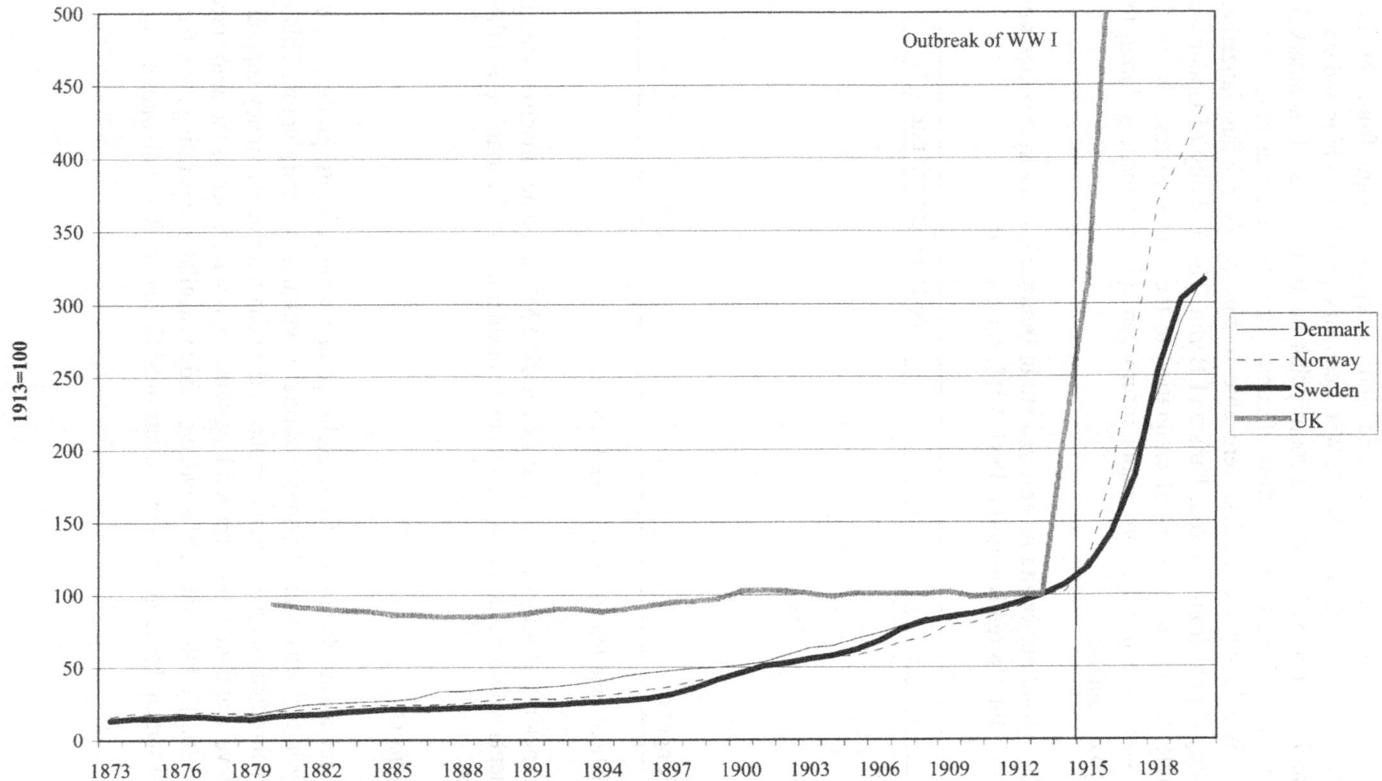

Figure 6.1 The money supply in Denmark, Norway, Sweden and the United Kingdom, 1873–1920. 1913=100

Comments: The money supply in the United Kingdom is shown for the period 1879-1915.

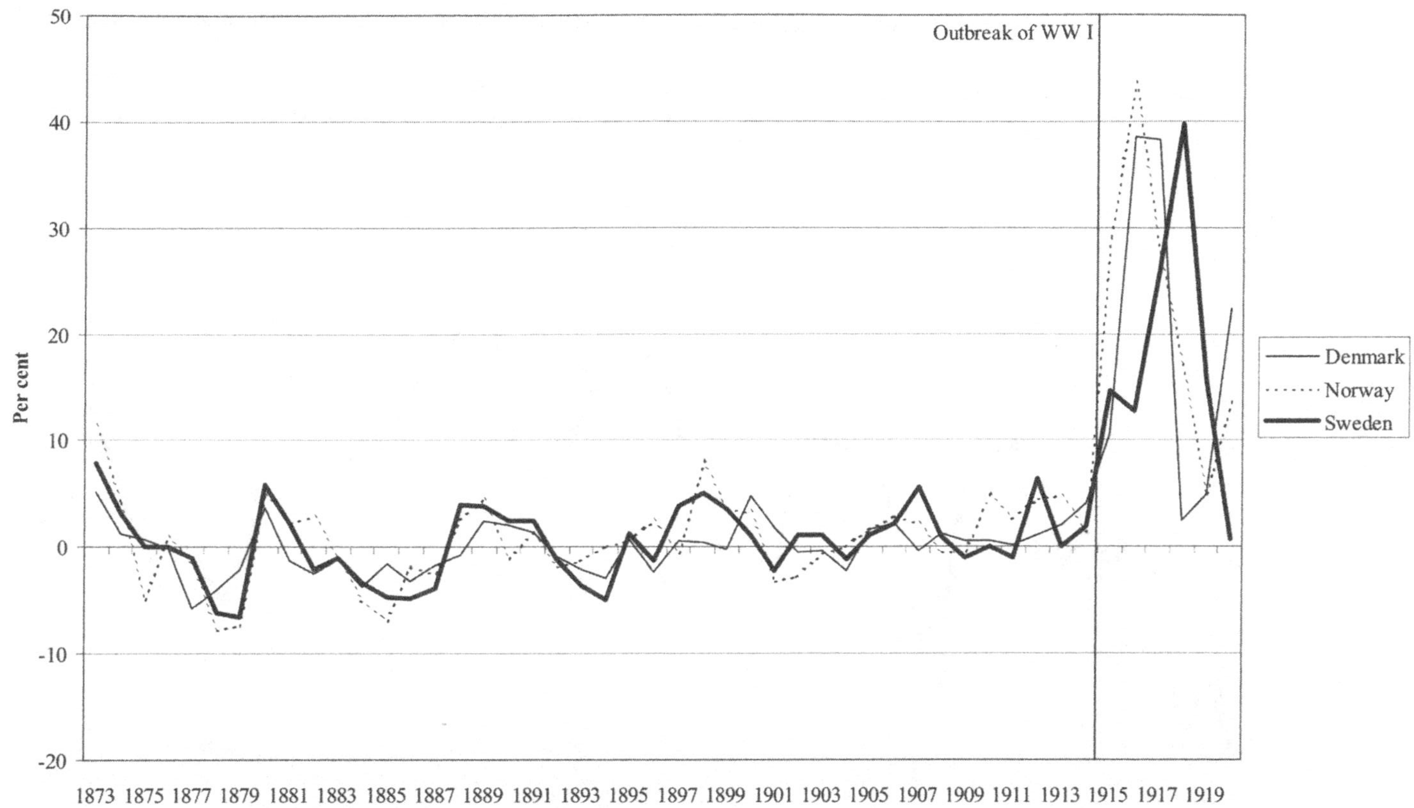

Figure 6.2 The rate of inflation in Denmark, Norway and Sweden, 1873–1920 (per cent)

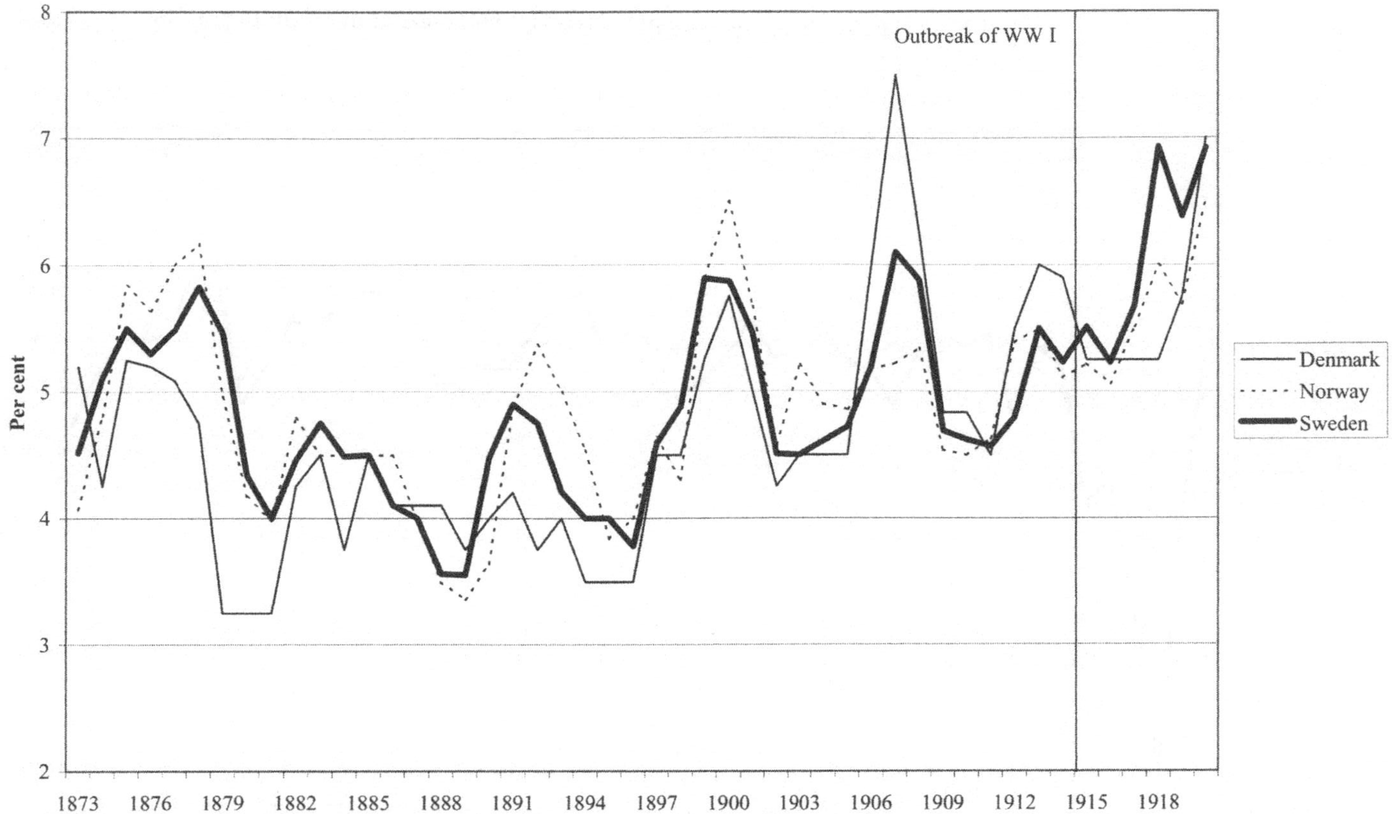

Figure 6.3 **The discount rate in Denmark, Norway and Sweden, 1873–1920 (per cent)**

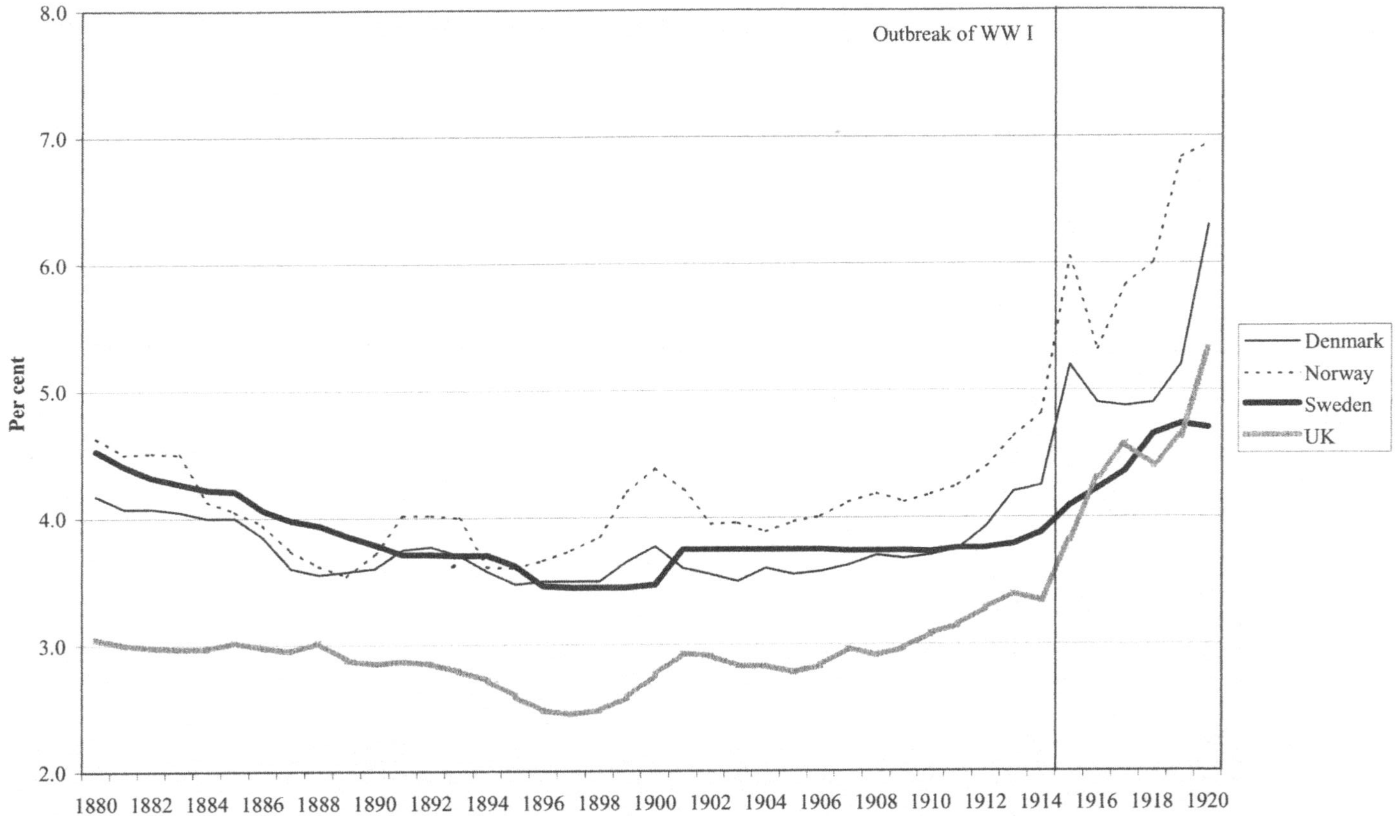

Figure 6.4 **The long-term rate of interest in Denmark, Norway, Sweden and the United Kingdom, 1880–1920 (per cent.)**

Figure 6.5 **The krona/dollar rate of the Danish, Norwegian and Swedish currency, 1880–1930**

The long-run behaviour of the money supplies in the three countries is displayed in Figure 6.1 for the period 1873–1920, normalized to 1 for 1913. The rate of growth was roughly identical within the union, around 5 per cent per year.[14] After the outbreak of war, the pattern changed significantly. Money supply expanded at an extremely rapid pace, particularly in Norway where it more than quadrupled in six years. The Scandinavian countries experienced a rapid process of monetization and of financial sophistication during the classical gold standard, as witnessed by the high rate of money-supply growth compared to the United Kingdom. This is evident from Figure 6.1 as well, demonstrating the almost constant level of the British money supply prior to 1914.

The price levels of SMU members exhibited the same long-run pattern as all countries adhering to the classical gold standard. There was a secular fall from 1873 to around 1896, followed by a slight secular rise prior to the First World War. The annual rate of change in the price level – oscillating around zero – co-varied closely across the union (see Figure 6.2). During booms the rate of change was as a rule positive; during depressions it was negative. Changes in the price level were mean-reverting during the classical gold standard.

The behaviour of prices was completely transformed with the outbreak of war in 1914. Inflation became rapid and divergent across the union, with Norwegian and Danish inflation leading Swedish. This divergence in inflation rates contributed to SMU's break-up.

As expected, the short-term interest rates, as indicated by the discount rates of the Scandinavian central banks in Figure 6.3, moved in a closely coordinated way. The rates were also of identical levels. The cyclical pattern in Figure 6.3 demonstrates that changes in the discount rate were used as a tool of monetary policy. Here the union members closely followed the Bank of England rate, which remained clearly below the rates of the Scandinavian central banks.

The long-term rates of interest among union members, shown in Figure 6.4, reveal a pattern close to that of the short-term rate, secularly falling until the turn of the century, then gradually rising in unison. The outbreak of war was followed by a rapid rise in nominal rates. Figure 6.4 also displays the long-term rate in the United Kingdom, which remained at about one percentage point lower than the level in Scandinavia. This differential reflects Great Britain's role as centre of the financial system of the world. It served to induce a flow of capital from the centre to the Scandinavian countries prior to 1914.

Nominal exchange rates between the three countries remained 1:1:1 between 1873 and 1914, as the members used the same currency. Following the outbreak of war, they declared their currencies non-convertible into gold, so leaving the gold standard. Soon afterwards, the parity between the Scandinavian currencies was broken. The Danish and Norwegian currencies started to be traded below par – see Figure 6.5. Exchange rates diverged substantially during the war. Sweden officially returned to gold at the pre-war dollar rate in April 1924, the first country in Europe to take this step. Denmark and Norway eventually followed suit. At the end of the 1920s they

14 Correlations between annual growth rates of the money supplies within the union were high as well. See Table 1 in Bergman et al., 'rise'.

were all back on gold at their old parities. At that time, a resurrection of the union was considered. Real exchange rates were fairly stable during the classical gold standard as well – see Figure 6.6. However, after 1914 their volatility increased rapidly.

To sum up, nominal variables, such as money, prices and interest rates show – as expected – identical patterns across Scandinavia during the union period, demonstrating that the three countries constituted a common currency area as well as being members of the gold-standard 'club'. No attempt has, to my knowledge, been made to disentangle the effects on nominal variables of the union from the effects of being on the international gold standard.

Real effects

The consequences of the monetary union cum the gold standard on nominal variables are fairly straightforward to explain. However, the effects of the union on real variables, such as growth and trade, remain an open issue. Hardly any research has dealt with this aspect of the union.

It is safe to conclude that the gold standard and SMU contributed towards monetary and financial integration and sophistication within Scandinavia. By being on gold, the Scandinavian countries could most likely obtain financing from abroad on better terms than otherwise.[15] Within the union, financial systems expanded rapidly. Recent empirical work suggests a crucial link between finance and growth. A study in this tradition for Sweden indicates an independent role for financial factors behind economic growth from the mid-nineteenth century until the outbreak of the Second World War.[16] This result is consistent with the view that the gold standard contributed to economic growth prior to 1914.

Commonly, a monetary union is viewed as a way of increasing trade among its members. This is a major benefit of EMU as epitomized in the concept of 'one market – one money'. The effect of SMU on trade flows within Scandinavia is an open issue.[17] According to contemporary sources, border trade between members benefited, although the total extent of trade within Scandinavia declined during the period.[18] SMU was not combined with a free-trade area, thus limiting the benefits

---

15 This argument is developed and tested by M. Bordo and H. Rockoff, 'The gold standard as a "good housekeeping seal of approval"', in M. Bordo (ed.), *The gold standard and related regimes* (Cambridge, 1999).

16 P. Hanson and L. Jonung, 'Finance and growth: The case of Sweden 1834–1991', *Research in Economics*, 51, 1997, pp. 275–301.

17 See O. Krantz, 'Den svensk-norska unionens betydelse för Sveriges ekonomiska utveckling' ('The impact of the union between Sweden and Norway on the economic development of Sweden'), Meddelande från Ekonomisk-historiska institutionen, Lunds universitet, 49, 1987; and Henriksen et al., 'Scandinavian currency union'. Krantz concludes that the political union between Norway and Sweden had marginal effects on Swedish economic growth.

18 D. Davidson, 'PM rörande den skandinaviska myntkonventionen', report to the Riksbank, 6 February 1917, stresses the positive impact of the union on border trade.

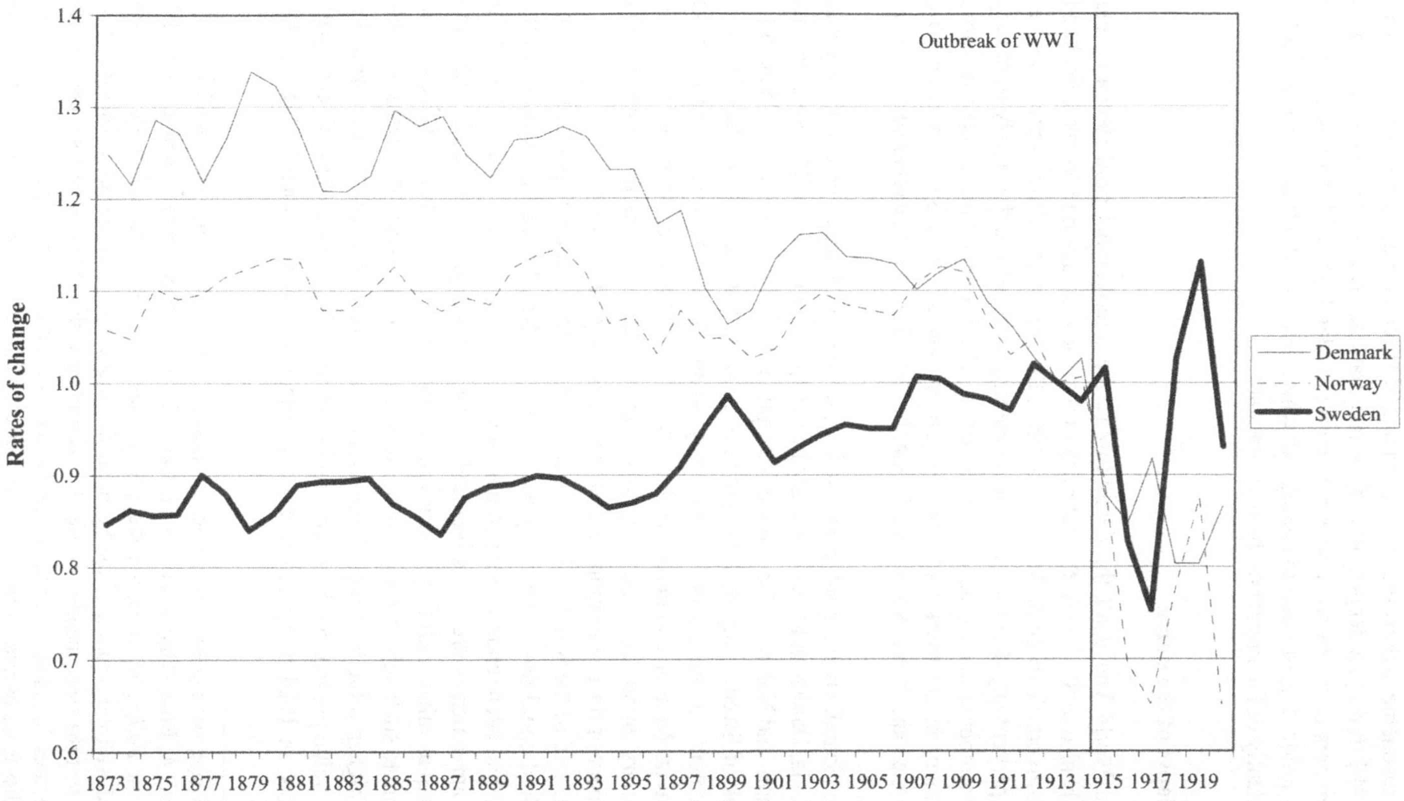

Figure 6.6 The real exchange rates of the Scandinavian currencies, 1880–1920. (1913=100)

of a common currency. Instead, tariffs were in force, raised first by Sweden, then by Norway, but Denmark remained a free trader.[19]

It is reasonable to draw the conclusion that SMU contributed positively to growth before 1914 through a deepening of financial markets. The Scandinavian countries were members of the international gold-currency standard in addition to forming a currency union. It is difficult to distinguish which effects SMU had on real variables independently of the impact of the gold standard.

The collapse of the union

The First World War dealt the deathblow to the international gold standard, and eventually also to SMU.[20] At the outbreak of war, Scandinavian notes were declared to be inconvertible to gold. At the same time, the export of gold was prohibited in order to prevent any drain of gold and, accordingly, growth in the supply of money in each member country ceased to be linked to gold. Monetary policy became more expansionary in Denmark and Norway than in Sweden. The Swedish krona rose *vis-à-vis* the Danish and Norwegian krona. In 1915, the official exchange rates were changed.

Since Scandinavian gold coins and gold were still legal tender throughout Scandinavia, Danish and Norwegian gold was exported to Sweden. The governments of Denmark and Norway often allowed exceptions to the prohibition of gold exports. The Bank of Sweden opposed this influx of gold. Negotiations took place to reach an agreement to put an end temporarily to the legal-tender status throughout Scandinavia. Neither Denmark nor Norway wished, however, to bring an end to the monetary union. Consequently, the outcome of the negotiations became a strict enforcement of the prohibition against the export of gold from 1917.

At the end of the war, the three Scandinavian currencies no longer had the same value. Gold could not move freely across their borders. In practically all respects, the SMU had been rendered inoperative by the war. The only remaining parts of the original agreement were that silver and copper coins represented legal tender and were of equal value in all three countries, and that the countries were entitled to mint and circulate such subsidiary coins in unlimited amounts. Since the Swedish coins were of higher value than their Danish and Norwegian counterparts, the currencies of lower value poured into Sweden – an illustration of Gresham's law. To cope with this inflow, in 1924 a supplementary agreement was made, which laid down that

19 Using econometric techniques to measure the impact of monetary unification on trade flows, A. Rose, 'One money, one market: The effect of common currencies on trade', in *Economic Policy*, 30, 2000, found significant positive effects. Such effects do not appear associated with the creation of the Scandinavian monetary union, however. One reason is probably that the three members were already trading with each other in a system of fixed exchange rates, based on silver as the specie metal, before switching to gold. Another reason may be that Rose overstates the impact of currency unification. See T. Persson, 'Currency unions and trade: how large is the treatment effect?', in *Economic Policy*, 33, 2001.

20 A detailed account of the breakdown of the union is given by Talia, 'Monetary integration', see also Bergman et al., 'Rise'.

each country, regardless of the 1873 currency agreement, could only mint silver and copper coins that were legal tender within its borders. The coins valid throughout Scandinavia were successively withdrawn. For all practical purposes, the union ended through the agreement of 1924.

Was the union successful?

Was the union a successful one? The answer is both yes and no. It was successful in establishing a common monetary area, contributing to nominal convergence and facilitating financial flows and financial sophistication. The krona, the currency denomination of the union, is still used in all three former SMU members. Compared to other decentralized monetary unions prior to 1914, like LMU, SMU functioned smoothly; in short, it appeared successful.[21]

SMU was not accompanied by co-operation in other fields. Perhaps most damaging, Scandinavia did not become a free-trade area while the union was effective, reducing the benefits of monetary unification. SMU also failed in the sense that it collapsed during the First World War. It lacked centralized co-ordination of monetary policies. If such a mechanism had been in place, it is tempting to conclude that SMU would have most likely survived the monetary turmoil of the First World War. Instead, each country and each central bank acted independently in economic and financial affairs, with no attempts to co-operate.[22]

A current and well-respected contemporary commentator on monetary events in Scandinavia, Knut Wicksell, looked favourably upon SMU. When the union was breaking up during the First World War, as part of the collapse of the gold standard, Wicksell actually proposed that it should be re-organized as a monetary union based on fiat money with a common central bank and a common inter-Scandinavian interest-rate policy. His recommendations reveal a modern approach:

> I repeat: after the suspension of the free minting of gold where it is concerned, it lies completely in the power of each individual country, and therefore of each and every one of the Scandinavian countries separately, to regulate the value of its money and the level of its prices freely.[23]

---

21 M. De Cecco, 'European monetary and financial cooperation before the First World War', in *Rivista di Storia Economica*, 9, 1992, pp. 55–76, here p. 67, gives a clear yes, announcing that the Scandinavian monetary union was 'the most successful of all European currency unions' in the pre First World War period.

22 A comparative study based on the archives of the central banks of the three Scandinavian countries would give us a better picture of the extent of monetary and financial cooperation among the central banks. Such a study is lacking. Talia, 'Monetary integration', is a first step in this direction.

23 K. Wicksell, 'The Scandinavian Monetary System after the [First World] War', orginally published as "Det skandinaviska penningväsendet efter kriget" i Bidrag till frågan om ett ekonomiskt närmande mellan de skandinaviska länderna. Inlägg av skandinaviska ekonomer (1917), translated and published in B. Sandelin (ed.), Knut Wicksell. Selected essays in economics, vol. 2 (London and New York, 1999).

However, in his opinion the three countries had so much in common that it was preferable that they should jointly frame their monetary policies, that is, set interest rates to stabilize prices. He recommended that a common central bank be set up for the three countries, a goal modelled upon the United States Federal Reserve System.

> I cannot really see any decisive obstacle to the establishment of a true central bank for all three countries, with its seat in Gothenburg, say. In my opinion, such a bank ought, first, to be a purely state (i.e. here, interstate) institution.

He concluded that 'joint future action by the Scandinavian countries on monetary matters is likely to offer good prospects'.[24] In the mid-1920s, Wicksell stated explicitly that he wanted SMU to be re-established:

> I, for my part, firmly believe in such a union. This monetary union … may be said to have constituted a small-scale pattern for that future regulation of the world's monetary system on a uniform basis which so long has been a favourite idea of economists.[25]

Resurrecting the union?

SMU collapsed due to the impact of the First World War. Monetary developments among the members of the union became too divergent, as seen from the evolution of money, prices and exchange rates in the charts. However, gradually, the Scandinavian countries returned to the gold standard at the pre-war dollar parity rate; Sweden in 1922–4, Denmark and Norway during the second half of the 1920s. By the end of the 1920s the three countries were all back at the same parity rates as prior to 1914.

The return to gold sparked an interest in re-establishing the union. However, the breakdown of the international gold standard during the 1930s put an end to any plans of this sort. The three Scandinavian countries belonged to the Sterling bloc in the 1930s. The Second World War, with the German occupation of Denmark and Norway, prevented further monetary cooperation. After 1945, Denmark and Norway became early members of the IMF system. Sweden joined in 1951.

Following the collapse of the Bretton Woods system, the three countries chose different exchange-rate systems. Denmark moved towards the ERM system and the euro system. After a series of devaluations during the 1970s and 1980s, Sweden adopted a floating exchange rate combined with inflation targeting in 1992–3. Norway stayed at a pegged exchange rate until March 2001, when it adopted inflation targeting.

---

24 Wicksell's positive opinion about the Scandinavian monetary union is also evident in K. Wicksell, 'Den skandinaviska myntunionens återställande', unpublished manuscript from 1923, in L. Jonung, T. Hedlund-Nyström and C. Jonung (eds.), Att uppfostra det svenska folket. Knut Wicksells opublicerade manuskript (Stockholm, 2001).

25 K. Wicksell, 'The monetary problems of the Scandinavian countries', 1925, translated and reprinted in K. Wicksell, *Interest and Prices*, translated by R. F. Kahn (New York, 1965).

At the opening of the twenty-first century, the three countries appear much more divergent monetarily than during the nineteenth century. Finland is the only Nordic country that belongs to the euro area. The optimal currency area approach suggests that the Nordic countries – that is Denmark, Norway, Sweden and Finland – have much in common today. They satisfy a large set of the standard criteria for forming a successful monetary union. Compared to the rest of Europe, they display among themselves a high degree of factor mobility, similar production structures, similar cyclical fluctuations and close to identical preferences concerning economic policies in general. They have much in common concerning culture, history and religion.[26] Thus, the three Scandinavian countries could be expected to be able to co-operate closely in monetary matters.[27]

This picture suggests that it was easier to accomplish monetary unification in a world of a metallic standard. The establishment of the monetary union in 1873–5 was regarded as a practical arrangement to facilitate the standardization of the coinage and adapt the Scandinavian monetary systems to international developments. Political considerations played a minor role – as opposed to the present situation. Then the control of the money supply, and thus the conduct of monetary policy, was outside the realm of the political system. The central banks of the Scandinavian countries were politicized during the period after 1945. The ECB system is an attempt to take monetary policy out of the immediate control of the national political body. This idea was easier to accept in Scandinavia during the nineteenth century than it is today.

26 See L. Jonung and F. Sjöholm, 'Should Sweden and Finland Form a Monetary Union?, in *The World Economy*, 22, 5, July 1999, for a test centred on Finland and Sweden using the optimal currency area approach.

27 The predictive power of the theory of optimal currency areas is commonly regarded as low. This seems to hold for the Nordic countries as well. See M. Hutchison and U.M. Bergman, 'Northern Light: Does Optimal Currency Area Criteria Explain Nordic Reluctance to Join EMU?', in J. von Hagen and M. Widgren (eds), *Regionalism in Europe: Geometries and Strategies After 2000* (Amsterdam, 2001).

CHAPTER 7

The Gold Standard: A Review from the Periphery

Pablo Martín-Aceña

Introduction

The period from 1880 to 1914, known as the heyday of the gold standard, was a remarkable one in world economic history. It was an era of globalization, marked by remarkable economic growth, substantial transfers of productive resources and rapid technological change. Under its aegis, a widespread system of fixed exchange parities was maintained from the 1880s until 1914. Entirely voluntary participation in the gold standard was a notable aspect of this regime, and despite a number of international crises, it functioned with surprising smoothness. Moreover, it appears to have done so with little, if any, international cooperation.

This legendary international monetary regime emerged during the late nineteenth century, when the majority of countries switched from bimetallism and paper to gold as the basis for their currencies. As an international standard, the key rule was the maintenance of gold convertibility at a previously established parity. The fixed price of gold ensured fixed exchange rates that, in turn, provided a nominal anchor to the international monetary system. Thus, an economy is said to be on the gold standard when its monetary unit's gold content is fixed by law. In addition, the institutions issuing fiduciary money are under legal obligation to exchange, at any time, any amount of gold specie for fiduciary currency, and vice versa, while any amount of bullion will be coined on request by the mint. Finally, the authorities must allow unrestricted international movements of specie and bullion and, more generally, free capital mobility. Using current terminology, the gold standard is an exchange regime characterized by a fixed exchange rate, free convertibility and perfect capital mobility.

As Bordo has indicated, gold was chosen as the basis for the monetary regime because of its desirable properties.[1] It is durable, readily recognizable, storable, portable, divisible and easily standardized. Especially important is that changes in its stock are limited, at least in the short run, by high production costs, making it costly for any government to manipulate. More important, gold was both a commodity money and a commodity money standard, which, through the operation of the competitive market, ensured a tendency towards long-run price stability.

---

1 M. Bordo, 'The Classical Gold Standard: Some Lessons for Today', *Federal Reserve Bank of St. Louis Review*, 63, 5, 1981.

A good measure of the gold standard's success was the breadth of its geographic ambit. During the 1850s only two countries adhered to the gold standard – Britain and Portugal – but at its zenith, just before the First World War, it is estimated that 28 states had linked their currencies to gold and a further 11 were officially, though not in practice, on gold. The former included all the then major political and economic global powers. Altogether, the population existing under a convertible metallic standard based upon gold must have numbered something like 900 million – in Europe, Asia, the Americas, Africa and Oceania.

Table 7.1 Monetary systems of the world, 1868

Country	Standard	Convertibility
Europe		
United Kingdom	Gold	Yes
France	Bimetallic	Yes
Belgium	Bimetallic	Yes
Switzerland	Bimetallic	Yes
Italy	Bimetallic	No
German states	Silver	Yes
North, South and Hanse towns, Bremen	Gold	Yes
Netherlands	Silver	Yes
Denmark	Silver	Yes
Norway	Silver	Yes
Sweden	Silver	Yes
Austria	Silver	No
Russia	Bimetallic	No
Greece	Bimetallic	No
Spain	Bimetallic	No
Portugal	Gold	Yes
Romania	Bimetallic	No
North America		
United States	Bimetallic	No
Canada	Gold	Yes
Central America		
Mexico	Silver	No
Nicaragua	Bimetallic	Yes
Guatemala	Bimetallic	No bank of issue
Honduras	No specific system	No bank of issue
Salvador	No specific system	No bank of issue
Costa Rica	Bimetallic	Yes

South America		
Peru	Bimetallic	No
Chile	Gold	Yes
Brazil	Gold	No
Venezuela	Bimetallic	No
Argentina	Bimetallic	No
Asia and Pacific		
India	Silver	Yes
China	Silver	Yes
Indonesia	Silver	Yes
Japan	Silver	No
Siam	Silver	No bank of issue
Philippines	Bimetallic	No bank of issue
Australia	Gold	Yes
Middle East		
Ottoman Empire	Gold	No
Egypt	Gold	Yes
Persia	Bimetallic	No

Eichengreen and Flandreau have shown how the geography of the gold standard changed dramatically between 1868 and 1908.[2] In Table 7.1 it is apparent that in the first year only two European nations, Britain and Portugal, and a few non-European countries (Canada, Chile and Egypt) were on gold, while the rest of the world was basically bimetallic or adhered to a silver standard. After 1900 (Table 7.2) the picture had altered almost entirely. Virtually all of Europe had joined the gold standard, with Spain the only exception. Furthermore, most of the world beyond Europe had also gone over to gold, with the few exceptions including China, still on silver, bimetallic Persia and a few Latin-American nations.

2 B. Eichengreen and M. Flandreau, 'The Geography of the Gold Standard', in J. Braga de Macedo, J., B. Eichengreen and J. Reis (eds), *Currency Convertibility. The gold standard and beyond* (London, 1996).

Table 7.2 Monetary systems of the world, 1908

Country	Standard	Convertibility
Europe		
United Kingdom	Gold	Yes
France	Gold	Yes
Belgium	Gold	Yes
Switzerland	Gold	Yes
Italy	Gold	Not technically, but stable currency
Germany	Gold	Yes
Netherlands	Gold	Yes
Denmark	Gold	Yes
Norway	Gold	Yes
Sweden	Gold	Yes
Austria	Gold	Not technically, but stable currency
Russia	Gold	Yes
Greece	Gold	Not until 1910 (Gold Exchange Standard)
Spain	Gold (silver coinage prohibited)	No
Portugal	Gold	No
Romania	Gold	Yes
North America		
United States	Gold	Yes
Canada	Gold	Yes
Central America		
Mexico	Gold	Yes
Nicaragua	Gold Exchange Standard	No
Guatemala	Silver (no free movement of silver)	No
Honduras	Silver	Yes
Salvador	Silver	Yes
Costa Rica	Gold	Yes
South America		
Peru	Gold	No
Chile	Gold	No
Brazil	Gold	No
Venezuela	Gold	No
Argentina	Gold	Yes

Asia and Pacific		
India	Gold Exchange Standard	Yes
China	Silver	Yes
Indonesia	Gold Exchange Standard	Yes
Japan	Gold Exchange Standard	Yes
Siam	Gold Exchange Standard	Yes
Philippines	Gold Exchange Standard	Yes
Australia	Gold	Yes
Middle East		
Ottoman Empire	Gold Exchange Standard	Yes
Egypt	Gold	Yes
Persia	Bimetallic/Silver	Yes

The origin of this universal gold regime harks back to the early years of the eighteenth century, when Isaac Newton, Master of the British Mint, set a high silver price for the gold guinea in 1717. This drove full-bodied silver coins out of circulation, as predicted by Gresham's law. An Act of 1798 foreshadowed further development away from bimetallism and toward the full gold standard by suspending the free coinage of silver and limiting the legal tender of silver coin to £25. The Coinage Act of 1816 authorized the gold sovereign; its content confirmed the mint price of a standard ounce of gold that had been recognized since the mid-eighteenth century. Silver money was subordinated to gold and its legal-tender power further limited to payments only up to £2. However, the paper pound's continuing non-redemption and gold's market quotation at a premium above its theoretical value deprived the 1816 coinage law of its full significance for a while. Finally, an Act of 1819 required the Bank of England to make its notes redeemable in gold bars at the coinage price of gold by May 1821 and in coin by May 1823. Actually, full redemption in coin was achieved in 1821, but at the cost of rapid credit contraction, further price deflation, industrial distress and widespread unemployment. The 1819 Act had also repealed restrictions on melting of coin and the export of coin and bullion. The 'paper pound' was equivalent to the gold sovereign, and Britain was on a full gold standard.

As has been indicated, for half a century between 1820 and 1870 the geography of the gold standard remained unchanged, with only two countries, Great Britain and Portugal, registered in the 'gold club'. Bimetallism reigned in the major European nations, the United States and Latin America, and the Orient. Then, during the early 1870s, a movement toward an international monetary regime based on gold gained momentum. What factors decided the monetary authorities of so many countries to abandon bimetallism or silver monometallism? Why were so many more nations on gold in 1910 than in 1880?

Going onto gold

According to Milward, there seem to be at least four categories of explanation for the general move to the gold standard.[3] The oldest, particularly favoured by monetarist theorists, relates the origin of the gold standard to changes in the relative supply of the two precious metals: gold and silver. An increase in the supply of the latter relative to gold, starting in the 1860s and continuing until 1900, forced countries interested in stable prices and currency values to switch from a silver standard to a gold standard or, where a bimetallic standard operated, to tie the currency effectively to gold. A second argument rests on contemporary political economy and the influence of those political groups that desired monetary stability. De Cecco and Gallarotti have argued that landowners, farmers, exporters and debtors preferred silver because falling prices benefited their interests, while gold, by contrast, became the choice of manufacturing, the urban classes and financial sectors.[4] Where these latter groups predominated, the gold standard succeeded earlier and was eventually imposed. It can be shown that, with the spread of industrialization, came a shift in the balance of power between urban and rural interests. As manufacturers and financiers gained the upper hand, gold was adopted and silver abandoned as the basis of the monetary system. In fact, industrialization went *pari passu* with monetary stabilization, and as the most advanced nations adopted the gold standard, the rest of the world followed suit. In other words, the more countries shifted to gold, the more appealing the option became for the remainder.

A third category of explanation looks at a specific diplomatic and political set of circumstances. Flandreau, for example, locates the origin of the gold standard in the defeat of France in its war against Prussia.[5] The German Empire used the indemnity paid by the French government to create a new national currency based on gold and, at the same time, gave up its traditional bimetallic commitment. A fourth argument brings out, on the one hand, the advantages to commercial policy which could be derived from adhering to the gold standard and, on the other, the fact that the adoption of gold monometallism made foreign investment easier and more secure, something particularly attractive for nations with aspirations to build a modern and industrial economy.

In Europe and in other regions of the world, the chain of events that led towards the gold standard can be laid out in the following way. As already discussed, the German Empire took the first step in the erection of the gold standard as an international regime in 1871. Within the German states the silver standard had enjoyed large support due to its many advantages, such as the stability of exchange rates in trade with Russia and Austria, but this had waned as a consequence of inflation when these trading partners had gone off silver and onto inconvertible paper. The indemnity that

---

3 A.S. Milward, 'The origins of the gold standard', in J. Braga de Macedo, B. Eichengreen and J. Reis (eds), *Currency Convertibility. The gold standard and beyond* (London, 1996).

4 M. De Cecco, *Money and Empire. The International Gold Standard, 1880-1914* (London, 1974); and G.M. Gallarotti, *The Anatomy of an International Monetary Regime. The Classical Gold Standard* (Oxford, 1995).

5 M. Flandreau, 'Central Bank Cooperation in Historical Perspective: A Sceptical View', in *Economic History Review*, 50, 4, 1998.

Germany received in 1871–3 as the victor in the Franco-Prussian War provided the resources needed to carry out a currency reform. A new gold-based currency unit, the mark, was adopted, and Germany used her indemnity to purchase gold on a substantial scale. With German gold purchases, and following silver discoveries in Nevada and other mining areas, bimetallic countries were faced with a precipitous decline in the (gold) price of silver. Their response was to suspend silver coinage and convertibility, starting with the Netherlands, Denmark, Norway and Sweden, and then spreading to France and other members of the Latin Monetary Union (Belgium, Switzerland, Italy and Greece). Gold became the monetary standard in every European country except those that retained inconvertible paper.

In the cases of Austria-Hungary and Russia, after a long record of paper-money inflation interrupted by periods of stabilization on silver, they were driven off their traditional silver standard during the mid-nineteenth century by issues of paper money made to meet the expenses of revolutions and wars.[6] Then, as silver depreciated on world markets from the 1870s, the value of the silver contained in the standard gulden and rouble threatened to sink down to the purchasing power of the paper units. Once the value of silver began sinking still lower, owners of silver bullion could have taken advantage of the guaranteed market provided by the free coinage of silver into gulden and roubles. Silver would have poured into Austria-Hungary and Russia, inflating their money supplies and pulling down the purchasing-power and foreign-exchange values of their currency units in step with their declining values. To forestall this unwelcome development, both countries suspended the free coinage of silver, Austria-Hungary in 1879 and Russia in 1893. Thus, Austria-Hungary commenced a period of 13 years, and Russia of four years, during which their national currency units were 'hanging in the mid-air', with values exceeding that of its traditional metallic content. In 1892 Austria-Hungary began adopting a gold-exchange standard, replacing the paper gulden with a gold crown worth half as much. Russia, after building up a gold reserve, moved onto a gold standard in 1897.

The United States also moved gradually towards the international gold standard. In 1873, when Congress omitted the silver dollar from the list of coins to be minted, the country was still using inconvertible greenbacks, dating from the Civil-War inflation. This Act, labelled 'the Crime of 1873', marked the end of bimetallism as the legal standard from which the inconvertible paper had been regarded as a temporary, wartime departure. A return to convertibility now meant gold monometallism, which took place in 1879 when the federal government decided to end the greenback period, which marked the resumption of convertibility at the dollar's pre-war gold content.

Beyond Europe and the United States, events also favoured the adoption of the gold standard. In India, a traditional silver-standard nation, the exchange rate between the rupee and sterling had been fairly stable. But with the decline of silver from the 1870s, the rupee:pound rate experienced widening fluctuations. In 1893, the Indian government suspended the free coinage of silver to check further

6 L.B. Yeager, 'Fluctuating Exchange Rates in the Nineteenth Century: The experience of Austria and Russia', in R.A. Mundell and A.K. Swodoba (eds), *Monetary Problems of the International Economy* (Chicago, 1969).

depreciation. However, the rupee continued to sink for a while in partial sympathy with silver until it briefly reached a low point of barely more than half its earlier gold value. Until 1898, the rupee resembled the gulden and the rouble in having a scarcity value greater than the bullion value of its silver content. Then, with the adoption of the gold exchange standard, it was pegged against sterling at two-thirds of its earlier value, involving official intervention on the foreign-exchange market to maintain the chosen rate. Similar measures put other Oriental currencies on gold, such as Japan, which adopted the gold standard in 1897, the Philippines and others. In Latin America, several countries still had inconvertible paper money. But the gold standard was now the target and the prevailing idea of a 'normal' currency standard. Going back to silver was no longer a live issue.

The operation of the gold standard

Since the eighteenth century, one of the fundamental issues raised by the study of the 'classical' gold standard's functioning has been how prices, money and real activity adjust when the economy's external position experiences disequilibrium. According to the well-known explanation offered by David Hume, external imbalances, particularly on the trade account, give rise to movements of gold between countries that will ultimately correct the initial disequilibrium. An economy facing a trade surplus, for example, will experience an inflow of the precious metal, whereas an economy facing a deficit will experience an outflow. The Humean framework further assumes a circulation exclusively of specie, or at least a fixed relationship between fiduciary currency and gold holdings, so that changes in the stock of the latter imply immediate changes in the money supply. Variations in the money supply, in turn, alter the price level in the manner described by the quantity theory of money. All other things being equal, an increase in the money supply generates a one-to-one increase in the price level. This adjustment process relies heavily on changes in the price level, induced by changes in the money supply, and, thus, price flexibility is crucial for the restoration of equilibrium.

A natural expansion of the Humean analysis is the extension of the IS-LM framework to the open economy.[7] This model captures two additional elements: the interest rate and the level of income. In a gold-standard environment, the model predicts that an exogenous increase in exports – or domestic expenditure – produces a hike in the domestic interest rate, and thus a balance-of-payments surplus. This is due to both a higher level of exports and capital inflows attracted by the higher return on domestic assets. In the absence of sterilization, these capital inflows are monetized. The money supply rises and the domestic interest rate returns to the international level, thus further increasing the level of income. The external gap – in this case a surplus – is closed by a higher level of imports caused by the rise in income. It is interesting to note that the model also predicts that, in the case of a negative external shock, the virtuous circle just described can turn into a vicious

7 J.M. Fleming, 'Domestic Financial Policies under Fixed and under Floating Exchange Rates', IMF Staff Papers, 9, 3, 1962; and R. Mundell, *International Economics* (New York, 1963).

one. A fall in exports reduces the domestic interest rate; there are capital outflows; the money supply goes down; and equilibrium is achieved at a level of income when imports are reduced to the new, and lower, export level. In this framework, changes in the interest rate depend on variations in the demand for money, as well as in the money supply. Here, contrary to the quantity theory, the income velocity of money is not constant.

The monetary approach to the balance of payments turns the above analysis upside down.[8] In this framework, a balance-of-payments disequilibrium arises from a 'notional' disequilibrium in the money market. Under a gold-standard regime, an excess demand for money generates a balance-of-payments surplus, whereas an excess supply of money gives rise to a deficit. In the first case, the economy attracts a balancing flow of gold, which helps to equalize the supply and the demand for money by satisfying the initial excess demand. In the second, an excess demand for goods arises and imports therefore increase to meet it. The consequent balance-of-trade deficit leads to an outflow of specie money, the supply of which reaches the level desired by the public. In this way the balance of payments itself becomes the mechanism of money market adjustment.

A fourth model, the so-called 'dependent economy model', incorporates most of these mechanisms but also adds complexity by assuming that the economy produces traded and non-traded goods.[9] The international price of traded commodities is set by the world market, and is thus a given for the individual economy. It is in this sense that the economy is 'dependent'. The price of non-traded goods is set domestically by demand and supply conditions. General equilibrium supply functions depend on relative prices and the economy's capital-labour ratio. Under these conditions, an increase in the relative price of traded goods shifts resources into this sector and *vice versa*. On the demand side, relative expenditure also depends upon relative prices, the scale variable being wealth or permanent income. In this instance, an increase in the relative price of traded goods will shift expenditure towards non-traded commodities. In this context, the domestic price of traded goods in terms of non-traded commodities (that is, the relative price of traded goods) becomes the driving force of the adjustment mechanism. Any disturbance, external or internal, has an impact on this relative price, and it has to adjust to restore equilibrium. Commodity arbitrage ensures that the domestic price of traded goods is equal to their international price multiplied by the nominal exchange rate, which in the context of the gold standard is fixed.

Attitudes towards the gold standard

Perceptions of the gold standard have varied greatly over time. The 1920s and 1930s were probably the years when, in retrospect, the image of smoothness, perfection

8 H.G. Johnson, 'The Monetary Approach to the Balance of Payments Theory', in J.A. Frenkel and H.G. Johnson (eds), *The Monetary Approach to the Balance of Payments* (London, 1976).

9 W. Salter, 'Internal and External Balance: The Role of Price and Expenditure Effects', *Economic Record*, 36, 1959.

and automaticity associated with the gold standard flourished most strongly. After 1945 the gold standard continued to mesmerize economists, politicians and public opinion in general, as well as to inspire various international attempts to establish fixed-parity mechanisms. By then, however, the scales were beginning to fall from the eyes of the informed public, with the realization that the facts had often been rather different from the myth constructed during the interwar period.

At times during the 'classical' gold standard, adjustment had not been so smooth, countries had often behaved selfishly and contrary to the 'rules of the game' that all were supposed to follow, and there had been considerable variation in the degree to which they had adhered to its defining principles. Some were fully on gold, others had had a 'limping' version of this standard, while a great many were only nominally on it, though in fact following some rule of inconvertibility. For instance, one might differentiate countries by the extent to which gold coins circulated internally. Gold coins formed an important part of the circulation in Britain, France, Germany and the United States, or Russia, Australia, South Africa and Egypt. It is also possible to distinguish countries on a full gold standard whose convertibility was automatic (Britain, Germany, the United States) from countries on a 'limping' gold standard where convertibility was at the option of the authorities (France, Belgium, Sweden).

Another differentiation arises if one considers countries according to their 'cover system', which linked the quantity of currency and coin in circulation to each country's gold reserve. There existed three main types of cover systems: fiduciary, proportional and a combination of the two. The fiduciary system allowed the authorities to create a certain quantity of unbacked currency (the fiduciary issue), while requiring remaining currency to be fully backed with gold. This was the case with Britain, Finland, Japan, Norway and Russia. The proportional system treated all currency alike but permitted the central bank to maintain a ratio of gold to currency issue of less than 100 per cent. This was the mode of coverage used in Belgium, Holland and Switzerland. Cover systems that combined features of both rules were adopted by Germany, Austria-Hungary, Italy and Sweden. In some countries, additional flexibility was built into the system by either permitting the note issue to exceed the legal limit upon payment of a tax or allowing reserves to fall below their legal minimum on the finance minister's authorization.[10]

The gold standard in the periphery

As explained, the gold standard was a very heterogeneous and flexible regime. However, the sense of the heterogeneity of experiences that has emerged in the vast body of literature built up over the last 50 or more years concerns more than simply form. It also has much to do with the preconditions and consequences of the gold standard. One line of research has focused on the relative ease, or difficulty, faced by different national economic structures in adhering consistently to the regime. The basic distinction in this respect arises between advanced, industrial

10 Eichengreen et al., 'Geography'.

core countries, for which it was relatively easy, and backward, primary-product-exporting peripheral countries, for which the domestic adjustments required now and then by the system were painful or even unbearable. The latter group, it is often concluded, were therefore involved with the gold standard for a shorter period and to a lesser degree, simply because the regime caused them far greater hardship than it did Britain, France, Germany or the United States.

A second line of enquiry concerns the advantage of being on the gold standard. It seems reasonable to argue that, if peripheral countries tried to endure the economic rigors that membership of this international 'club' required, it was because it held some advantages. Or rather, was it that they were merely innocent importers of an economic ideology that in reality was unsuited to them? The verity of the latter point is not easy to establish. Regarding the former, one view is that the gold standard was in fact a badge of good national behaviour in the monetary and financial domains, which enhanced access to international capital markets and lowered the cost of obtaining much-needed foreign investment for development.[11] Another is that the efficiency of this badge in signalling good behaviour was less than has been claimed, that some countries on the gold standard were unattractive to foreign investors while others, which were not on it, were able to obtain significant inflows of capital. A third approach is that, even if it was a credible indicator, its price was too high to justify this option in terms of the loss of output and slower productivity growth it entailed.

With notable exceptions, research on the gold-standard regime has been devoted to the countries of the core, and much less to peripheral nations. We know little of how the gold standard operated for non-industrial nations or, for instance, how easy or difficult it was for Latin-American and Mediterranean countries to maintain a viable fixed-exchange-rate regime or to sustain convertibility in the long run. A few years ago, Jaime Reis and I, with a group of scholars, made an attempt to examine the case of six peripheral countries – three from Latin America (Brazil, Chile and Colombia) and three from Europe (Italy, Portugal and Spain). We looked at the performance of the gold standard in these nations, and tried to answer some of the questions mentioned above. The remaining part of this article presents some of the conclusion that were reached.[12]

On the whole, the six countries surveyed faced considerable difficulties in maintaining their adherence to the gold standard. The 'automatic adjustment mechanism' that operated so well for core countries seems in peripheral cases to have been too onerous to permit a strict and sustained adherence to this monetary regime. Overall, the number of years that they were on a metallic standard (gold, silver or bimetallism) was less than those when an inconvertible paper currency obtained (see Table 7.3). On the other hand, considerable variation underlies this apparent regularity. The performance of Chile, Colombia and Portugal was reasonably creditable compared with the rest. At the same time, not all episodes of inconvertibility were identical. Some were marked by sharp fluctuations in the

11 M. Bordo and H. Rockoff, 'The Gold Standard as a "Good Housekeeping Seal of Approval"', in *Journal of Economic History*, 56, 2, 1996.

12 P. Martín Aceña and J. Reis (eds), *Monetary Standards in the Periphery. Paper, Silver and Gold, 1854–1933* (London, 2000).

exchange rate for protracted periods – for example, in Chile from 1880 to 1894 – while others, such as Italy and Spain before 1914, had quasi-fixed exchange rates for some time.

Table 7.3 Episodes of convertibility and non-convertible paper currency, 1850–1930

	Metallic standard	Non convertible currency
Brazil	1906–14	1850–1905
	1926–30	1914–25
Chile	1850–78	1878–94
	1895–8	1898–1925
	1925–30	
Colombia	1850–85	1885–1922
	1922–30	
Italy	1885–93	1861–84
	1928–30	1894–1928
Portugal	1854–91	1891–1930
Spain	1850–83	

The first point to note about these peripheral economies is that, relative to the core, their external sectors were of paramount importance. During the gold-standard years, the dynamism of these countries depended very much on their export industries. Both the growth rate and general business conditions were strongly influenced by their leading export sectors, which usually, moreover, comprised only a few commodities. Factor endowments – natural resources and unskilled labour – were relatively abundant compared with the mature economies. Consequently, their comparative advantage lay in goods whose production was relatively intensive in the use of these two inputs. It comes as no surprise, then, that exports from the peripheral countries consisted mainly of relatively unprocessed agricultural and mining products, while their imports were mostly industrial, intermediate and capital goods, as well as capital-intensive services such as shipping.

It seems reasonable to assume that world markets for the kind of commodities exported by peripheral economies were almost perfect. There were millions of consumers, and even if a commodity was produced in only a few places in the world, that was by multiple, competitive suppliers. If that was so, then prices generated in this kind of market will have followed a random walk, meaning that the index of export prices for any peripheral economy was more volatile than the index of its import prices. They exported few commodities but imported a wide variety. This type of economy therefore also tended to face highly volatile terms of trade, and was consequently subject to macroeconomic instability. Furthermore, under these circumstances maintaining convertibility required the prices of non-traded goods to show the same degree of flexibility as those of traded goods. If they did not, an external shock would be transmitted to the real economy, probably with the direct consequences previously outlined. The best way of partially isolating the economy from external upheavals was to have a floating exchange-rate regime, obviously a contradiction with adherence to a metallic monetary standard.

A second problem relates to the functioning of the international capital market. Nineteenth-century peripheral countries normally experienced a shortage of investment capital due to a combination of low savings rates and low income levels. This made the absolute amount of domestic savings insufficient for financing growth, and in order to expand over the long run, they needed to borrow abroad substantially and continuously. Servicing of the external debt became a sizeable item on the current account, and was financed by growing export earnings and a system of revolving credit. A result was that the level of investment expenditure, and thus of aggregate demand, came to depend strongly upon the conditions prevailing in the international capital market. A worsening of these conditions, leading to higher international interest rates and the drying up of funds, therefore had serious consequences for these economies.

A third problem relates to the nature of the financial system. There were almost as many different arrangements in this field as there were countries on the planet, a fact illustrated by the variety evinced by the six countries studied. The most relevant distinctions are simple – whether there was monopolistic, or multiple competitive, issue of bank notes; whether any institution agreed to perform central-bank-type functions; and the degree of severity of the regulations governing banking activity. The role of the financial system, particularly with regard to the transmission mechanism, was important for our analysis. An external imbalance sets in motion a series of processes that ultimately induce the changes in relative prices needed to restore internal and external equilibrium. The first and direct effect is on the stock of high-powered money, via the outflow of specie and bullion, but the transmission of this effect to the rest of the financial system, and eventually the real economy, is contingent upon the particular financial arrangements prevailing in the economy. If there is a monopoly for issuing fiduciary currency under stern reserve backing regulations, or if there is widespread circulation of metallic coin, the effect will take place rapidly. If there is a situation of competitive banks of issue where fudging with the backing is allowed, this effect might never take place.

All six countries exemplified the difficulties that their peripheral status created as they sought to manage monetary affairs according to the acceptable norms of the time – convertibility and a metallic standard. The Latin-American economies, however, experienced these disadvantages to a much greater extent than their counterparts in the European periphery. They suffered from much greater exchange-rate instability and, when forced off the metallic standard, experienced much greater difficulties in returning to convertibility. This can readily be seen when we consider the application of the dependent-economy model to either group. All were price takers on the world market for their exports and imports. Moreover, export industries were usually the most dynamic sectors of the economy, and their expansion introduced capitalist practices and business innovations to the rest of the economy. The main export commodities, however, had pronounced cycles. During good years the quantities demanded rose rapidly, as did prices, but unfortunately for these economies producers generally increased their supply and provoked a price fall, as happened with coffee, nitrate, rubber and quinine, among others. Sometimes the depressive side of the cycle was accompanied by a reduction in world demand, thus exacerbating the effect of the price decline. Export prices for each of these economies were therefore more volatile than was the case for the core economies. The South American peripheral economies differed from the European in two further respects. They were large in the sense that they produced a considerable share of the world supply of their main export commodity: coffee and rubber in the case of Brazil and Colombia, and nitrate and copper in Chile. And often their main export commodity accounted for more than 50 per cent of the country's total exports. In contrast Italy, Spain and Portugal had far more diversified exports, while none of their export commodities had a dominant world position, and exports played a lesser role in their overall economic effort.

The story told by the six countries studied also indicates that the first effect of a crisis on the current account was currency overvaluation. When this was maintained for a sufficiently long period of time, a severe financial crisis ensued and convertibility was abandoned, as occurred in Chile in 1878, Colombia in 1885 and Portugal in 1891. In the case of Brazil, periodic attempts to return to convertibility during the nineteenth century were foiled by the end of an export commodity cycle or by a severe drop in the price of coffee. In other words, the root of the problem in all these situations was that the price of non-traded goods did not show the flexibility needed to ensure simultaneous internal and external equilibrium.

The intensity of these effects was not, however, always the same, and again seems to have been less for the European segment of our sample of countries. Some economies could be 'out of line' in this way for longer periods than others, and could even survive until the next export cycle, while others were more fragile. Being able to enjoy balancing capital inflows, generated for example by governments obtaining foreign loans even when internal conditions were unattractive to investors, was one key to this. Another was the receipt of an increasing flow of invisibles such as emigrant remittances. These elements are especially important for understanding the evolution of the Italian and Portuguese balance of payments and their exchange-rate variations. In the case of Portugal, remittances were between one-third and one-half of the value of total exports, and they grew steadily until the late 1880s. Indeed, it was only when Brazil's economic and political problems had a negative impact on them that a serious exchange crisis arose (in 1891). For Italy too, remittances were important in keeping the external account balanced; to such an extent, indeed, as to make Italy a creditor country by the turn of the century. Thus, variations in the international interest rate had a less dramatic effect than for the other countries studied. In fact, it seems likely that Italy was even able to siphon off gold from the rest of the world during crises, in the same way as the core countries are supposed to have done.

The financial system naturally also played a crucial role in the working of the adjustment mechanism. Generally speaking, the closer the relationship between the balance of payments and the money supply, the faster was the economy's response to an external imbalance. In the simplest case of commodity money and in the absence of fiduciary currency, the relationship between the balance of payments and the money supply is direct and immediate. Consequently, the price of non-traded goods may respond quickly to an external imbalance. However, this was not always so. During the years that Portugal was on the gold standard, the bulk of its money stock was gold coin, a fairly large proportion of which was British sovereigns. Yet, until the immense crisis of 1891, there does not seem to have been a clear relationship between the balance of payments and the stock of circulating coins, the reason being that a large amount of hoarding acted as a buffer. Portugal did not have a developed capital market, and the hoarding of gold was one of the most important forms of saving available to the public. Just what was the cause and what the effect is not easy to determine, and clearly relates to national preferences for forms of liquidity and saving, institutional constraints and national cultural characteristics. In any case, it was a situation in which external imbalances could have been met by a change in savings behaviour instead of a change in the money supply. Hence, there was no pressure on domestic prices to adjust to the new conditions. The Colombian example, until 1885, is similar. The bulk of the money stock comprised silver coin and, as in Portugal, the lack of a capital market forced people to save by hoarding bullion. However, lack of access to the international capital market made the relationship between the balance of payments and the money stock quite immediate, with domestic prices adjusting in response to the external conditions.

As these economies developed, domestic capital markets began to emerge and the need for fiduciary currency became apparent. By the 1870s, all six countries were more or less rapidly developing a note issue based on a legal obligation to redeem these monetary instruments in specie. The regulations for the backing of these notes varied from country to country. The 1860 Chilean banking law did not require any backing, whereas the Italian and Spanish regulations were very clear about the necessity for it. An explicit backing requirement directly connects the balance of payments with the monetary base but not necessarily with the money supply. For the latter to occur, there must be a strict relationship between the base and the stock of money. This often failed to happen, as shown by money multipliers that were far from constant. Variations in the public preference for currency and in the reserve:deposit ratio could alter the multiplier significantly. During times of financial stringency, when the preference for currency rose, the multiplier would fall. During periods of economic and financial expansion, if the rules regarding the reserve cover of deposits were lax or non-existent, the reserve:deposit ratio would be lowered and the multiplier would rise. The Chilean experience of the 1870s shows how severing the relationship between the balance of payments and the money stock could delay for years the price adjustments needed to restore internal and external equilibrium. In most cases, such a lag ended in an immense balance-of-payments-cum-financial crisis.

In all the countries, financial crises, bank failures and, above all, the government's needs to secure easy credit for its fiscal requirements prompted the creation of a monopoly for issuing fiduciary currency. In general, this was given to a privately-owned bank of issue that was willing to finance the government, within certain limits. With the passage of time, it evolved into a central bank. The rules established for this included a strict backing requirement, so that the balance of payments could at last be directly linked to the monetary base. Even so, the outcome varied a great deal from country to country depending on how these arrangements came about. This could mean a weak link to the money supply and a delayed response by domestic prices to external imbalances.

In Brazil and Chile the alternative to a central bank of issue was the setting of monetary rules. In both cases, the intention was to keep the domestic interest rate stable, following the 'real bills' doctrine. In Chile this was very successful because the government's financial needs did not disrupt the system but in Brazil these needs forced the banking sector to abandon the rule and thus inflation became embedded. There is a strong contrast in this respect with what happened in the European countries. Once Italy, Portugal and Spain had abandoned convertibility, their respective monetary policies seem to have been consistently geared to the restoration of convertibility, but at the nominal rate of exchange that had prevailed before the crisis. Policy therefore had to be stringent and follow a proxy-gold-standard norm. In all three cases, the nominal exchange rate was revalued during the early twentieth century and, until 1914, stayed close to the historical parity. With conditions so favourable, and bearing in mind the advantages it was supposed to bring, the question this poses is why none of these countries sought formally to re-establish the gold standard.

Why reject the gold standard?

At present we can only speculate about the reasons for this somewhat paradoxical option. As in several other instances, as yet we have no answers for what is obviously one of many fascinating questions relating to the history of monetary standards in the countries of the periphery. I can here address only the particular case of Spain, one of the nations that attempted to join the gold standard on several occasions but failed in every attempt.

Between 1902 and 1912 the government and parliament discussed a series of projects aimed at introducing the gold standard, with full redemption of Bank of Spain notes. The first move in this direction was made in January 1902, when the Minister of Finance submitted a proposal. This was to create an independent issuing department within the Bank of Spain and gradually to repay the public debt in circulation, as well as to effect a similar reduction of banknotes in the hands of the public. At the same time, in an effort to strengthen the metal reserves, the authorities tried to make it compulsory for customs duties to be settled in gold or foreign currency. But the minister's plans were thwarted by the Bank of Spain, whose management disliked the idea of increasing the metallic coverage of banknotes and reducing the quantity of notes in circulation.

The second attempt was also made in 1902, when a new Minister of Finance presented two laws to reform the monetary system. The first was aimed at reorganizing the issue system, modifying the composition of the Bank of Spain's assets and limiting the fiduciary circulation. Simultaneously, the Treasury agreed to return to the Bank, over a period of ten years, the total amount of outstanding floating debt in its portfolio. In addition, the rules on specie reserves were modified, strengthening the gold guarantee for banknotes in circulation. The second law once and for all banned silver purchases by the state, which also put an end to its policy of silver coinage. This was clearly an anti-inflationary policy, since it did away with one of the government's traditional means of creating money. Of course, the ultimate objective of all these measures was to reduce the quantity of money and thus improve the exchange rate of the peseta. However, the full implementation of these measures was hindered once more by the Bank of Spain, whose management always resisted any deflationary policy. In addition there were significant differences of opinion between the members of the Board of the Bank and the high civil servants of the ministry with regard to the application of the 1902 laws.

In 1903, there was yet another attempt to stabilize the exchange rate of the peseta and return to gold convertibility. The project included opening an exchange office at the Bank, whose task would be to buy and sell foreign currency on behalf of the Treasury. It was initially endowed with 400m. pesetas, plus funds from a foreign loan that was yet to be negotiated. However, the project collapsed after the fall of the government that supported it. During the ensuing decade four more projects were discussed, all designed to introduce the gold standard. The first was presented in October 1906, and three more followed in November 1908, January 1912 and December the same year. All sought to completely redeem the floating debt held by the Bank of Spain, to replace silver with gold as part of the specie guarantee for bank notes and to set the limits on future increases in fiduciary circulation. It was also proposed to create a gold fund by which to stabilize and defend the value of the peseta through intervening on the foreign-exchange market, something that would have ultimately led to the introduction of the gold standard. But yet again, none of these projects reached fruition.

The failure of all these attempts is difficult to explain. Perhaps one reason lay in the opposition of the Bank of Spain, which was not prepared to support the Ministry of Finance and assume its responsibilities. The members of the Board of the Spanish central bank refused on many occasions to use the gold reserves to sustain the peseta exchange rate, and thought that the stabilization of the currency was the government's task. It is also true that the political situation was not conducive to any of the stabilization plans. On the contrary, the rapid succession of governments, the doubts and unjustified fears and the fragility of the parliamentary coalitions hampered serious discussions and impeded the approval of a convertibility law. Although all were in theory in favour of the gold standard, the fact is that the regime was never adopted.

CHAPTER 8

The Bretton Woods Agreements: A Monetary Theory Perspective

Filippo Cesarano

The Bretton Woods monetary system is a highly controversial topic in international economics. During the quarter of a century after the Second World War, the largest industrialized countries experienced high growth accompanied by stable exchange rates and prices, constituting the best overall macroeconomic performance since the inception of the gold standard.[1] On the other hand, the Bretton Woods regime displayed a number of weaknesses – an inadequate adjustment mechanism, controls on capital movements, the adjustable peg and a possible incoherence between liquidity provision and gold convertibility – that eventually proved to be fatal. Acknowledging this contrasting evidence, Barry Eichengreen wittily remarked: 'Even today, more than three decades after its demise, the Bretton Woods international monetary system remains an enigma'.[2]

Viewed from the broader perspective of the evolution of monetary institutions, the Bretton Woods construction was part of the epoch-making transition from commodity money to fiat money. This was a momentous transformation that was gradually completed over the period stretching from the outbreak of the First World War to the suspension of the dollar's convertibility on 15 August 1971. Bretton Woods was the final stage of this lengthy process, a last, ephemeral attempt to maintain a link with commodity money. In fact, the very origin of the post-war monetary setting displays a peculiar feature. Distinguishing between a monetary *system* and a monetary *order*, Mundell[3] identified only three instances of a monetary order: the Roman-Byzantine,

1 M.D. Bordo, 'The Bretton Woods International Monetary System: A Historical Overview', in M.D. Bordo and B. Eichengreen (eds), *A Retrospective on the Bretton Woods System* (Chicago, 1993), p. 27.

2 B. Eichengreen, *Globalizing Capital. A History of the International Monetary System* (Princeton, 1996), p. 93.

3 'A system is an aggregation of diverse entities united by regular interaction according to some form of control. When we speak of the international monetary system we are concerned with the mechanisms governing the interaction between trading nations, and in particular between the money and credit instruments of national communities in foreign exchange, capital, and commodity markets. The control is exerted through policies at the national level interacting with one another in that loose form of supervision that we call co-operation. An *order*, as distinct from a system, represents the framework and setting in which the system operates. It is a framework of laws, conventions, regulations, and mores that establish the setting of the system and the understanding of the environment by the participants in it.

spanning almost 1,200 years from Julius Caesar to the fall of Constantinople; the gold standard; and Bretton Woods, with each displaying rather different characteristics. The Roman-Byzantine order was the product of imperialistic power, whereas the gold standard emerged from an historical process. In contrast, the Bretton Woods monetary order was a project elaborated by experts, an unprecedented event in monetary history that made the Bretton Woods architecture unique.

An immediate implication of this distinctive feature is the central role of theory. Drawing up a monetary plan requires knowledge of the principles underlying a monetary economy, and although political interests may come to bear, the end product reflects the designers' theoretical framework. In fact, owing to the early appropriation of the issuing function by a monopolist, namely the government, monetary thought exerted a strong influence upon both the design and the management of monetary institutions, even in ancient times when knowledge was rudimentary and rather scanty.[4] This influence was constrained by the commodity standard, but after the diffusion of fiduciary payment media and the advance of monetary economics from the mid eighteenth century, the impact of theory progressively increased. In the late nineteenth century, leading economists suggested innovative monetary schemes and, in the aftermath of the First World War, the quest for monetary reform gained momentum. In general, theory helps to shape the rules of the game, which in turn define the distinctive properties of a given monetary set-up.

Analysing the main theoretical contributions made during the inter-war years is essential for understanding both the origin and the basic characteristics of the Bretton Woods monetary order. From a theoretical perspective, the interpretation of Bretton Woods as the final stage of the transition from commodity money to fiat money clearly emerges. In fact, the various factors put forward to account for the end of Bretton Woods can be reduced to just one: the influence of monetary theory upon the development of the monetary system. In this respect, the Great Depression can be viewed as the 'defining moment'[5] in that it marks a watershed in the evolution of the state of the art. The different approaches to the subject before, and after, 1929 are examined here, showing their relationships with the key features of the Bretton Woods monetary order and the determinants of its demise.

A monetary order is to a monetary system somewhat like a constitution is to a political or electoral system. We can think of the monetary system as the *modus operandi* of the monetary order.' R.A. Mundell, 'The Future of the International Financial System', in A.L.K. Acheson, J.F. Chant and M.F.J. Prachowny (eds), *Bretton Woods Revisited* (London, 1972), p. 92, italics in the original.

4 F. Cesarano, 'Monetary Systems and Monetary Theory', *Kredit und Kapital*, 32, 2, 1999, pp. 192–208.

5 A recent collection of papers bearing this title, M.D. Bordo, C. Goldin and E.N. White (eds), *The Defining Moment. The Great Depression and the American Economy in the Twentieth Century* (Chicago, 1998), analyses the main changes brought about by the crisis of the 1930s, focusing, however, on economic policy rather than theory.

The critique of the gold standard

After the First World War, policymakers' overriding concern was to re-establish the gold standard. In 1918, the Cunliffe Committee called for Britain's return to gold to restore sound monetary and financial conditions, the prerequisite for economic stability. This recommendation was grounded on two basic principles of classical monetary theory: metallism, which considered it a necessary requisite of money to consist of, or be 'covered' by, a commodity;[6] and the equilibrium hypothesis, which assumed the self-adjusting property of the economy and, particularly, of the international monetary mechanism. With regard to the latter, Hume's specie-flow model is the *locus classicus*, but has continuously given rise to controversies since its publication and even before, witness Oswald's critical assessment.[7]

From a theoretical viewpoint, Hume's analysis is commonly thought to violate the law of one price, a key assumption of the modern monetary approach. From an empirical standpoint, the absence of large price differentials and the presence of conspicuous gold flows between countries each allegedly falsifies Hume's hypothesis. Both criticisms, however, are based on the traditional, textbook version of his model, which misinterprets it. On closer examination, Hume's essay maintains the law of one price, and rather than analysing the dynamics of the adjustment process, shows that market forces prevent a departure from long-run equilibrium.[8] This alternative interpretation portrays the gold standard as a homeostatic system hinging on a highly credible fixed parity, quite consistent with the empirical evidence.

The smooth functioning of the gold standard corroborated the hypothesis that it was an optimal monetary system, the crowning achievement of repeated efforts to dispose of centuries-long tampering with the currency by government. Essential to its successful operation were three 'implicit rules'.[9] First, the restoration rule – that is, the re-establishment of parity after a period of suspension in application of the escape clause to overcome major shocks[10] – solved the time-inconsistency problem of monetary policy, thus enhancing the system's credibility. Second, Bagehot's rule efficaciously tackled an incipient gold drain with an interest rate increase since, given highly credible fixed parities, very small interest rate differentials were sufficient to trigger substantial capital inflows. Third, the common price level was determined by the demand for, and supply of, gold, making the system entirely symmetrical because no country could affect the purchasing power of money. All in all, the successful performance of the gold standard stemmed from the efficacy of its implicit rules,

6 J.A. Schumpeter, *History of Economic Analysis* (Oxford, 1954) p. 288.

7 D. Hume, 'Of The Balance of Trade', in E. Rotwein (ed.), *David Hume. Writings on Economics* ([1752], Madison, 1970). J. Oswald of Dunnikier, 'Letter to Hume, 10 October 1750', in E. Rotwein (ed.), *David Hume. Writings on Economics* ([1750], Madison, 1970).

8 F. Cesarano, 'Hume's Specie-Flow Mechanism and Classical Monetary Theory: An Alternative Interpretation', in *Journal of International Economics*, 45, June 1998, pp. 173–86.

9 R.I. McKinnon, 'The Rules of the Game: International Money in Historical Perspective', in *Journal of Economic Literature,* 31, March 1993, pp. 1–44, here pp. 3–4.

10 M.D. Bordo and F.E. Kydland, 'The Gold Standard As a Rule: An Essay in Exploration', in *Explorations in Economic History*, 32, October 1995, pp. 423–64.

which were closely interrelated in that the enforcement of one of them enhanced the effectiveness of the others. In fact, the implicit rules were the basis of the chief properties of the gold standard – credibility, stability and symmetry – although this link was more complex than a simple one-to-one correspondence.

However, during the last quarter of the nineteenth century, economists had cast serious doubts on the optimality of the gold standard. On the one hand, advances in price theory exploded the notion of the value of gold as a natural phenomenon and, instead, made it depend on demand and supply forces in the same way as any other price.[11] On the other, the undesirable effects of deflationary pressure stimulated various proposals aimed at price-level stabilization.[12] Although coming from eminent economists, these proposals had hardly any impact on policymakers, whose attitude was rather adverse to innovation in monetary arrangements. Indeed, the cultural lag separating theorists from central bankers is a constant feature of the evolution of the monetary system, with far-reaching implications for its design.

The major problems inherited from the First World War – huge public debts, substantial and differentiated price-level increases, a fall in gold production[13] and war reparations – made the rapid reinstatement of the gold standard, particularly of the restoration rule, hardly sustainable by most countries. The Genoa Conference, April 1922, was an attempt to solve these problems through the gold-exchange standard, which called for coordination between central banks to stabilize the value of gold.[14] Yet only a few policymakers conformed to the Genoa Resolutions, whereas many continued to abide by the gold-standard model. This discrepancy between innovative arrangements and central bank behaviour was one of the chief factors that eventually undermined the monetary system.

---

11 D. Laidler, 'Rules, Discretion and Financial Crises in Classical and Neoclassical Monetary Economics', ms., April 2001, p. 19.

12 To mention just a few representative examples: Jevons suggested the tabular standard introduced earlier by Lowe. Marshall, instead, argued for symmetallism, defining the unit of account as a weighted basket of gold and silver. Walras proposed issuing a divisionary money (billon régulateur) in order to stabilize the money stock. Finally, Wicksell deserves to be mentioned because, in contrast with the other schemes that were all variations on the commodity standard theme, he argued for cutting the link with gold altogether, a 'first step towards the introduction of an ideal standard of value.', K. Wicksell, *Interest and Prices* ([1898], New York, 1965), p. 193.

13 According to R. Nurkse, *International Currency Experience. Lessons of the Inter-War Period* (Geneva, 1944), p. 27, gold output decreased by a third between 1915 and 1922.

14 'These steps [balancing of budgets; adoption of gold as a common standard; fixing of gold parities; cooperation of central banks, etc.] might by themselves suffice to establish a gold standard, but its successful maintenance would be materially promoted [...] by an international convention to be adopted at a suitable time. The purpose of the convention would be to centralize and coordinate the demand for gold, and so avoid those wide fluctuations in the purchasing power of gold which might otherwise result from the simultaneous and competitive efforts of a number of countries to secure metallic reserves. The convention should embody some means of economizing the use of gold by maintaining reserves in the form of foreign balances, such, for example, as the gold exchange standard or an international clearing system.', Ibid., p. 28.

In the academic world, several aspects of commodity money were criticized on theoretical grounds, although the policy argument stressing the barrier against government interference proved an ultimate defence. Inconvertible paper money, therefore, was usually discarded, with the notable exception of Wicksell.[15] In any case, the goal of price stability became the starting-point of the analysis.[16] It led to consideration of a monetary-setting alternative to the gold standard, a 'managed' money instead of a 'natural' money. However, the state of the art presented a rather variegated picture and no common view of the monetary system emerged. Resorting to a heroic simplification, three main strains of thought can be distinguished. The prevailing idea was to shift to managed money while simultaneously maintaining a link with gold. At each side of this middle-of-the-road position, there were two extreme approaches. The radical, chiefly represented by Keynes, favoured the abandonment of commodity money, assigning to the central bank wide discretionary powers to stabilize prices and employment. The conservative, mainly followed by Austrian economists like Mises and Hayek, stuck firmly to the gold standard.

Ralph Hawtrey, a noted exponent of the mainstream and a protagonist of the Genoa Conference, stressed the necessity of resorting to fiduciary media to satisfy the demand for money. He referred to the gold-exchange standard as 'the favourite of currency theorists'.[17] The danger of over-issuing was pointed out, but eventually it was the deflationary pressure produced by the conspicuous accumulation of gold by the United States and France that proved fatal to the monetary system. Central bankers, not deeming the gold-exchange standard as credible as the gold standard, remained faithful to the latter's paradigm. Consequently, while cooperation was essential for stabilizing the value of gold, the necessary meeting of central banks to undertake it never took place.[18] Indeed, from the very beginning, the gold-exchange

15 In his classic on quantity theory, I. Fisher, *The Purchasing Power of Money* ([1911], New York, 1963), ch. 13, recognizes the theoretical soundness of fiat money, but rejects it because of the likelihood of government's meddling with monetary stability. Anticipating Friedman's simple rule, he critically considers a 'simple way' of stabilizing the price level. 'It is true that the level of prices might be kept almost absolutely stable merely by honest government regulation of the money supply with that specific purpose in view. One seemingly simple way by which this might be attempted would be by the issue of inconvertible paper money in quantities so proportioned to increase of business that the total amount of currency in circulation, multiplied by its rapidity, would have the same relation to the total business at one time as at any other time. If the confidence of citizens were preserved, and this relation were kept, the problem would need no further solution. But sad experience teaches that irredeemable paper money, while theoretically capable of steadying prices, is apt in practice to be so manipulated as to produce instability', Ibid., p. 329.

16 A.C. Pigou, *Industrial Fluctuations* (London, 1927), pp. 251–7; D.H. Robertson, *Money* ([1928], Cambridge, 1970), p. 116; G. Cassel, *The Theory of Social Economy* ([1932b], New York, 1967), p. 510.

17 R.G. Hawtrey, 'The Gold Standard', in *Economic Journal*, 29, December 1919, pp. 428–42, here p. 437.

18 Montagu Norman's testimony before the Macmillan Committee is, in this respect, rather eloquent. 'It always appeared impossible, during those years when we were waiting, to summon such a conference for the excellent reason that the people would not come. They would not come, not because they were unwilling to co-operate, but because they were

standard was considered 'with misgiving and suspicion as an academic proposal of doubtful practicability'.[19] Such widespread scepticism can be understood since the introduction of an activist policy in place of an 'automatic' mechanism involved such a momentous mutation that even those favouring the new system displayed a great deal of caution. The novel tasks given to central banks marked the birth of modern monetary policy, whose implementation raised complex theoretical questions that are still debated.[20] Moreover, there was great concern about losing the shield against government interference provided by the gold standard.[21] Both theoretical and political difficulties heightened central bankers' conservative attitude, which contrasted with the change in behaviour required by the Genoa Resolutions. Initially, the policies of the United States and the United Kingdom were coherent

---

unwilling to face the publicity and the questionings in their own countries, which would arise if they attended any such conference, and all the attempts that I made to that end failed.', quoted in R.G. Hawtrey, *The Gold Standard in Theory and Practice* ([1927], London, 1947), p. 102. According to Hawtrey, the meeting of central bankers would have had a meaning quite different from the preceding ones. 'Another international conference! What, will the line stretch out to the crack of doom? But here there is a difference. The calling in of the central banks is a recognition of the principle that currency policy is ultimately credit policy, for the direction of credit policy is the special function of a central bank', R.G. Hawtrey, 'The Genoa Resolutions on Currency', in *Economic Journal*, 32, September 1922, pp. 290–304, here p. 291.

19 Ibid., p. 295.

20 'Stabilisation cannot be secured by any hard-and-fast rules. The central banks must exercise discretion; they must be ready to detect and forestall any monetary disturbance even before it has affected prices. The policy can only be perfected by long experience. Nor can it be assumed that perfect stabilisation of internal purchasing power is always reconcilable with perfect stabilisation of the foreign exchanges. The maintenance of the exchanges within a small fraction of parity, which is of the essence of the scheme, may involve a small departure of the internal purchasing power of the unit from the norm in one or more countries. A suitable compromise must be arrived at by the central banks among themselves, but it is no use to under-estimate the difficulty of preserving an even course under such conditions.', Ibid., p. 300. In this regard, Keynes too shows a prudent attitude. '[A]n internal standard, so regulated as to maintain stability in an index number of prices, is a difficult scientific innovation, never yet put into practice.', J.M. Keynes, *A Tract on Monetary Reform* (London, 1923), p. 156.

21 'We must remember the enormous impetus to which any banking system is subject, both from within and without, towards increasing continually the volume of its loans, and the formidable difficulty of so regulating the supply of money as really to meet the legitimate needs of trade. We must remember, too, the pressure exerted upon Governments in the name of the consumer to provide this and that – coal or railway-transport or house-room – by some means or other below its economic cost. It is not surprising if both bankers and Governments in their more responsible moments desire to have some charm more potent than a mere metaphysical index-number both to elevate before the people and to contemplate in the privacy of their own cells. There are the same arguments against disturbing the simple faith of the banker and the City journalist (the politician perhaps has none) as against disturbing that of the pious savage. If a gold standard had never existed, it might be necessary to invent something of the kind for their benefit', Robertson, *Money*, pp. 121–2. Recalling the peculiar experience of stone money on the island of Yap, Robertson remarks: 'Just so gold is a fetish, if you will, but it does the trick', Ibid., p. 123.

with the gold-exchange standard. However, in the late 1920s, the gulf between the innovative model that had emerged at Genoa and central bankers' lack of adaptation or downright hostility to the new mode of thought increased. This brought about the subsequent monetary turmoil.

The goal of purchasing-power stability, which contrasted with price-level determination in the gold market, broke the third implicit rule and, therefore, opened a fissure in the gold standard. A further, more conspicuous, crack followed from the critique of the restoration rule. Its enforcement would have produced a substantial deflation in most countries, thus raising the real value of public debt and depressing output and employment. *Prima facie*, going back to the pre-war parity entailed a once-and-for-all adjustment of monetary equilibrium. Yet, from a modern point of view, it also affected monetary policy as a continuous process since it prevented the time-inconsistency problem. Hence, the critique of the restoration rule undermined the credibility of the gold standard, as well as the stabilizing role of capital movements stemming from Bagehot's rule. Thus, all the implicit rules of the gold standard were impaired, as were their related properties – stability, credibility and symmetry – not easily reproduced in another monetary setting. In fact, the attempt to compensate for the loss of credibility of the gold-exchange standard by increased cooperation failed, simply because cooperation under the gold standard resulted from a high degree of credibility. Once the rules of the gold standard were called into question, the very characteristics of the system were spoiled, and it was hard to reinstate them by other devices.

Departing from the mainstream, Keynes interpreted monetary reform in a radical way, arguing for a bending of the rules of the monetary system with a view to stabilizing prices and employment.[22] This approach, turning upside down the gold-standard model, characterized his research programme on the subject. Clearly, the theoretical framework supporting this idea changed as Keynes's monetary thought progressed from the *Tract* to the *Treatise*, to the *General Theory* and beyond, but the leitmotiv remained the same. Instead of constraining the policymaker's behaviour by means of rigid rules, modify the latter in order to implement activist economic policy. The resort to debasement during the Middle Ages was, thus, considered positively 'as a method of carrying into effect a preference for stability of internal prices over stability of external exchanges'.[23] The chief advantages of the gold standard, that is long-run purchasing-power stability and insulation from political interference, were rejected simply by acknowledging the existence of a 'managed' currency in place of a 'natural' one.[24] Considering a 'pious hope'[25] the possibility of successfully carrying out the cooperation required by the gold-exchange standard, Keynes refused half-way solutions, which he deemed inferior to either the gold standard or fiduciary money, and embraced a modern conception of monetary policy, not, however, based

22 Keynes, *Tract*.
23 Ibid., p. 163.
24 Ibid., pp. 172–3.
25 Ibid., p. 174.

on 'a precise, arithmetical formula'.[26] Taking a radical position, Keynes called for cutting the link with gold altogether and allowing substantial discretion in monetary policy.[27]

At the other end of the academic spectrum, Austrian economists such as Mises and Hayek opposed any degree of discretion in monetary management and staunchly defended the gold standard. Albeit sharing the target of stable prices, Mises stressed the difficulty of attaining it, owing to the lack of knowledge of the monetary transmission mechanism – the argument, together with long and variable lags, for Friedman's 'simple rule'. Furthermore, it was argued that discretionary monetary policy led to government abuses and, thus, much higher costs than those deriving from the lack of money stock controllability in the gold standard.[28] Interestingly, Mises,[29] starting from a diametrically opposite position, arrived at the same conclusions as Keynes, namely that the two extreme models, the gold standard and fiat money, were to be preferred to the hybrid gold exchange standard. This is also Milton Friedman's opinion in his classic essay on flexible exchange rates.[30]

---

26 Ibid., p. 186. '[S]ince I regard the stability of prices, credit, and employment as of paramount importance, and since I feel no confidence that an old-fashioned gold standard will even give us the modicum of stability that it used to give, I reject the policy of restoring the gold standard on pre-war lines. At the same time I doubt the wisdom of attempting a "managed" gold standard jointly with the United States, on the lines recommended by Mr. Hawtrey, because it retains too many of the disadvantages of the old system without its advantages, and because it would make us too dependent on the policy and on the wishes of the Federal Reserve Board.', Ibid., p. 176.

27 'It is desirable, therefore, that the whole of the reserves should be under the control of the authority responsible for this, which, under the above proposals, is the Bank of England. The volume of the paper money, on the other hand, would be consequential, as it is at present, on the state of trade and employment, bank-rate policy and Treasury Bill policy. The governors of the system would be bank-rate and Treasury Bill policy, the objects of government would be stability of trade, prices, and employment, and the volume of paper money would be a consequence of the first (just – I repeat – as it is at present) and an instrument of the second, the precise arithmetical level of which could not and need not be predicted. Nor would the amount of gold, which it would be prudent to hold as a reserve against international emergencies and temporary indebtedness, bear any logical or calculable relation to the volume of paper money; – for the two have no close or necessary connection with one another. Therefore I make the proposal – which may seem, but should not be, shocking – of separating entirely the gold reserve from the note issue', Ibid., pp. 195-6.

28 L. von Mises, *The Theory of Money and Credit* ([1912], Indianapolis, 1980), pp. 268–71. The 1934 English translation of von Mises is based on the second German edition published in 1924.

29 Ibid., p. 432.

30 M. Friedman, 'The Case for Flexible Exchange Rates', in M. Friedman, *Essays in Positive Economics* (Chicago, 1953), p. 164; also M. Friedman, 'Real and Pseudo Gold Standards', in *Journal of Law and Economics*, 4, October 1961, reprinted in M. Friedman, *Dollars and Deficits. Inflation, Monetary Policy and the Balance of Payments* (Englewood Cliffs, N.J, 1968), pp. 150–1.

Hayek's case for the gold standard rested on the analysis of business cycles[31] and of monetary policy.[32] He underscored the notion of neutral rather than stable money,[33] so that money should not disturb optimal resource allocation as determined in the general equilibrium model. The neutrality principle, however, is hard to translate into a policy norm, given price rigidity and unpredictability. While price stability would tamper with general equilibrium, a declining price level stemming from productivity increases entailed no costs and avoided distortions in factor allocation. Criticizing Cassel's and Pigou's call for an elastic currency, Hayek, like Mises, emphasized the lack of knowledge of the monetary transmission mechanism, and argued for a constant money stock, albeit with changes allowed to compensate for velocity variations.[34]

The difficulties inherited from the First World War led to a rethinking of the basic features of the monetary system along the lines discussed at the Genoa Conference. The gold exchange standard was assumed to maintain the essential properties of the gold standard, but in reality impaired credibility. Hawtrey's conjecture to offset this credibility loss with more intensive cooperation was at odds with both the innovations introduced into monetary arrangements and central bankers' cultural background. In fact, the suggestion of stabilizing the price level sowed the seeds of spoiling the properties of the pre-war monetary system irremediably. Accordingly, the reformed gold standard eventually collapsed, leaving no common view about the optimal design of monetary institutions. A protagonist of this transformation in the state of the art was Keynes. Explaining these developments with the diffusion of managed money, Hayek traced its origins back to the transition from the gold-specie standard to the gold-bullion standard. The main point was the role of the monetary authority, that is whether or not it could regulate the quantity of money. In this regard, the United Kingdom's abandonment of the gold standard in September 1931 was a watershed in monetary history and the product of a new theoretical paradigm, chiefly due to Keynes.[35]

---

31 F.A. von Hayek, *Monetary Theory and the Trade Cycle* ([1933b], New York, 1966).

32 F. A. von Hayek, *Prices and Production* ([1931], New York, 1967).

33 F. A. von Hayek, 'On "Neutral Money"', in R. McCloughry (ed.), *Money, Capital & Fluctuations* ([1933a], London, 1984).

34 Hayek, *Prices*, pp. 121–4.

35 'This abandonment of the gold standard undoubtedly implies a final break with the unique tradition of more than two hundred years, on the basis of which Britain has repeatedly returned to the gold standard at the cost of great sacrifices, even after periods of temporary shock to its currency unit. This time the sacrifices which had been made since 1921 were in vain, because the responsible authorities were unwilling or unable to exact what probably would have been the smaller sacrifices necessary to ensure the long-term position of the pound. The greatest responsibility for this, however, must be borne by those who initially opposed the return to the gold standard. For although their position was justifiable at that time, they did not abandon it even when the gold standard had been restored at its former parity, and fought with the utmost vigour against all the measures necessary if that standard were to be finally consolidated. It is beyond all doubt that they found an increasingly more receptive hearing within the management of the Bank. If one wanted to describe the abandonment of the gold standard in Britain as "the economic consequences of Mr Keynes", and there

The Great Depression and the search for an alternative monetary system

The Great Depression had a major impact upon the economics profession, and led to a general rethinking of the monetary system. The critical assessment of the gold standard after the shock of the First World War weakened the metallist doctrine, one of the two foundations of the classical model. The length and severity of the 1930s depression undermined the second, viz. the equilibrium hypothesis, thus enhancing the acceptance of managed money.

During the 1930s, while support for the gold standard faded, economists were divided over the equilibrium hypothesis. Keynes was the most notable exponent of the critical view, taking, as during the previous decade, a radical position on both economic theory and monetary reform. The mainstream, instead, stuck to the classical model, and arrived at a monetary explanation of the Great Depression, anticipating Milton Friedman's 'inescapable [conclusion]: ... monetary contraction or collapse is an essential conditioning factor for the occurrence of a major depression'.[36] In his Rhodes Memorial Lectures, Gustav Cassel, stressing the different nature of the 1929 crisis with respect to pre-war business cycles, identified its basic characteristic in the price level's sharp fall, which was a monetary phenomenon and, therefore, admitted only a monetary explanation.[37] Following this line of thought, Hawtrey emphasized the dynamic aspect of central bank policy, and thus the danger of disturbing equilibrium through untimely action. Starting from the relationship between the quantity of money and nominal income, Hawtrey put the case for stabilizing the money supply on more solid ground, referring to both assumptions underlying Friedman's simple rule: the presence of lags and the lack of knowledge of the transmission mechanism.[38] Hawtrey also stressed the depression's international character, showing how, in the absence of monetary cooperation, mistaken monetary policies were transmitted to other countries. In particular, the absence of concerted action to implement monetary expansion proved fatal to the gold-exchange standard.[39] The accumulation of gold by the United States and France stopped the adjustment process from the very outset and set off a deflationary process.[40] At the basis of such behaviour was central bankers' distrust of innovations in monetary arrangements departing from the gold standard, thus showing the permanence of a cultural divide between policymakers and economists.[41] In any case, monetary mismanagement, owing to either a violation

---

are many reasons to do so, I believe that even today J.M. Keynes would still regard such a statement not as criticism but as praise.', F.A. von Hayek, 'The Fate of the Gold Standard', in R. McCloughry (ed.), *Money, Capital and Fluctuations* ([1932], London, 1984), pp. 132–3.

36 M. Friedman, 'Why the American Economy is Depression-Proof', in M. Friedman, *Dollars and Deficits. Inflation, Monetary Policy and the Balance of Payments* ([1954], Englewood Cliffs, N.J, 1968), pp. 82–3.

37 G. Cassel, *The Crisis in the World's Monetary System* (Oxford, 1932a), pp. 41–9.

38 R.G. Hawtrey, *The Art of Central Banking* ([1932], London, 1970), pp. 280–2.

39 R.G. Hawtrey, *Economic Destiny* (London, 1944), pp. 88–9.

40 Cassel, *Crisis*, pp. 63–72.

41 David Williams gives a good description of central bankers' conservative attitude in the 1920s. 'Once the chief results of the gold exchange standard had been achieved – stabilization of exchange rates and the strengthening of monetary reserves – there was

of the gold standard rules or a failure to cooperate and stabilize the money stock, accounted for major downturns in economic activity which, coherently with the equilibrium hypothesis, required a monetary therapy.

In the mid-1930s, this analysis became widely accepted, witness the contributions to Irving Fisher's Festschrift volume.[42] The starting-point was the necessity of reducing the amplitude of cyclical fluctuations since a sharp increase in output caused a subsequent recession and an unstable growth path.[43] The policy recipe was to stabilize the money supply, which, though not eliminating income fluctuations entirely, could reduce them to within small limits.[44] Accordingly, monetary arrangements, in contrast with the commodity standard, must allow control of the money stock.[45] However, while the departure from the rigid rules of the gold

---

increasing pressure by some important countries to revert to a gold bullion standard. The gold exchange standard was never accepted as anything but a temporary palliative by France; Germany and the smaller countries of West and Central Europe had a strong desire to hold as much gold as was possible. The gold exchange standard in the 'twenties was regarded not only as an expedient, but as a temporary expedient', D. Williams, 'The 1931 Financial Crisis', *Yorkshire Bulletin of Economic and Social Research*, 15, November 1963, pp. 92–110, reprinted in M. Thomas (ed.), *The Disintegration of the World Economy Between the World Wars*, vol. 2 ([1963], Cheltenham and Brookfield, 1996), p. 95.

42 A.D. Gayer (ed.), *The Lessons of Monetary Experience* (London, 1937).

43 In this regard, the Fed chairman, Marriner Eccles, notes: 'Those who believe in nature taking its course argue that there are forces that tend to restore the flow of income when it is disturbed. ... The answer to this argument is that it is true as far as it goes, but it does not go far enough. It assumes a condition of stable national income, and this is precisely the condition that is absent during a general downswing. ... Similarly, in depressions, when incomes are falling, a reduction in prices may fail to stimulate demand. This is particularly likely to happen if a further continued fall in prices is generally expected. Thus a departure from stability, although it may set in motion corrective forces, also unfortunately produces intensifying and aggravating ones. Our recent experience is grim witness to the fact that these latter forces may far outweigh the corrective forces for an impossibly long period. Before the self-generating forces of deflation in the last depression were exhausted or were offset by positive government action, the national income had been cut in half, and a sixth of our population was being supported out of public funds. Now that we are on the upswing, the self-generating forces of revival might carry us into another boom unless we are prepared to take corrective action in time', M.S. Eccles, 'Controlling Booms and Depressions', in A.D. Gayer (ed.), *The Lessons of Monetary Experience* (London, 1937), pp. 7–8. See J.W. Angell, 'The General Objectives of Monetary Policy', in A.D. Gayer (ed.), *The Lessons of Monetary Experience* (London, 1937), pp. 52–3; A.H. Hansen, 'Monetary Policy in the Upswing', in A.D. Gayer (ed.), *The Lessons of Monetary Experience* (London, 1937), p. 89; J.H. Williams, 'International Monetary Organization and Policy', in A.D. Gayer (ed.), *The Lessons of Monetary Experience* (London, 1937), p. 26.

44 Angell, 'Objectives', p. 83.

45 'The criminal characteristic of the money and banking systems that have hitherto existed in nearly all modern countries is that they have been inherently unstable within wide limits, and that they have usually worked to *intensify* fluctuations in both directions rather than to damp them down. In so-called good times, when the total money volume of economic activity is increasing, most money and banking systems also greatly increase the quantity of circulating money; indeed, this is one of the favorite ways of augmenting the current volume

standard, suggested by Keynes much earlier,[46] was generally accepted,[47] there was no unanimous opinion about the design of a new monetary setting, a daunting task after the monetary gyrations following the 1929 crisis. Various suggestions were put forward to improve the working of the gold-exchange standard – cancel war debts, re-establish freedom in international trade and capital movements and reduce the demand for gold reserves[48] – but an essential condition remained the stabilization of the value of gold through cooperation. The scepticism surrounding the accomplishment of this objective prevented the formulation of detailed proposals for reconstructing the monetary system. Wide credence was given, instead, to the conception of monetary policy as a continuous process aimed at preventing major cyclical fluctuations in order to maintain price and output stability.[49]

As during the 1920s, the range of opinions remained highly variegated,[50] but the state of the art's centre of gravity permanently shifted away from an 'automatic'

---

of new private investment rapidly. But the increase in the quantity of money, if regarded by the business community as 'normal,' is itself likely to intensify the changes which are already under way. ... All this taken alone might not be a conclusive condemnation. But if expansion does at last cease, and gives way to the beginning of contraction, the money and banking system suddenly turns about, and now intensifies the general *fall.* As bank investments are sold and as bank loans are called or allowed to run off, the quantity of money declines; this decline and the circumstances out of which it arises engender new fear, and accentuate the fall in expectation and the rise in idle balances of cash which are developing anyway; the growing struggle for business solvency compels many liquidations of inventories and other holdings, which further increases the banks' desire to reduce their commitments, and thus further contracts the quantity of money; and thus a downward spiral of interactions is initiated. Once well under way, as is only too familiar, the decline can go to disastrous lengths before it is checked', Angell, 'Objectives', pp. 83–5, italics in the original.

46 Keynes, *Tract.*

47 Mlynarsky clearly describes the change in the state of the art. 'The classical doctrine of the automatic standard was thus opposed by the conception of a managed currency. More and more economists were accepting the principles of the new school. Today Keynes appears to have the greatest number of adherents; according to him the gold parity should be changed from time to time. Foreign-exchange quotations should fluctuate within limits broader than those of the gold points, for instance within 5 per cent of a given parity. The issue of bank notes should be severed from gold movements and controlled only from the point of view of stabilizing the purchasing power of money as the most important consideration. Without going into technical details, and without discussing the shortcomings or advantages of the new doctrine, it can be stated that it is a complete reversal of the Ricardian theory and hence quite revolutionary with regard to the classical doctrine', F. Mlynarsky, 'Proportionalism and Stabilization Policy', in A.D. Gayer (ed.), *The Lessons of Monetary Experience* (London, 1937), p. 272.

48 Cassel, *Crisis*, pp. 89–92.

49 Angell, 'Objectives', pp. 52–3.

50 Viner makes this point. 'In the late 1930's probably no country was wholly satisfied with the existing monetary situation. But there was no agreement as to the directions in which improvement was to be sought. Some wished for a return to the rigid pre-1914 gold standard, without fundamental change therein. Others dreamed of a new kind of gold standard – an internationally managed one designed to produce both stability of the exchanges and stability of world price levels, so as to cure the great defect of the traditional gold standard, that it made

monetary mechanism. However, the pursuit of domestic targets through a managed money might conflict with the maintenance of a fixed parity,[51] eventually leading to the link with gold being cut. This conclusion, once regarded as seemingly 'shocking', was accepted a decade later by all economists arguing for a viable managed money. As Cassel remarked: 'Clearly, the only way to a permanent stabilization of the world's monetary system is to make the supply of credit entirely independent of the gold reserves of central banks'.[52] This question may be viewed as the origin of the policy 'trilemma'[53] – also called the inconsistent trinity, or irreconcilable trilogy, or eternal triangle. In this, only two of the following three elements can be included in choosing a policy regime: fixed exchange rates, free capital movements and independent monetary policy aimed at domestic goals. This is indicative of the complex problems, both theoretical and institutional, that arose from the abandonment of the gold standard during the early 1930s. To give a cursory example: while Cassel fully grasped the one-way bet offered by a gold parity that was not credible,[54] thus anticipating Friedman's criticism of the Bretton Woods system,[55] several other problems remained unsolved. Economists, venturing into uncharted waters, did not arrive at a clear idea for the design of future monetary arrangements.[56]

Following the impact of the Great Depression, the mainstream moved towards the position taken by Keynes roughly a decade before. However, Keynes was now proposing more innovative monetary schemes. His *Treatise on Money*, although widely criticized from a theoretical point of view, suggested a monetary setting

---

the world subject to sustained deflationary or inflationary price trends resulting from fortuitous developments in the discovery of gold fields and in the technology of gold mining. Still others, and especially the totalitarian countries, sought a permanent and complete divorce of their monetary systems from gold and a further extension and intensification of exchange controls administered on a national basis and with narrowly nationalistic and indeed, in some cases, openly aggressive objectives.', J. Viner, 'Two Plans for International Monetary Stabilization', in J. Viner, *International Economics* ([1943], Glencoe, Ill., 1951), p. 194. See also Angell, Objectives, pp. 53–4.

51 Keynes, *Tract*, ch. 4.

52 G. Cassel, *The Downfall of the Gold Standard* ([1936], New York, 1966), p. 229.

53 M. Obstfeld and A.M. Taylor, 'The Great Depression as a Watershed: International Capital Mobility over the Long Run', in M.D. Bordo, C. Goldin and E.N. White (eds), *The Defining Moment. The Great Depression and the American Economy in the Twentieth Century* (Chicago, 1998), pp. 354–5.

54 Cassel, *Downfall*, pp. 240–1.

55 Friedman, 'Case', pp. 163–4.

56 Two specific proposals, though subject to various criticisms, may be an exception: Fisher's 100 per cent reserve requirement: I. Fisher, 'The Debt-Deflation Theory of Great Depressions', in *Econometrica*, 1, October 1933, pp. 337–57, and I. Fisher, *100 per cent Money* ([1935], New Haven, 1945), pp. 133–4, with a view to dampening fluctuations in the money multiplier, and thus in the money supply, and Benjamin Graham's and Frank Graham's commodity reserve currency, substituting a basket of commodities for a single one as the standard in order to avoid the defects of the gold standard and preserve all its advantages, B. Graham, *Storage and Stability* (New York, 1937), and F.D. Graham, 'The Primary Functions of Money and Their Consummation in Monetary Policy', in *American Economic Review. Papers and Proceedings*, 30, March 1940, part 2, pp. 1–16.

consistent with the implementation of autonomous economic policy and the maintenance of stable exchange rates.[57] Widening the gold price fluctuation band to 2 per cent would discourage capital movements, and make it possible to manoeuvre short-term interest rates for internal purposes. The high capital mobility of the gold standard had to be avoided because, in an economy characterized by rigidities, it would produce serious imbalances.[58] The control of capital movements provided a solution to the policy trilemma that was to be part of the British position during the Bretton Woods negotiations. In the final chapter of the *Treatise*, two plans were proposed: a more limited one, mostly tracking the Resolutions of the Genoa Conference, and a more radical one, based on the establishment of a supranational central bank.

After the Great Depression, Keynes's main contributions were to economic theory, not monetary institutions. In contrast with the received view that identified the cause of the crisis with monetary mismanagement in an equilibrium model, he rejected the equilibrium hypothesis.[59] The foundations of this approach were

---

57 J.M. Keynes, *A Treatise on Money* (London, 1930), vol. 2, pp. 300–6.

58 'If we deliberately desire that there should be a high degree of mobility for international lending, both for long and for short periods, then this is, admittedly, a strong argument for a fixed rate of exchange and a rigid international standard. What, then, is the reason for hesitating before we commit ourselves to such a system? Primarily a doubt whether it is wise to have a Currency System with a much wider ambit than our Banking System, our Tariff System and our Wage System. Can we afford to allow a disproportionate degree of mobility to a single element in an economic system which we leave extremely rigid in several other respects? If there was the same mobility internationally in all other respects as there is nationally, it might be a different matter. But to introduce a mobile element, highly sensitive to outside influences, as a connected part of a machine of which the other parts are much more rigid, may invite breakages', Keynes, *Treatise*, vol. 2, pp. 334–5.

59 In a radio broadcast with the eloquent title 'Poverty in Plenty: Is the Economic System Self-Adjusting?', Keynes divides economists into two groups according to their positive or negative answer to the question. Including himself in the second one, he claims to have found a basic weakness in the orthodox model. 'Now *I* range myself with the heretics. I believe their flair and their instinct move them towards the right conclusion. But I was brought up in the citadel and I recognize its power and might. A large part of the established body of economic doctrine I cannot but accept as broadly correct. I do not doubt it. For me, therefore, it is impossible to rest satisfied until I can put my finger on the flaw in that part of the orthodox reasoning which leads to the conclusions which for various reasons seem to me to be unacceptable. I believe that I am on my way to do so. There is, I am convinced, a fatal flaw in that part of the orthodox reasoning which deals with the theory of what determines the level of effective demand and the volume of aggregate employment; the flaw being largely due to the failure of the classical doctrine to develop a satisfactory theory of the rate of interest', J.M. Keynes, 'Poverty in Plenty: Is the Economic System Self-Adjusting?', in D. Moggridge (ed.), *The Collected Writings of John Maynard Keynes, vol. 13* ([1934], London, 1973), p. 489, italics in the original. In a previous passage, Keynes lucidly expounds the main principles of the classical position underlying the malfunctioning of the monetary system. 'Professor Robbins [...] stresses the effect of business mistakes under the influence of the uncertainty and the false expectations due to the faults of post-war monetary systems. These authorities do not, of course, believe that the system is automatically or immediately self-adjusting. But

developed in the *General Theory* which, given its policy implications, was to play a key role in shaping the design of monetary institutions. He dealt with the latter topic in two essays reflecting the vision of his *magnum opus*. The scheme outlined in *The Means to Prosperity* is the institutional counterpart of an analysis investigating the conditions for economic recovery, and anticipates many features of the Bretton Woods system. Besides providing abundant credit and maintaining a low long-run interest rate, a public expenditure programme must be implemented to trigger output expansion.[60] In the monetary proposal, an international authority issues gold notes, obtainable by countries against gold bonds according to quotas determined on the basis of gold reserves. Voting power is proportional to quotas. The main aim is to stabilize the price level by fixing the interest rate and controlling the creation of gold notes. In Keynes's words, the plan involved 'a qualified return to the gold standard',[61] allowing parity variations and a widening of the gold points up to 5 per cent to discourage capital movements. In a subsequent paper,[62] two kinds of problems were distinguished: short-run fluctuations and a persistent disequilibrium. The former could be tackled with the policies indicated in the *Means to Prosperity*. The latter, mainly related to either a divergence between wage and efficiency increases, or more general causes – such as a lack of confidence or the possibility of war – required a parity change. The article's message was to eschew credit contraction to cure a 'fundamental international maladjustment'.[63] This was a concept analogous to the 'fundamental disequilibrium' of the Bretton Woods agreements because, in the absence of a decrease in nominal wages, monetary restriction would raise unemployment.

The Great Depression was indeed a turning point because it delivered a fatal blow to the theoretical model underlying the gold standard. Before 1929, criticism of the latter was confined to the academic world in its search for a more stable monetary set-up, but had little or no impact on policymakers. In fact, as has been shown, central bankers' unwavering trust in the gold-standard model was a main factor in the monetary gyrations of that period. After 1929, the state of the art's centre of gravity definitely moved towards managed money, and even policymakers began to distance themselves from gold-standard orthodoxy. In this regard, there are striking differences between the results of the Cunliffe Committee in 1918 and those of the Macmillan Committee in 1931. The former stressed the benefits of the gold standard and the necessity of the return to gold, whereas the latter argued for a managed money aimed at not only maintaining parity but also stabilizing prices and employment, thus revealing a fracture in the approach to monetary arrangements. Clearly, such a major paradigm shift occurred at different speeds according to

---

they do believe that it has an inherent tendency towards self-adjustment, if it is not interfered with and if the action of change and chance is not too rapid', Ibid., p. 487.

60 J.M. Keynes, 'The Means to Prosperity', in D. Moggridge (ed.), *The Collected Writings of John Maynard Keynes, vol. 9* ([1933], London, 1972), pp. 353–5.

61 Ibid., p. 362.

62 J.M. Keynes, 'The Future of the Foreign Exchanges', in D. Moggridge (ed.), *The Collected Writings of John Maynard Keynes, vol. 21* ([1935], London, 1982).

63 Ibid., p. 367.

the relative degree of conservatism of the protagonists.[64] Even abstracting for a moment from both Keynes's downright rejection of the equilibrium hypothesis and the message of the *General Theory*, mainstream economists definitely rejected the 'automatic' gold standard, although they did not have a unanimous view about how to reform the monetary system.

The Bretton Woods agreements: designing the post-war monetary order

After the unsuccessful attempt of the Tripartite Agreement in September 1936, the objective of reconstructing the monetary system was pursued by the major powers from the outbreak of war. Germany's *Neuordnung*[65] was intended to replace the gold standard and London as the main financial centre by introducing a clearing mechanism in continental Europe. The Keynes Plan and the White Plan, issued respectively in April and July 1943, countered the German project. They eventually led to the Joint Statement of April 1944, the document that constituted the basis of the Bretton Woods conference.

The British Ministry of Information contacted Keynes as early as November 1940 to criticize the German proposal. However, he appreciated this scheme, built on Schacht's idea of a clearing system, and argued in the first draft of his Plan for 'a refinement and improvement of the Schachtian device'.[66] The starting-point was to eliminate the dysfunctionality of the inter-war monetary system by doing without an international money altogether through the 'banking principle', that is bank

---

64 Contrasting the results of the Genoa and London conferences, respectively influenced by the Cunliffe and Macmillan Committees, Clarke stresses this point. 'Although both the Genoa and London conferences must be classed as failures, the records of the negotiations and the memoirs of participants provide a fascinating account of the interaction between economic developments and international monetary thought. At Genoa the traditional gold-standard view, as formulated by British thinkers, was accepted almost without question. Eleven years later this view was championed primarily by the French and other continental Europeans but was rejected in practice by the United States, Britain, and the countries that were to comprise the sterling area. With this shift in monetary views came two other crucial changes. At Genoa the aim was a unified monetary system based on parities fixed in terms of gold – a system in which domestic economies would have to adjust in order to maintain international equilibrium. By 1933 only the inflation-scarred Continental Europeans were clinging to the traditional order of priorities, while Britain and the United States gave domestic recovery precedence over external stability. The further outcome of London was to accelerate international monetary disintegration, with the sterling area, the European gold bloc, and the United States each dealing as best it could with its special regional problems', S.V.O. Clarke, *The Reconstruction of the International Monetary System: The Attempts of 1922 and 1933*, Princeton Studies in International Finance, no. 33 (Princeton, 1973), p. 2.

65 W. Funk, *Wirtschaftliche Neuordnung Europas* (Berlin, 1940).

66 *CW* 25, p. 24, References to Keynes's *Collected Writings* are indicated as *CW* followed by the volume number. According to R.E. Lüke, 'The Schacht and the Keynes Plans', *Banca Nazionale del Lavoro Quarterly Review*, March 1985, pp. 65–76, the central idea of the Keynes Plan goes back to a monetary reform presented by Schacht at an international conference in February 1929.

clearing. The Keynes Plan, reflecting Mill's 'ideal case'[67] and Wicksell's 'organized credit economy',[68] extended a main tenet underlying monetary evolution, that is the development of less costly payment media, to an international context, while searching for optimal macroeconomic solutions.

The Plan opens with a quest for autonomous domestic policy, thus calling for a monetary system, managed by a supranational central bank, consistent with this objective. In order to avoid competitive devaluations and favour a return to multilateral trade, exchange rates are fixed but can be varied in the event of external imbalances. Furthermore, the money stock is independent of the vagaries of the gold market, and creditor countries are involved in the adjustment process to assure symmetry. Credit facilities prevent the monetary mechanism from causing a fall in economic activity, and controls on capital movements create sufficient room for manoeuvre to implement domestic policies.

The kernel of the Plan is best illustrated by Keynes himself in a comment on Hayek's revival of the commodity reserve currency. The Clearing Union solved the two main problems of the gold standard, namely the lack of control over the money supply and the unemployment effects of the adjustment mechanism, by, respectively, working through the velocity, not the quantity, of money, and allowing autonomous price and wage policies to maintain employment. An external disequilibrium requires a change in domestic policies and, if this proves unfeasible, an exchange rate variation. With respect to the gold standard, therefore, the Keynes Plan turned the design of the monetary system upside down in that the latter, instead of being a constraint, allowed economic policy to pursue domestic targets.[69]

The Keynes Plan, albeit original and radical like his previous proposals, contained various weaknesses. The most delicate aspect was the independence of economic policy in the presence of the adjustable peg, which was to be reconciled by capital controls. Their efficacy is, however, disputable. Moreover, the establishment of a supranational central bank raises the problem of apportioning the decision-making power, which is likely to be concentrated in one or just a very few countries. This limitation is of a political nature but also has economic implications. In a context of waning monetary discipline and discretionary policies in a fixed-exchange rate regime, it creates a gap in the scale of sovereignty, thereby undermining credibility

67 J.S. Mill, *Principles of Political Economy*, W. Ashley (ed.), ([1848], New York, 1987), p. 524.

68 Wicksell, *Interest*, [1898], pp. 62–101.

69 'The fundamental reason for thus limiting the objectives of an international currency scheme is the impossibility, or at any rate the undesirability, of imposing stable price-levels from without. The error of the gold-standard lay in submitting national wage-policies to outside dictation. It is wiser to regard stability (or otherwise) of internal prices as a matter of internal policy and politics. Commodity standards which try to impose this from without will break down just as surely as the rigid gold-standard', J.M. Keynes, 'The Objective of International Price Stability', in *Economic Journal*, 53, June–September 1943, pp. 185–7, here p. 187; F.A. von Hayek, 'A Commodity Reserve Currency', in *Economic Journal*, 53, June–September 1943, pp. 176–84.

and the system's other properties.[70] At the country level, the sanctioning power of the International Clearing Union may prove insufficiently effective to keep the system viable, given the pursuit of full employment policies. The inflationary potential of the Keynes Plan thus does not derive from an intrinsic defect of its rules,[71] but rather from the lack of an adequate disciplining mechanism squaring the adjustable peg with activist economic policies.

The innovative character of the Keynes Plan contrasted with the conservative approach of the White Plan. An International Stabilization Fund supplies financing facilities to member countries, which contribute their quotas in gold, currencies and government bonds. The monetary unit is the unitas, equivalent in value to $10 of fine gold. The excessive accumulation of credit balances is met by the scarce currency clause instructing the Fund to purchase and distribute the scarce currency among member countries. A variation in the exchange rate is admitted in the event of a 'fundamental disequilibrium'.

The objectives of the two Plans were analogous – trade multilateralism, stable exchange rates, activist stabilization policies and symmetry in the adjustment process – but the instruments to attain them differed. The Keynes Plan aimed to overcome the slow and costly adjustment of the gold standard with a clearing system making overdraft facilities available to debtor countries. Quotas fixed the limit of debt and credit positions, whereas in the White Plan, quotas were effectively deposited. Underlying the American position, there was an adversity to all potentially inflationary features, such as overdraft facilities and the introduction of an international money – the bancor – too radical an innovation to pass the politicians' approval.[72] The White Plan, in fact, reflected a more conservative vision, stressing the principle of free trade and capital movements, and trying to maintain a role for gold in the system. These objectives were consistent with America's huge gold reserves, strong competitiveness and high net credit position.

After their publication, both proposals were critically reviewed. In general, the White Plan was considered similar to the gold-exchange standard, and thus inadequate for overcoming inter-war problems, while the Keynes Plan was deemed inflationary. According to Lutz, neither had a mechanism to prevent policies from

---

70 In the concluding section of the Plan, Keynes is aware of this criticism but plays it down, deeming the surrendering of sovereignty by member countries 'no greater … than in a commercial treaty', J.K. Horsefield, *The International Monetary Fund 1945–1965: Twenty Years of International Monetary Cooperation, vol. 3, Documents* (Washington, 1969b), p. 36. This argument, however, does not fully consider the implications of establishing a supranational monetary authority, particularly on the consistency of the rules of the game of the International Clearing Union.and their enforcement.

71 After the circulation of the first draft in a restricted circle, Hawtrey objected to the mild penalties against persistent debtors (*CW* 25, pp. 40–2). In the final version, therefore, a series of rigid limits is set for debtors, including a generalized reduction of quotas in the event of 'an excess of world purchasing power', Horsefield, *Monetary Fund*, vol. 3, p. 25.

72 J.K. Horsefield, *The International Monetary Fund 1945-1965: Twenty Years of International Monetary Cooperation, vol. 1, Chronicle* (Washington, 1969a), p. 30.

leading to a fundamental disequilibrium.[73] Though based on gold, its role was 'quite unnecessary or even a nuisance under both schemes',[74] whose viabilities were doubtful, given the contrast of activist policies with a fixed-exchange-rate regime.[75] On the contrary, Viner took a positive view and, albeit pointing out some limitations, was favourable to a monetary reform including the best elements of each proposal.[76] The Joint Statement carried out such a melding in a way that was heavily biased towards the American position. This widely held view, however, neglects the influence of Keynes's thought on economic policy design and on post-war monetary arrangements.

Albeit recognizing the predominance of the United States in the negotiations, Keynes worked hard to assure the success of the reform. In his House of Lords speech, he considered the Joint Statement to be 'a considerable improvement on either of its parents', though lacking 'certain features of elegance, clarity and logic' of the Clearing Union plan.[77] After pointing out several advantages of the joint proposal, he emphasized the primacy of domestic targets *vis-à-vis* exchange rate stability, so that economic policy was not directed at maintaining parity as in the gold standard but at full employment.[78] This change in policy perspective stands out in Article I of the Bretton Woods Articles of Agreement acknowledging the epoch making paradigm shift produced by the *General Theory.*

The architects of the Bretton Woods monetary order sought to re-establish a symmetrical adjustment mechanism, as well as multilateral trade, in a fixed-exchange-rate regime, while allowing the pursuit of independent domestic policy. The policy trilemma was solved by maintaining capital controls and, in the long

---

73 F.A. Lutz, *The Keynes and White Proposals*, Essays in International Finance, no. 1 (Princeton, 1943), p. 17.

74 Ibid., p. 20.

75 Concluding his article, Lutz remarks: 'It is interesting to step back and to look at the plans as a whole. Unlike the classical economists, most modern economists do not favor solutions of economic problems which are based on principles. Instead they advocate, in each concrete instance, measures devised ad hoc which, if ingenious from a technical point of view, may contradict other measures devised in other fields. The result is that the pattern of economic policy of modern governments is far from being a model of logical consistency', Ibid., pp. 20–21.

76 Viner, 'Plans', p. 215.

77 *CW* 26, p. 10.

78 'The plan not merely confirms the de-thronement [of gold] but approves it by expressly providing that it is the duty of the Fund to alter the gold value of any currency if it is shown that this will be serviceable to equilibrium. In fact, the plan introduces in this respect an epoch-making innovation in an international instrument, the object of which is to lay down sound and orthodox principles. For instead of maintaining the principle that the internal value of a national currency should conform to a prescribed *de jure* external value, it provides that its external value should be altered if necessary so as to conform to whatever *de facto* internal value results from domestic policies, which themselves shall be immune from criticism by the Fund. Indeed, it is made the duty of the Fund to approve changes which will have this effect. That is why I say that these proposals are the exact opposite of the gold standard. They lay down by international agreement the essence of the new doctrine, far removed from the old orthodoxy.' (*CW* 26, pp. 18–9).

run, by resorting to changes in parity, when the reversal of policies proved unable to correct external imbalances. Hence, in the spirit of the treaty, exchange rates were kept stable in the short run to avoid the beggar-thy-neighbour policies of the 1930s, and flexible enough in the longer term to square with autonomous domestic policies.

However, after the 1949 devaluations, the game began to be played with fixed exchange rates, giving rise to the fixed-rate dollar standard of 1950–70.[79] This development, arising from the necessity of both facilitating the operation of the European Payments Union and enhancing the credibility of post-war anti-inflation policies, made the system much more similar to the gold-exchange standard. Not only were parity variations regarded as exceptional, but gold had far from lost its role. This was not just a mere legislative matter regarding the Bretton Woods rules,[80] but characterized policymakers' behaviour.

Major countries came to accumulate substantial gold reserves, something that continued until the early 1960s. Indeed, the very idea of a fiat-money standard was somewhat alien to central bankers, as shown by the deep concern for the dollar convertibility constraint and the related Triffin dilemma. However, since the United States controlled the home price level, the growth of demand-determined reserves held by other countries, mainly in United States Treasury bonds, was not a threat to the American gold stock. Hence, one can agree with McKinnon's conjecture that the fixed-rate dollar system could have continued indefinitely, had the United States maintained a stable purchasing power and demonetized gold.[81] Yet, neither condition was met, again due to the determining influence of economic theory.

First, at the heyday of Keynesian economics, no country would have renounced the pursuit of domestic targets other than the price level. Certainly not the United States, which, playing the role of the *nth* country in Mundell's redundancy problem,[82] could hardly have been expected to renounce the extra degree of freedom in order to uphold the viability of the international monetary system. Second, the decision to demonetise gold would have been difficult for the holder of the largest gold reserve to take. There was no schizophrenic attitude, therefore, on the part of the centre country, whose behaviour simply reflected the prevailing state of the art and the overwhelming strength of its economy *vis-à-vis* the rest of the world.

Bringing all these factors together, it appears that the post-Second-World-War monetary order was doomed, since the rules by which the game was eventually played were inconsistent. Keeping a link with gold while concurrently pursuing

79 McKinnon, 'Rules', sections 2–3.

80 'Bretton Woods ratified the gold-exchange standard, it did not legislate a dollar standard', J. Williamson, 'On the System in Bretton Woods', in *American Economic Review. Papers and Proceedings*, 75, May 1985, pp. 74–9, here p. 75.

81 McKinnon, 'Rules', p. 39. The implicit assumption underlying McKinnon's hypothesis is that the seignorage gained by the US was considered by other countries as a price to pay in exchange for the service of guaranteeing the system's stability.

82 R.A. Mundell, 'The Redundancy Problem and the World Price Level', in R.A. Mundell, *International Economics* (New York, 1968).

autonomous domestic policies necessarily led to the system's collapse.[83] It is not by chance that increasing concern about the viability of monetary arrangements dates from the early 1960s, when capital movements began to be liberalized, and official dollar liabilities held by foreign central banks exceeded, in 1964, the United States' gold reserve. The policy trilemma, then, had no solution, and seeking refuge in the convertibility constraint was as illusory as it was erroneous.

The central role of theory, thus, comes out once more in the epilogue of the Bretton Woods story. Not only was there a repeat of the divide between policymakers' conservative thinking and economists' more progressive analytical framework, but also the latter was not sufficiently advanced to fully grasp the problem of the international monetary system in its entirety. As McKinnon rightly remarked in connection with the failure of the post-Second World War monetary setting: 'Understanding what the rules actually are, and the obligations of the various players, can be extremely important'.[84] And, in the case in point, it was precisely an incomplete understanding of the Bretton Woods viability conditions that brought about the demise of the system. In fact, Friedman's far-sighted suggestion to introduce flexible exchange rates and treat gold like any other commodity was regarded as a curiosity. With the possible exception of the United Kingdom, the fiscal and monetary discipline followed by countries other than the United States reflected a traditional habit of mind and was coherent with the system's stability. On

83 The possible inconsistency between fixed exchange rates and domestic economic policy had already been pointed out immediately after the Bretton Woods conference. In the symposium published by the *Review of Economic Statistics* in November 1944, Halm remarks: 'It will be one of the most delicate tasks of the Fund to arbitrate the conflict between the principle of exchange stability and the principle of non-interference with domestic policies. Since these two principles characterize the positions of the gold standard and of Lord Keynes respectively, one cannot be surprised to find the Fund Agreement rather obscure in this respect and inclined to leave it to the Board and the Executive Directors gradually to solve by experience and according to given circumstances what cannot be crystallized in unequivocal formulae right at the beginning', G.N. Halm, 'The International Monetary Fund', in *Review of Economic Statistics*, 26, November 1944, pp. 170–5, here p. 172. Frank Graham's comment is more caustic: 'It would seem that, after all this, we might have learned that we cannot both have our cake and eat it. We should know that we must either forgo fixed exchange rates *or* national monetary sovereignty if we are to avoid the disruption of equilibrium in freely conducted international trade or the system of controls and inhibitions which is the only alternative when the internal values of independent currencies deviate – as they always tend to do – from what was, perhaps, a correct relationship when the fixed rates of exchange were set up. Yet the old error was, to all intents and purposes, again repeated in the International Monetary Organization which did not much curtail national monetary sovereignty. It is true that some concessions were made to the consequent demand for flexibility in exchange relationships. But there is, nevertheless, a strong bias in the statute toward the ideal of rates maintained unchanged for an indefinitely lengthy period, and not even the slightest provision for the adoption, by the various participating countries, of the congruent monetary policies without which a system of fixed exchange rates simply does not make sense', F.D. Graham, *The Cause and Cure of 'Dollar Shortage'*, Essays in International Finance, no. 10 (Princeton, 1949), p. 6, italics in the original.

84 McKinnon, 'Rules', p. 39.

the contrary, the centre country failed to provide an effective anchor. However, even the most virtuous policies might not have been sufficient to assure viability, given the inadequacies of the prevailing analytical view of sticking to gold convertibility and to the Triffin dilemma.[85]

Finally, an answer can be given to the Bretton Woods enigma posed by Eichengreen, raised in this article's opening paragraph. Initially, economic growth was sustained by trade expansion and domestic policies that did not create instability, given pervasive capital controls and huge American gold reserves. When both these factors faded away, the constraints of the system – fixed exchange rates and gold convertibility – became binding. Furthermore, they clashed with the policy design of the centre country, which was no longer in line with the function of anchoring the system. Enhanced by a laggard state of the art, irresolvable inconsistencies eventually emerged and caused the end of the post-war monetary setting.

Conclusions

The Bretton Woods monetary order had the unique characteristic of being a project designed by experts and, therefore, lends itself to examination from a monetary theory perspective. However, the advance of monetary economics is not continuously and promptly translated into monetary reform. The state of the art can either fall behind or be ahead of the actual institutional framework. Such temporal discrepancies are often eliminated by the impact of exogenous shocks on the received view. Hence, the aftermath of the First World War enhanced the critique of the gold standard, and subsequently the effects of the Great Depression produced a decisive step towards managed money and the search for an innovative monetary system.

This challenging task became a priority after the outbreak of the Second World War. The ruling paradigm of Keynesian economics, which emphasized activist economic policy in pursuit of full employment, influenced the approach of the Bretton Woods negotiators, though the institutional structure of the new setting maintained some of the features of the traditional gold-exchange standard. Indeed, central bankers' conservative attitude, lagging behind theoretical advances, was the cause of the inertia in monetary arrangements throughout the twentieth century. The asynchronous evolution of theory and institutions brought about the inconsistencies that plagued the Bretton Woods system and eventually led to its collapse. In fact, most of the factors commonly put forward to account for the end of Bretton Woods – the structural flaws in its design, namely the gold-exchange standard and the adjustable peg, the failure of the United States to stabilize the price level after 1965 and the pursuit of domestic policy targets by other industrial countries[86] – mainly reflected the major shift in the state of the art during the inter-war period and the related contrast with conservative modes of thought.

All things considered, the influence of monetary theory on the evolution, and viability, of monetary arrangements was decisive. The properties and the success

85 The EMS, lacking any link to gold and allowing frequent exchange-rate realignments, worked somewhat better than Bretton Woods, at least until September 1992.

86 Bordo, 'Bretton Woods', p. 83.

of the gold standard were founded on the metallist doctrine and the equilibrium hypothesis of the classical model. The rejection of both inverted the principles underlying the monetary system and paved the way for the epoch-making transition to fiat money. The Bretton Woods monetary order was the last stage of this process, a last ephemeral attempt to maintain a link with commodity money while stressing the role of activist economic policies.

CHAPTER 9

The European Monetary System[1]

Michael Artis

Introduction

By any standards the European Monetary System (EMS) was a remarkable invention. It can now be seen to have paved the way for the creation of European Monetary Union. Yet that ambition did not figure in the declarations with which the EMS was launched in 1979. It began life as a response to a distrust of American leadership of global monetary affairs. Its immediate aim – to create a zone of monetary stability in Europe – seemed relatively modest. EMS arrangements conveyed a desire to do this on a symmetric basis, and it was hailed as an innovator in this respect.

Early experience caused one influential observer (Samuel Brittan of the *Financial Times*) to describe the EMS as 'a mere crawling peg'. Yet, not much later, the French government had performed the Mitterand 'U-turn', the EMS turned into a counter-inflationary framework and the investment in symmetry was liquidated in favour of pegging the Deutschmark (DM), provoking a new description of the EMS as (merely?) 'a Greater DM Area'.

Of course, this evolution just mirrored the transition of industrial economies at large from a 'Keynesian' to a 'monetarist' orientation, with the modification that the nominal anchor that monetarism proposed to find in the money supply, or its growth rate, could be found in the exchange rate. Put slightly differently, it seemed possible to import the reputation of the low-inflation partner through pegging the exchange rate, saving time on the alternative creation of a counter-inflationary reputation at home. This passage to the era of the 'hard EMS' involved the residual use of the flexibility that it provided, and before the speculative crises of 1992 and 1993, EMS was advertised as a paragon among exchange-rate systems – hard yet flexible, preserving conditions of competitiveness from arbitrary misalignment yet also projecting a counter-inflationary influence. It appeared capable of making these gains even while capital controls were liberalized. Realignments had been effected without exciting ruinous speculation. With this record, it came to serve as a model for exchange-rate system 'blueprints' at the global level.

But nemesis follows hubris. In 1992 and 1993 there came the first of the decade's waves of speculative foreign-exchange crises, that affecting the EMS, followed by the Mexican, south-east Asian and Russian crises. For the EMS, the crisis was resolved, first, by the widening of the fluctuation bands to ±15 per cent (which did not

1 I am indebted to Luca Onorante for speedy research assistance and to Antti Suvanto for encouraging comment.

seem much different from floating) and, eventually, by the creation of the European Monetary Union. This evolution has led to the current fashion for the 'hollowing-out hypothesis' – the notion that there is no middle ground between more or less free floating and 'completely' fixed exchange rates, as in currency boards, dollar- (or euro-)ization and monetary union.

In what follows, the first task is to amplify the description of the EMS's evolution. Then, along the way, some counter-factual questions are posed. These are always difficult to frame; after all, everything is path-dependent in some degree, and what has happened is what happened, not something else. But posing them is a way of provoking reflection and, perhaps, of gaining a surer understanding of what was unfolding. One can think of a lot of questions to ask in this regard. A selection will be posed as the article progresses.

The beginning

The EMS was founded by the Council of Ministers' meeting in December 1978. The official declaration said that its purpose was:

> to establish a greater measure of monetary stability in the Community' and that it 'should be seen as a fundamental component of a more comprehensive strategy aimed at lasting growth with stability, a progressive return to full employment, the harmonization of living standards and the lessening of regional disparities in the Community.

The deeper background is well described in Gros and Thygesen,[2] and in Ludlow,[3] which also concerns itself in detail with the contribution of the national authorities to the EMS's design.

The chief features of the design were: the designation of central rates in a currency grid and a band of fluctuation for the currencies participating in the Exchange Rate Mechanism (ERM) of the System; the creation of a new currency unit – the ecu; provisions relating to symmetrical marginal intervention and the availability of credit for this purpose; the explicit allowance made for a realignment of the central rate; and the creation of a 'divergence indicator'. The size of the fluctuation band, at ±2.25 per cent, was taken from the preceding experience of the ill-fated 'Snake' experiment. Italy (a non-participant in the 'Snake') was granted a wider (±6 per cent) band, and this treatment was subsequently to be extended to all new entrants to EMS (the full list is noted in Table 9.1). The fluctuation band was applied to all the central cross rates of members of the ERM.

2 D. Gros and N. Thygesen, *European Monetary Integration* (2nd ed., Harlow, 1998).
3 P. Ludlow, *The Making of the European Monetary System* (London, 1982).

Table 9.1 Realignment dates and central DM parities in the ERM

	Realignment Dates					
	NG/DM	FF/DM	BF/DM	IL/DM	DK/DM	IP/DM
13 Mar 1979	1.08370	2.30950	15.7164	457.314	2.82237	0.263932
24 Sep 1979	1.10537	2.35568	16.0307	466.460	2.96348	0.26921
30 Nov 1979	-	-	-	-	3.11165	-
23 Mar 1981	-	-	-	496.232	-	-
5 Oct 1981	-	2.56212	16.9125	539.722	3.28279	0.284018
22 Feb 1982	-	-	18.4837	-	3.38433	-
14 Jun 1982	-	2.83396	19.2693	578.574	3.52817	0.296090
21 Mar 1983	1.12673	3.06648	20.0285	626.043	3.63141	0.323703
22 Jul 1985	-	-	-	679.325	-	-
7 Apr 1986	-	3.25617	20.4252	699.706	3.70332	0.333416
4 Aug 1986	-	-	-	-	-	0.362405
12 Jan 1987	-	3.35386	20.6255	720.699	3.81443	0.373281
8 Jan 1990	-	-	-	748.217	-	-
15 Sep 1992	-	-	-	802.488	-	-
2 Feb 1993	-	-	-	Out	-	0.414757
8 Feb 1993	Margins of the ERM broadened to ±15% except for the Dutch guilder					
25 Nov 1996	-	-	-	990.004	-	-
16 Mar 1998	-	-	-	-	-	0.402676

Other events occurring during the EMS are:

13 Mar 1979 inception of ERM; 12 Sep 1987 Basle-Nyborg Agreement; 19 Jun 1989 entry of Spain; 8 Jan 1990 reduction of the Italian margin; 8 Oct 1990 entry of United Kingdom; December 1991 Maastricht Summit; 6 Apr 1992 entry of Portugal; 2 Jun 1992 negative outcome of the Danish referendum on Maastricht; June 1992 Irish referendum on Maastricht; 25 Aug 1992 French polling result indicating a small majority of French voters in favour of the ratification of the Maastricht treaty; 14 Sep 1992 devaluation by 7 per cent of the Italian lira; 17 Sep 1992 withdrawal of Italy and Britain from the ERM; 20 Sep 1992 positive outcome of the French referendum on the Maastricht Treaty with a slim majority (the 'petit oui'); 23 Nov 1992 devaluation by 6 per cent of the Spanish peseta and the Portuguese escudo; 1 Feb 1993 devaluation by 10 per cent of the Irish pound; 13 May 1993 devaluation of the Spanish peseta and the Portuguese escudo; 2 Aug 1993 ERM bands widened to ±15 per cent except for the Dutch guilder; 7: Jan 1995 entry of the Austrian schilling; 1995 entry of Finland; 24 Nov 1996 reentry of Italy; 16 Mar 1998 entry of Greece; May 1998 Brussels Summit announcing the bilateral parities between the European currencies for 31 Dec 1998.

Source: Bessec, 'Mean reversion'.

The ecu, a cocktail of EMS-member currencies, was introduced as a *numéraire*, and played an important role in the divergence indicator. This was designed explicitly to isolate the currency that stood out from the rest since it would 'flash' when a currency (whether weak or strong) passed a threshold of 75 per cent of its maximum possible divergence against the ecu. The flashing of the indicator would signal a presumption of corrective action on behalf of the currency in question. The credit provisions underlay a symmetrical requirement, on both the weak and the strong currency, for foreign-exchange intervention at the margin. The country of the weak currency would be able to borrow, without prospect of refusal, from the country of the strong currency in order to support its intervention. (It was not then public knowledge that the Bundesbank, opposed to participation in the EMS, had successfully sought from the German government an assurance that, if the financing obligations arising from participation should prejudice its domestic obligations to ensure stability, it could repudiate those obligations.) The principal credit mechanism, the so-called very-short-term financing facility, required repayment to be made within 45 days. Subsequently, facilities were extended to cover intra-marginal intervention and with a repayment period of 60 days in the Basle-Nyborg agreement of 1987.

The symmetrical features of the system attracted positive appraisal from all who had been brought up on Triffin's masterly assessment of the weaknesses of the Bretton-Woods regime.[4] Hitherto, there had been no effective arrangements to enforce adjustment equally upon the very strong as upon the weak currencies in an exchange-rate system. The failure of the 'scarce currency' clause in the Bretton-Woods agreements was well known. All told, the formal arrangements strongly reflected a very Keynesian approach to exchange-rate system building.

Despite this and despite the absence of any explicit reference to an EMU objective, it was clear however even at the time that EMU ambitions were still entertained by some for the new system. Such had, after all, been explicit in the launching of the ill-fated Snake experiment (which followed the Werner Report's suggestion for a narrowing of the intra-European fluctuation margins),[5] to which the EMS was successor. The bad experience with the 'Snake' counselled a more subdued passage towards the same end, a pragmatic conclusion that proved well justified by events.

Of course, there were still other important, comparable motivations present, if hard to discern in the written declaration, two among them most important. First, the interest in the Community in a set-up for exchange rates that would limit arbitrary variations in competitiveness was obvious. This was not just a matter of making sense of the setting of prices within the CAP (much stressed by Giavazzi and Giovannini[6]) – the Community's first and most important policy as such. More important, the continuation of arbitrary changes in competitiveness always threatened to provoke accusations of 'competitive devaluations', in the limit to unravel the lowering of protectionist barriers within Europe. Second, there was a palpable German interest in an arrangement that would defuse the pressure on the DM and its cross rates with its European neighbours, whenever the dollar entered a weak spell. The Commission had occasion to lay out these more pragmatic arguments (without referring to the specific German interest) in the evidence it provided to a Committee of the House

---

4 R. Triffin, *Gold and the Dollar Crisis* (New Haven, 1960).

5 Prior to this the Smithsonian realignment of the Bretton-Woods system had specified a fluctuation margin of ±2.25 per cent against the dollar, implying that the margin for intra-European cross rates was effectively ±4.5 per cent.

6 F. Giavazzi and A. Giovannini, Limiting Exchange Rate Flexibility (Cambridge, Mass., 1989).

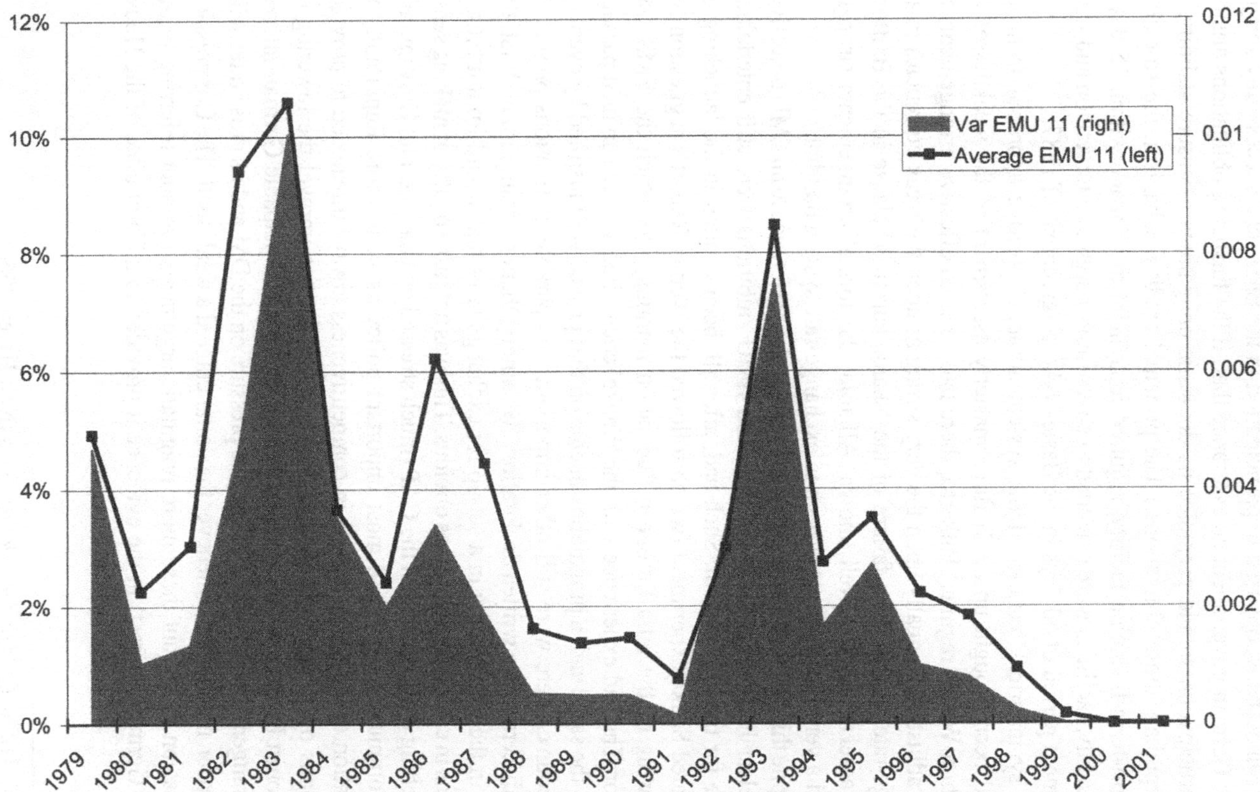

Figure 9.1 **Exchange rate variability. Nominal exchange rates with DM. Per cent yearly changes (mean and variance)**

of Lords in 1983,[7] when it also asserted that 'the EMS as it is now derives part of its strength from being conceived as a stage toward full European monetary union'.[8]

However, EMS's first years featured a large number of realignments. At this point its characterization as a crawling peg did not seem unreasonable.

The evolution of the system

Table 9.1 shows the timing and size of the currency realignments (*vis-à-vis* the DM) of the original members of the ERM with, in the note, information on the dates of entry, and subsequent history, of the later members. The frequency of realignments during the first years is obvious and contrasts sharply with what later unfolded. Most of those countries that subsequently entered had practised a policy of shadowing the DM (or the ecu) prior to joining, so the device employed in Figures 9.1 and 9.2 of looking at the collective behaviour of current EMU members (excluding Greece) is a convenient one. Figure 9.1 shows the development of the cross-section variance of the change in bilateral DM exchange rate, as well as the mean. Clearly, both fall sharply until the crises of 1992 and 1993, when there is a sharp increase, followed subsequently by a further decline. The same is true for the rate of inflation. The period opens with a high mean and high variance for this variable, both falling rapidly, and in this case, without noticeable effect from the speculative crises.

A historical division of the EMS's evolution into five parts can be proposed on the basis of these data: first there was a 'crawling peg' period, which ended in 1983 with the Mitterrand 'U-turn'. Then there was the transition to 'the hard EMS', with some further, but less frequent, realignments, up until 1987. Then there were no realignments, other than the formal one associated with the reduction in the lira's fluctuation band from ±six per cent to ±2.25 until the crisis period of 1992–3. The speculative crises consitituted the fourth period, followed by the fifth and final period that led to the formation of the European Monetary Union.

From 'crawling peg' to 'hard EMS'

Measuring the stabilizing effect

During the first two subperiods of this history, a question can be posed as to how far the reduction in the variance of exchange rates was due to the operation of the ERM as such, or could have happened anyway. Of course, when considering the whole of theEMS's duration including the transition to EMU itself, it is obvious that this is an otiose question. No other countries in this period reduced exchange-rate fluctuations between themselves to the extent of forming a monetary union. But for the earlier EMS periods, the issue still has some interest. A number of papers have

7 Select Committee of the House of Lords, The European Monetary System (London, 1983), HMSO.

8 Ibid., p. 82.

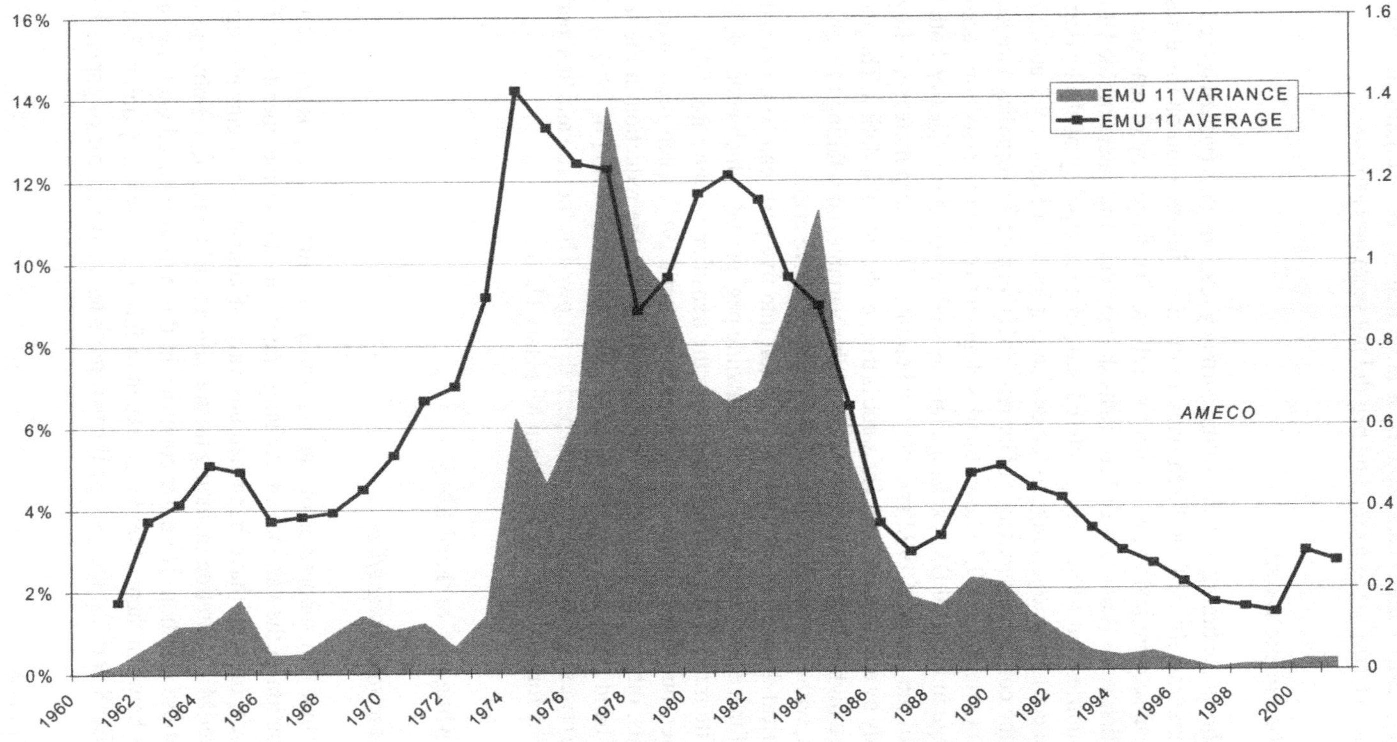

Figure 9.2 **Inflation convergence. Inflation rate in EMU 11**

been devoted to this question.[9] They all concluded positively, to the effect that the ERM had had a stabilizing effect on European exchange rates (most specifically European bilateral DM rates). Furthermore, they conclude that this reduction in volatility had not been purchased at the cost of transferring volatility elsewhere (for example into interest rates), nor of destabilizing overall effective exchange rates.[10] Finally, it appears that the volatility-reducing effects of the EMS applied as much to real as to nominal rates. The methodology used in these studies was in essence very simple: a comparison is made, for some measure of exchange-rate volatility, between the experience of the ERM countries before and after the introduction of the ERM, and the experience of a control group of non-ERM countries over the same 'before' and 'after' periods. The stabilizing effect was found to be strengthening through time as the ERM moved to the realignment-free period.

EMS as a target zone

The next issue to arise is how this was brought about. To a later generation of researchers, a good part of the answer seemed to lie in the 'target zone' literature. In his original article, which laid the foundations for this literature, Krugman illustrated how a credible target zone would produce a 'honeymoon effect'.[11] The credibility of the central rate would determine that, as the exchange rate approached the limit of the band of fluctuation, expectations would increasingly harden to pull it back towards the centre of the band. Applications of the *simple* target zone model to the EMS data produced somewhat unsupportive results.

Contrary to predictions, the inverse relationship between interest-rate differentials and the position of the exchange rate inside the band was not generally observed. Furthermore, exchange rates seemed to spend most of their time well inside the band instead of near the edges, as predicted by the simple model with its assumption of marginal intervention commitments and perfect credibility. Central banks seemed to take the view, pragmatically, that allowing the exchange rate to stray too near the

---

9 H. Ungerer, O. Evans and P. Nyberg, 'The European Monetary System: the experience 1979–82', International Monetary Fund Occasional Papers, no. 19, May 1983; H. Ungerer, O. Evans and P. Nyberg, 'The European Monetary System – recent developments', International Monetary Fund Occasional Papers, no. 48, 1986; M.J. Artis and M.P. Taylor, 'Exchange rates, interest rates, capital controls and the European Monetary System: assessing the track record', in F. Giavazzi, M. Micossi and M. Miller (eds), *The European Monetary System* (Cambridge, 1988); M.J. Artis and M.P. Taylor, 'The Achievements of the European Monetary System', in *Economic and Social Review*, 20, June 1989, pp. 121–45; L. Sarno, 'Exchange rate and interest rate volatility in the European Monetary System: some further results', in *Applied Financial Economics*, 7, 1997, pp. 255–63.

10 This is not at all obvious. Stabilizing exchange rates against the DM might very well have meant destabilising rates against the dollar and to such an extent as to destabilize the effective exchange rates of at least some ERM countries. In fact, M. Fratianni and J. von Hagen, *The European Monetary System and European Monetary Union* (Oxford, 1992) concluded that this had happened although Artis et al., 'Exchange Rates', disagree.

11 P. Krugman, 'Target zones and exchange rate dynamics', in *Quarterly Journal of Economics*, 106, 1991, pp. 311–25.

edge of the band would be more likely to excite expectations of a realignment than to arouse stabilizing speculation. Most intervention in the ERM was intra-marginal (researchers could be chided for not taking this into account immediately since this feature of the operation of the system was well-known).[12]

Clearly, also, the EMS was not perfectly credible as in the simple model. Uncovered interest parity could not be relied upon to allow for interest rates to fall as the exchange rate approached the edge of the band.[13] Yet, for most of the time,[14] interest rates and forward exchange rates met Svennson's 'simplest test'.[15] The forward rate would be within the band (the most notable exception being for the Italian lira), and the interest rate would lie within its 'credibility band' for reasonable horizons,[16] and credibility could be seen to grow through time. On Svensson's more exacting 'drift-adjusted' method, the results are less favourable. But Williamson (rightly) makes much of the observation that, in the EMS, forward rates did not change one for one with the spot rate,[17] a characteristic of more freely floating systems, indicating that the system did have something of the key feature of anchoring expectations which is the core of the target-zone model.

Achieving purchasing-power parity

The stabilizing effects of the EMS, as indicated above, stretched to real exchange rates, where it helped to remove the tendency towards misalignment (prolonged periods of real exchange-rate departure from equilibrium) that seems to be a feature of floating-rate regimes. EMS managers were able to make timely realignments that restored competitiveness even whilst the 'normal' fixity of the nominal rate could be used as an ingredient in counter-inflationary policy.

This 'double act' was one of the EMS's great achievements. In the normal way, exchange rates vary far from preserving purchasing-power parity. Also, in the normal way, an attempt to use a hard exchange-rate policy as a nominal anchor sooner or later runs into the problem posed by the fact that its imperfect credibility results in a loss of competitiveness. Yet, as Figure 9.3 shows – the Ff exchange rate is shown

---

12 See S. Mastropasqua, M. Micossi and R. Rinaldi, 'Interventions, sterilization and monetary policy in European Monetary System countries, 1979–87', in F. Giavazzi, M. Micossi and M. Miller (eds), *The European Monetary System* (Cambridge, 1988).

13 In the full credibility model, as expectations are anchored, it might be expected that as the exchange rate approached the edge of the band it would be increasingly expected to fall back to its central value – hence, via uncovered interest parity, interest rates did not need to rise, but could fall compatibly with preserving the current central rate and bands.

14 L.O. Svensson, 'Assessing target zone credibility. Mean reversion and devaluation expectations in the ERM 1979–92', in *European Economic Review*, 1993, pp.763–802.

15 L.O. Svensson, 'The Simplest Test of Target Zone Credibility', IMF Staff Papers, 38, September 1991, pp. 655–65.

16 Given UIP these conditions amount to the same thing.

17 J. Williamson, 'Crawling Bands or Monitoring Bands: how to manage exchange rates in a world of capital mobility', in *International Finance*, October 1998, 1, pp. 59–79.

as 'representative' – real exchange rates in the ERM varied far less than real dollar rates, a result which Axel Weber has also obtained using more formal methods.[18]

The role of capital controls

It is clear that the capital controls were useful in providing time for realignment decisions to be made, and in easing the pressure on domestic interest rates. The differential between onshore and offshore interest rates would respond very visibly to expectations of a realignment (see the various papers contained in the *European Economy* for May 1988 which was devoted to the liberalization issue). As a means of realigning without attracting speculation, parity changes were urged in which the band around the new central rate would overlap with the band around the previous central rate. Then no discrete change in the exchange rate, with its attendant enormous profit opportunities, need be involved (Kenen estimated that over 70 per cent of realignments were of this type).[19]

The capital controls were probably helpful to the authorities in gaining a reputation for credible management and timely realignments, and in allowing them to prevent the build-up of unsustainably uncompetitive positions. But the controls leaked, and they could only apply to outflows of domestic residents' capital. They could not prevent the liquidation of non-residents' positions in the domestic currency. The fact that they were removed cannot, therefore, be assumed to be the underlying cause of the 1992 and 1993 crises. Given the much greater volumes of international capital then available, as well as the underlying problems that had become evident in at least two major countries, even had these controls remained, they might well have been, sooner or later, overwhelmed.[20]

The EMS as a disinflationary framework

Giavazzi and Pagano famously advertised the advantages of exchange-rate targeting as a counter-inflationary policy,[21] and it is widely accepted that the EMS was used as a framework within which countries strove, successfully, to bring down the high

18 Which he also attributes to the conscious policy of the EMS managers. More recently still, M. Bessec, 'Mean reversion versus adjustment to PPP: the two regimes of exchange rate dynamics under the EMS, 1979–1998', paper presented at the World Conference Econometric Society, Seattle, 2000, has obtained further supportive evidence. She uses a Markov-switching model to identify two EMS regimes, one identified with periods of calm and mean reversion, the other with turbulent periods (around realignments) when the exchange rate seems to hunt for its PPP parity.

19 P.B. Kenen, *Managing Exchange Rates* (London, 1988).

20 Still, it should be pointed out that more than one economist warned against the removal of capital controls on the grounds that it would invite a speculative strain on the EMS that it might not be possible to handle (see, for example, C. Wyplosz, 'Capital Flow liberalization and the EMS: a French perspective', in *European Economy*, 36, May 1988, pp. 85–104).

21 F. Giavazzi and M. Pagano, 'The Advantage of Tying One's Hands. EMS Discipline and Central Bank Credibility', in *European Economic Review*, 32, 1988, pp. 1055–82.

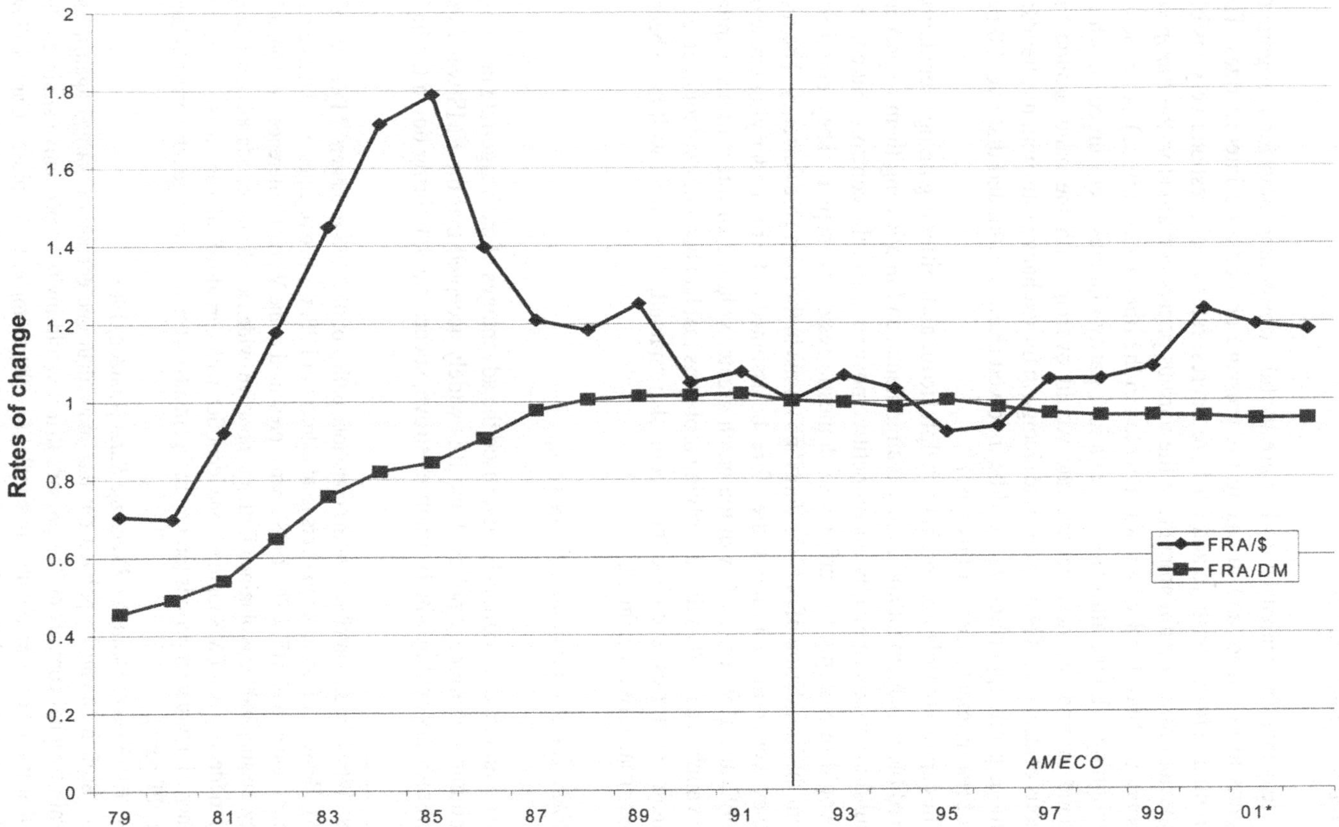

Figure 9.3 Real exchange rates for the French Franc

rates of inflation that had prevailed at the start of the regime. Politically, the existence of this framework, with the accompanying peer-pressure on governments and policymakers, must have made the conquest of inflation easier. In countries strongly sympathetic to European ambitions, the belief that these required a concerted effort at inflation reduction must have helped to validate the introduction of counter-inflationary policies. Such claims, though, should be distinguished from the stronger claims associated with this line of argument, which are much harder to verify.

These stronger claims suggest that EMS enabled the importation of a credibility effect, which would have lessened the unemployment cost of the reduction in inflation (in the framework of the expectations-augmented Phillips curve, the short-run schedule simply falls).[22] Several researchers have tried to verify whether such an effect can be found, with in the aggregate only small success. Artis and Ormerod, Kremers, and Anderton, Barrell and McHugh are representative.[23] The latter paper includes the comment 'ERM membership alone did not engender belief, harsh policies had to be implemented to gain the reputation of anti-inflation resolve', though Kremers is more positive, illustrating that country experience was not uniform. This conclusion is underlined by Weber's study of credibility, which found EMS-related gains only for some smaller countries: the Netherlands, Denmark and Ireland are cited.[24]

The EMS as a 'Greater DM zone'

Since the 'counter-inflationary' framework rationalization for the EMS turns on there being an anchor country with a good counter-inflationary record and, therefore, a 'hard currency', distinguishing this rationalization from the cruder picture of the EMS as a 'DM Area' is hardly possible. Once again, extreme versions of the hypothesis (where Germany's policy shows no regard for other EMS members whilst other EMS members' policies reflect only German interests) can be ruled out,[25] but more relaxed ones are strikingly confirmed. Most notably, perhaps, there is the study by Artis and Zhang of interest-rate linkages with the United States.[26] Earlier studies, using earlier

22 In the 'New Keynesian' version, as G. Mankiw, 'The Inexorable and Mysterious Trade-Off Between Inflation and Unemployment', in *Economic Journal*, 111, May 2001, pp. C45–C61, shows, a credible future fall in inflation should inspire a current fall in unemployment. The absence of such observations can count against the importance of credibility effects.

23 M.J. Artis and P. Ormerod, 'Is there an EMS Effect in European Labour Markets?', in S. Collignon S. and C. Johnson (eds), *The Monetary Economics of Europe: Causes of the EMS Crisis* (London, 1994); J. Kremers, 'Gaining Policy Credibility for a Disinflation: Ireland's experience in the EMS', IMF Staff Papers, 37, March 1990, pp. 116–45; R. Anderton, R. Barrell and J. McHugh, 'Nominal convergence in European wage behaviour: achievements and explanations', in R. Barrell (ed.), *Economic Convergence and Monetary Union in Europe* (London, 1992).

24 A. Weber, 'Policy-makers' reputation in the EMS disinflation', in *European Economic Review*, 36, 1992, pp. 1473–92.

25 Fratianni et al., *European Monetary System.*

26 M. Artis and W. Zhang, 'The Linkage of Interest Rates within the EMS,' in *Weltwirtschaftliches Archiv*, 134, 1, 1998, pp. 117–32.

sample periods, found no evidence of German dominance in this respect, instead confirming that the United States was the dominant interest-rate setter. Artis and Zhang, benefiting from a data set that included the period after unification, show that after this episode, when German and United States behaviour parted company, Europe indeed followed the German lead. The fact that it did so is strong testimony to the extent to which the rest of Europe had chosen to be bound to Germany in financial affairs, since the German-unification shock remained more idiosyncratic than goods-market integration might have suggested that it would be.

The crises, 1992–3

The speculative crises that struck the system in 1992 and 1993 destroyed the 'Hard EMS', and they destroyed the prospect of the route to EMU being through the narrow bands of the ERM. As it proved, they did not destroy the countries' ability to get to the destination of EMU, but simply required a different route to be followed.

Much has been written about these crises and, in particular, the recent re-appraisal by Eichengreen should be mentioned.[27] This conducts its post-mortem in the light of the intervening experience of foreign-exchange-rate crises in emerging markets, whereas Kenen undertakes its appraisal in the light of a comparison with the breakdown of the Bretton-Woods system.[28] Eichengreen shows, very clearly, that a single explanation is likely to be inadequate.[29] We now know that contagion can spread a crisis rapidly.

The main features, it can now be appreciated, are probably these. First there is the competitiveness problem. Subsequent experience has shown how nominal-exchange-rate pegging, conducted with a view to bringing down inflation, sooner or later encounters the difficulty that its incomplete credibility poses a problem of falling competitiveness. Deteriorating current accounts and relative prices eventually overtake the combination of high interest rates and steady, if not appreciating, nominal exchange rates that characterize the first stage of the policy. Countries that embark on a high-exchange-rate policy from a position of high unemployment may, first, attract plaudits for their strong commitment. Later, this is increasingly seen as a foolhardy 'ride on a tiger's back'. Second, in the case of the EMS, where a *system* of exchange rates was involved, there may be – and actually was – a problem of co-ordination present that does not arise in unilateral exchange-rate-targeting regimes. Third, in the case of EMS, the passage to EMU enshrined in the Maastricht Treaty – only arrived at towards the end of 1991 – may have added an additional feature encouraging a belief in the 'self-fulfilling' expectations nature of a currency raid.

How do these features play out? First, it is rather clear that the Italian and British currencies were both under a competitive pressure. The weakness of the lira was signalled well in advance of the crisis, with the forward rate outside the band. The

27 B. Eichengreen, 'The EMS Crisis in retrospect', CEPR Discussion Papers, no. 2704, February 2001 (Centre for Economic Policy Research, London).

28 P.B. Kenen, 'What have we learned from the EMS Crises?', in *Journal of Policy Modeling*, 17, 1995, pp. 449–61.

29 Eichengreen, 'The EMS Crisis'.

British case is less obvious; the crisis was not signalled any earlier than two weeks before it broke. However, it is clear enough that sterling had entered at too high an exchange rate, and that, whilst membership of the ERM had not prevented a reduction in interest rates in the United Kingdom, the reduction had been insufficient. The problem had not been brought to a head, however, because of the hope invested in a sequence of forecasts showing that the upturn was around the corner (the Prime Minister spoke of the 'green shoots of recovery' being witnessed in spring 1992).[30] Implicit in the focus on these forecasts was a presumption that the situation could not go on as it was. The continual disappointment of these expectations was, therefore, bound to bring trouble.

The second feature, that of the co-ordination problem arising in a system, is explored intensively in Buiter et al.[31] Most economists then agreed (and retrospect has not changed opinions) that the German unification shock required a revaluation of the DM – or a relative rise in the German price level. As the Bundesbank was quite unwilling to acknowledge that a rise in German prices would be an acceptable solution, the problem was how to bring about the change in the exchange rate. The main difficulty in this connection seemed to be the excessive investment in reputation that the hard EMS model had encouraged. It is commonly agreed that the Bundesbank would have reduced its interest rate to a greater extent had more countries agreed, with Italy, to devalue. But the investment in the hard exchange-rate policy prevented any country from moving; no country wished to display 'weakness'. The generally received report is that France was the leading country to resist the suggestion of devaluation.

The third factor stressed in crisis post-mortems is that the Maastricht Treaty conditions encouraged the emergence of self-fulfilling beliefs underlying multiple (two, at least) equilibria. The fact that the first signs of unease in the markets seemed to be associated with the negative Danish referendum over the Maastricht Treaty underlie this prejudice, which is worked out in some detail in Eichengreen and Wyplosz.[32] The idea is that, since the Treaty specified a 'no devaluation' exchange-rate criterion, a successful raid on a currency would quickly reveal that the government behind that currency would now see no reason to be so restrained about inflation and would gravitate quickly to another, lower exchange-rate, higher-inflation, higher-demand, equilibrium. This explanation could never apply sensibly to the United Kingdom, and subsequent events do not seem to support the alleged alternative equilibrium: countries that devalued did not choose higher-inflation, higher-demand paths.

Subsequent experience has also highlighted the relevance of contagion, of 'market structure' factors, of the influence that the actions of a major player can

30 For detail on the Treasury's forecasts see M.J. Artis, 'The United Kingdom', in J. Forder and A. Menon (eds), *The European Union and National Macroeconomic Policy* (London, 1998).

31 W. Buiter, C. Corsetti and P. Pesenti, *Financial Markets and European Monetary Cooperation* (Cambridge, 1998).

32 B. Eichengreen and C. Wyplosz, 'The Unstable EMS', Brookings Papers in Economic Activity, 1, 1993, pp. 51–124.

have on others and, indirectly, the importance of what central banks make known to be their views. In the case in point, it is clear that the actions of the Bundesbank led, if only through their interpretation by Goerge Soros,[33] in one case to the destruction of the United Kingdom's position and in the other to the survival (at least in 1992) of the French.

After the crises

The recurrence of further strain in 1993, even after the departure of Italy and the United Kingdom from the EMS, was eventually resolved by the widening of the bands to ±15 per cent. This removed the 'one-way bet' that encouraged speculation, and it did not lead to the recrudescence of inflation, nor to bad behaviour on the part of participants. However, it was also not the case that the fundamentals converged immediately. The only obvious difficulty that arose concerned the Spanish and Portuguese currencies, which in 1995 sustained an attack, and realigned downwards. Whether this was really necessary is disputed.

However, the wider bands were not much exploited, and it seems that a new 'soft' target zone replaced the older one, such that the financial press was justified in watching for deviations from the old band of ±2.25 per cent. Bartolini and Prati have offered a formal interpretation of this period.[34] They suggest that the system should be thought of as having targeted within a narrow band a moving average of current and past exchange rates, allowing the current rate to move to absorb speculative movement whilst maintaining a relatively rigid long-run target.

In its last phase, the EMS also absorbed the newcomer currencies of the Greek drachma and the Finnish markka as well as the re-entry of the Italian lira. This was a prolegomenon to the very last phase of transition, that between the choice of eligible currencies for the first wave of EMU in May 1998 and the start of the Union in January 1999. This phase was accomplished with a calmness that soundly defeated the sceptical expectations of some[35] and, in this sense, was a fitting commemoration of a subtle and successful system. More to the point, the tranquillity of this final phase of transition is testimony to the political commitment of the countries concerned to the realization of monetary union in Europe. The projection of this commitment onto the market ensured that there was no speculative strain, no testing of the technical defences that had been prepared (for the posssible new adherents to the Union, the United Kingdom and Sweden, the same assurance may not be forthcoming, and their transition will, accordingly, be the more risky).

The EMS thus proved to be a remarkably adaptive and flexible system. It adapted itself not only to the phasing-out of capital controls and the concomitant enormous

33 For some indicative quotations see M.J. Artis and M. Fratianni, 'The Lira and the Pound in the 1992 Currency Crisis: Fundamentals or Speculation?', in *Open Economies Review* (Special Issue), 7, Supplement, December 1996, pp. 573-600.

34 L. Bartolini and A. Prati, 'Soft exchange rate bands and speculative attacks: theory and evidence from the ERM since August 1993', *mimeo*, 1997.

35 W. Eltis, Britain, *Europe and EMU* (London, 2000), ch. 9; M. Obstfeld, 'EMU, Ready or not?', Princeton Essays in International Finance, July 1998.

increase in the size of the world capital market but also to the change in intellectual 'regime' as the world moved from a more or less strongly 'Keynesian' orientation to one that stressed the primacy of inflation control.

In one way, of course, the EMS is still alive, as it lives on in the shape of ERM 2: but this is another story.

CHAPTER 10

European Monetary Union: A Project of Promise and Risk

Paul De Grauwe

Introduction

The introduction of the euro was a major European historical event. It was probably the first time in the continent's history that a large-scale process of monetary unification was implemented without arms and bloodshed. For this reason alone it will stand as a model for the rest of the world when others consider moving in the direction of greater monetary unification. In this paper, first, the factors that made European Monetary Union (EMU) possible are analysed. Second, a view is taken of the future in order to analyse the steps required to make EMU a permanent success.

What factors explain the successful introduction of monetary unification in Europe?[1] One way to answer this question is to contrast the attempts at monetary unification made during the 1970s with the undertaking of the 1990s. The former failed while the latter was a success. Both started with a report, the Werner and the Delors reports, respectively. Each contained a blueprint for a monetary union in Europe. Each stressed a gradual transition process, the fixity of exchange rates over the transition, the need to control budgetary positions and the ultimate requirement that monetary policies be centralized. So why did the Werner Report fail to lead to EMU while the Delors Report led to success? One answer frequently given is that, with the collapse of the Bretton-Woods system, turmoil on the exchange markets broke down the fixed-exchange-rate system that European countries had attempted to organize. This setback killed the whole EMU project in the 1970s.

This explanation is not fully satisfactory. After all, the fixed-exchange-rate mechanism of the European Monetary System (EMS), seen in the context of the Delors Report as the necessary stepping-stone towards EMU, also collapsed under the onslaught of the speculative attacks of 1992–3. And yet this breakdown did not halt progress towards EMU. Why is it that practically the same events produced such different reactions on the part of policymakers? During the 1970s they responded by shelving the idea of EMU, whereas in the 1990s they went on towards EMU as if nothing had happened. The answer is that the political will to have EMU was low in the 1970s, but by the 1990s it had become a very strong commitment. It is this political commitment that saved EMU after the EMS crisis of 1992–3. The

1 S.F. Overturf, *Money and European Union* (New York, 1997); D. Gros and N. Thygesen, *European Monetary Integration* (New York, 1998).

question that arises is: what had changed between 1970 and 1990 to explain the development of a strong political will propelling EMU? The following elements provide an answer.

First, ideas had changed. Whereas during the 1970s the prevailing view had been that monetary policies and exchange rates were important instruments which national authorities should employ to stabilize the economy, this idea was very much discredited in Europe over the 1980s. It was replaced by the monetarist paradigm that stressed the ineffectiveness of money and the exchange rate in affecting output and employment in a permanent way. Furthermore, countries that had actively used the exchange-rate instrument (Italy, France) experienced a decline in the credibility of their macroeconomic policies, creating an inflationary bias and macroeconomic instability. This experience made these countries ripe for the jump into a monetary union.

Second, the internal-market programme further integrated European economies. Policymakers increasingly felt that trade distortions and conflicts would increase if countries were allowed to use the exchange-rate instrument. In addition, the experience of EMS suggested to policymakers that a system of pegged exchange rates would never permanently stabilize the exchange rates within Europe, thereby opening up the prospect of endemic exchange-rate crises.

Third, monetary union was seen by a number of countries, in particular France, as a way to wrestle monetary hegemony from Germany. In EMU, France, Italy and other European Union countries would be the equal of Germany, instead of being forced to follow the German diktat as had become the practice since the early 1980s. This last explanation, of course, leads to the puzzle of why Germany led itself to be seduced into EMU. With EMU, Germany lost its monetary power and a valuable brand name: the Deutschmark. I believe it will remain difficult to explain Germany's pro-EMU decision. Of course, one can refer to the quid pro quo whereby Germany accepted monetary union in exchange for an eastward widening of the EU. But this seems to be unsatisfactory as an explanation. In due time, Germany would have prevailed in opening up the EU's eastern borders.

In my opinion, the German decision to join EMU is one of these rare historical events that are very much influenced by one person, in this case, Helmut Kohl. Presumably, the Chancellor must have thought that the cost for Germany of losing its monetary power was more than compensated not only by EMU's economic benefits, but also and more importantly by non-economic gains. These have to do with the German Chancellor considering that EMU was an essential building block for European unification, which was in turn seen as an essential condition for maintaining peace in Western Europe. Whether this is true is impossible to say. It is certainly true that it dominated Helmut Kohl's mind.

Thus, in the end the practical idea of monetary unification prevailed and was implemented peacefully. Is this the end of the story? Some sceptics have argued that, ultimately, there will not be a happy ending but that, like many modern marriages, monetary unification can end in fighting and divorce.[2] History tells us

2 M. Feldstein, 'EMU and International Conflict', in *Foreign Affairs*, March–April, 1998.

that monetary unification must be part of a whole. One cannot simply centralize monetary decision-making without, at the same time, centralizing other parts of economic management and, possibly, political management. Why is this? The main reason is that centralizing monetary policy and creating one currency sets in motion centrifugal forces. These must be contained to prevent conflict and crises. What are these destructive centrifugal forces?

Centrifugal forces in a monetary union

Quite paradoxically, a monetary union engenders not only integrative but also centrifugal forces. Two of the latter will be analysed. The first one occurs in the long run; the second one can occur quite rapidly.

Long-run centrifugal forces

These can be described in the following way.[3] Monetary union reduces obstacles to trade and, therefore, increases the size of markets. This, in turn, allows firms more easily to capture economies of scale. In this connection, economists distinguish between internal and external economies of scale. Internal economies of scale refer to firms increasing the scale of their respective operations in order to augment profits through declining average costs. External economies of scale refer to the dynamics whereby firms (often small undertakings) cluster together to profit from the same scarce resources (like a pool of skilled labour). The best-known example of this effect is Silicon Valley. Both developments are important because they inevitably lead to specialization and also the regional agglomeration of economic activities. When companies increase in size, they merge or swallow other companies and concentrate the location of their activities in fewer places. Similarly, firms that cluster together create agglomeration of activities in certain regions and not in others.

Monetary union is likely to activate these developments so that a regional reallocation of economic activities is the probable outcome. This will create new areas of boom while condemning older regional centres to decline. All this has occurred previously within national economies. Consider, for example, the emergence and then the later decline of regions like Wallonia in Belgium, Lorraine in France, the Ruhr in Germany, and so on. Monetary union is likely to generate these processes on a greater scale so that regions (or countries), that once constituted the centre may become relegated to having a peripheral status and vice versa.

One may argue that since these problems have been weathered in the past, they will again in the future. However, the difference is that, previously, most European countries established national systems of redistribution and solidarity that tended to soften the blows and the social dislocations produced by such geographical economic restructurings. Presently, at the beginning of the twenty-first century, no such mechanisms exist at the European level.

3 See P. De Grauwe, *The Economics of Monetary Union* (Oxford, 2000).

Another difference is that future economic restructurings may involve large areas, or even the whole, of nation states, especially the small ones. This will create strong political conflicts as residents of nations, experiencing the negative effects of the regional reallocation of economic activities, come to blame the European construction for their misfortunes. These possible conflicts will be intensified by the lack of labour mobility. When in the past one region was affected negatively, outward migration usually provided the safety valve, but such mobility is currently very much absent in Euroland.

It should be stressed that future technological developments may help to reduce the effect of these centrifugal forces. In particular, the increasing service component of new technologies may dampen their adverse effects. More generally, the increasing share of services may reduce the forces set in motion by economies of scale and agglomeration effects, since service activities tend to be smaller in scale and more decentralized. Nevertheless, centrifugal forces will continue to do their work of generating conflicts.

Potential instabilities in financial movements

A second mechanism leading to the onset of centrifugal forces in Euroland may occur through financial flows. These can be described in the following way. EMU is certainly going to increase dramatically the degree of capital mobility within the euro area. The complete elimination of foreign-exchange risk, following the euro's introduction and the disappearance of regulatory constraints on the holdings of 'foreign'-euro assets, will lead financial institutions to increase very substantially their holdings of 'foreign'-euro assets. The result is to open up European financial markets in a more profound way than occurred during the 1980s, when most European countries eliminated systems of capital controls.

Within the context of this dramatic liberalization of Europe's financial markets, there is the fact that the regulatory and institutional environment has not yet been adapted to it. Prudential control continues to be undertaken at the national level, which handicaps the regulators in assessing the risk of the institutions under their jurisdiction. The conditions that could lead to financial disturbances are, therefore, present in the euro area, at least currently when institutions have not yet adapted to the new environment. This does not, of course, mean that crises must inevitably occur. In order to gauge the risk of such occurrence, let us analyse a particular scenario.

Suppose a country, say Spain, experiences a boom that is more dynamic than in the rest of Euroland. As a result, output expands more rapidly and prices rise faster in Spain than in other euro countries, while there is also a real-estate boom and general asset inflation in Spain. Since the European Central Bank looks at euro-wide data, its management can do nothing to restrain Spanish economic conditions. In fact, the existence of a monetary union is likely to intensify asset inflation in Spain. Unhindered by exchange risk, very substantial amounts of capital will probably be attracted to Spain from the rest of the euro area. Furthermore, Spanish banks, still the dominant institutions on Spanish financial markets, are pulled into the game, and increase their lending. The decisions of their managements are driven by the high rates of return produced by ever-increasing Spanish asset prices, and by the fact, that in a monetary union, they can borrow funds at the same interest rate as banks in Germany, France, and so on. After the boom comes the bust. Asset prices collapse, creating the possibility of a crisis in the Spanish banking system.

Is this prognostication too far fetched to be realistic? The United States monetary union provides many examples of such local booms and busts, followed by financial crises resolved only by large-scale bail-out operations. Scenarios of local booms and bust, like the one described, will almost certainly happen in Euroland. The important ingredient triggering the consequent crises is the existence of regional differences in rates of return on assets coupled with the fact that, in a monetary union, banks can borrow at the same interest rates.

We conclude that the centralization of monetary policies in Euroland will not lead to automatic convergence. On the contrary, the centralization of monetary policies may set in motion the dynamics of economic and financial divergence. The essential reason why these centrifugal forces will operate is that the nation states, with their own idiosyncrasies, have been kept almost totally intact, only one feature of the nation state, the ability to create money, having been taken away. If these centrifugal forces are left unchecked, they will create havoc in the monetary union. What can be done to avoid these unpleasant consequences?

Completing the union: the role of risk sharing

Centrifugal forces in a monetary union will not be easily checked. Their unpleasant consequences, however, can be mitigated if steps are undertaken to complete the union. These must comprise establishing institutions for sharing risk at the European level. Divergent movements in economic conditions, stimulated by Euroland's existence, will create hardship in some parts of the union and prosperity in others. In order to maintain the cohesion of the whole, risk-sharing institutions are essential. How can this be done?

Ideally, the centralization of a significant part of national budgets (including social security) could provide for a risk-sharing mechanism.[4] A centralized budget ensures that countries, or regions, affected by economic hardship automatically share in the fruits of other regions' economic success. Currently, however, budgetary policies remain firmly in the hands of the nation states. As a result, the Community budget is just too small to constitute the backbone of this kind of risk sharing at European level. This is certainly a great contrast with modern nation states, all of which have built up extensive risk-sharing mechanisms through centralized national budgets. These states' politicians have come to understand that risk sharing across their respective territories is essential for sustaining cohesion and a willingness to maintain national unity. Euroland is still far removed from such a realization.

The other main avenue for building institutions of risk sharing lays in the full integration of financial markets.[5] This may not be obvious at first sight. An example will make this clear. Consider a union between only two countries, say France

4 See M. Buti and A. Sapir, *Economic Policy in EMU: a study* (New York, 1998).

5 P. Asdrubali, B. Sørensen and O. Yosha, 'Channels of Interstate Risk-sharing: United States 1963-1990', in *Quarterly Journal of Economics*, 111, 1996, pp. 1081–1110; K. Lannoo

and Germany. Suppose also that their respective financial markets are completely integrated, so that there is only one common bond market and one common equity market, while their banking sectors are also totally integrated.

Let us concentrate first upon how an integrated bond and equity market facilitates risk sharing. Suppose that France experiences a negative economic shock while Germany receives a positive shock. As a result, French firms make losses, depressing stock prices of French firms. However, since the equity market is fully integrated, French stocks are also held by German residents, so that they share a part of the cost of the fall in French economic activity in France. Conversely, the boom in Germany raises stock prices of German firms. Yet, as these financial assets are also held by French residents, they enjoy some compensation for hard economic times in France. Put differently, an integrated stock market works as an insurance system, with the risk of a negative shock in one country shared by all countries. As a result, the impact of the negative output shock in one country on the income of its residents is mitigated.

A similar mechanism works through the operation of an integrated bond market. When firms in France make losses, with some going bankrupt, this lowers the values of outstanding French bonds. But, as some French bonds are held by German residents, they thereby also pay some of the price of economic duress in France.

An integrated mortgage market has comparable effects on the degree of risk sharing. When French real-estate prices fall as a result of the negative shock to France, this negatively affects the values of outstanding mortgage-backed bonds. The opposite occurs in Germany, and the positive shock there is likely to lead to a housing boom, increasing the values of German mortgage-backed bonds. Again, this will allow for risk sharing between France and Germany. Economically unfortunate French are compensated by holding a portion of German mortgage-backed bonds, while economically fortunate Germans share in French economic misfortunes through their investments in French mortgage-backed bonds.

Finally, the integration of the banking sectors also facilitates risk sharing. Suppose the banking sector is fully integrated. This means that banks operating in France and Germany are the same. Thus, Deutsche Bank has a large portfolio of French loans (made to French firms, consumers, home-owners), and similarly with Crédit Lyonnais in Germany. The negative shock in France has the effect of making a part of French loans 'non-performing', i.e. some French firms and consumers fail to service their debt. As a result, Deutsche Bank loses revenue. However, it has some compensation from better revenues in Germany, where the boom boosts the value of the outstanding loans. Similarly, Crédit Lyonnais has compensation for its losses on its French loans through higher profits from its German activities.

We conclude that, in a monetary union, financial-market integration provides different channels of risk sharing. These make it possible for the residents of countries (regions) affected by a negative shock to maintain their incomes at relatively high level (compared to output). The counterpart of this risk sharing is that residents of the booming country see their incomes increase at a lower rate than their output.

D. and Gros, *Capital markets and EMU*, Report of a CEPS Working Party, Centre for European Policy Studies (Brussels, 1998).

Recently, important empirical research has been undertaken to measure the importance of risk sharing among regions (countries) through financial markets. Researchers have found that financial markets in the United States allow for considerable risk sharing among American regions. In fact, they have come to the conclusion that this risk sharing through the market is at least as important as the risk sharing provided by the federal government budget.[6]

From the previous discussion, one can conclude that, in the absence of budgetary unification in Euroland, the only risk-sharing mechanism available comes from the integration of financial markets. The good news is that this kind of risk sharing will come automatically, driven by market forces. The bad news is that this risk-sharing mechanism, while benefiting the affluent, will be of little use to the poor who do not hold a well-diversified portfolio of stocks and bonds.

Conclusion

The introduction of EMU is a major undertaking, full of potential for a renewal of economic dynamism in Europe. At the same time, like all projects full of promise, it is a risky venture. The main danger arises from the probability that EMU could intensify divergences among its participating countries. We have identified two such centrifugal forces. One arises from increased market integration possibly leading to greater regional specialization and therefore to major reallocations of economic activities, whereby some regions, or states, will regress and others will progress. These tendencies have happened in the past. The distinctive new feature is that this may now happen at a larger scale that could involve entire nation states, especially the smaller ones.

A second risk stems from financial movements. These will be unleashed within Euroland through financial institutions and investors seeking the highest rates of return. Again, this will tend to favour some regions and countries, while others may be hit negatively by such movements.

Although EMU may unleash centrifugal forces, very little has been done to create institutions that will make risk sharing possible at the level of Euroland. This is a major shortcoming. A necessary condition for a union of nations (or of individuals) to be maintained is that there is a perception of distributive fairness. An essential ingredient in such a perception is the existence of risk sharing. The latter acts as a glue holding together nations (and individuals) that experience divergent economic conditions. Without risk sharing, a sense of belonging to the same collectivity cannot develop. This collective feeling is of great importance for maintaining the union.

Financial-market integration will go some way towards providing for such risk sharing. However, this will be insufficient, mainly because financial markets will deliver risk sharing for the affluent, while leaving the less affluent in the cold. A union of nations cannot be successful if only the affluent have the feeling that union institutions insure them against calamities.

---

6 Asdrubali et al., 'Channels'; J. Mélitz and F. Zumer, 'Interregional and International Risk Sharing and Lessons for EMU', CEPR Discussion Paper, no. 2154, May 1999.

There is a major responsibility of national governments to build Europe-wide systems of risk sharing. This must inevitably involve some form of budgetary centralization. Currently, however, there is no political momentum to move in this direction. This leaves the whole European monetary construction very vulnerable to economic disturbances. It is also the single most important threat to its long-run survival.

CHAPTER 11

From the Athenian Tetradrachm to the Euro: Some Concluding Remarks

Vítor Gaspar[1]

The contributions to this volume cover, broadly, three millennia of the history of coins and currency – their evolution from the invention of coin-shaped currency in the seventh century BC to the transition to the euro. Before considering the euro, it is important to stress that a wealth of facts and analyses are included in these contributions. In these concluding remarks, it is impossible to do justice to their authors. Instead, an attempt will be made to provide examples of links between the principles relevant for the design of the single monetary policy and the historical experience.

Governor Karatzas, National Bank of Greece, referred to coin and currency meeting the need to 'expedite and systematize commercial transactions'. James Tobin has remarked that

> Among the conventions of almost every human society in historical record has been the use of money, that is, particular commodities or tokens as measures of value and media of exchange in economic transactions ... The reason for the universality of money as a social institution is that it facilitates trade.[2]

The unit-of-account or score-keeping function of money has been emphasized by economists for centuries.[3] As James Tobin put it, 'money is similar to language, standard time, or the convention designating the side of the road for passing'.[4] This connection is made in the contributions of both Cécile Morrisson and Juan Carlos Martinez. They emphasize the link between coinage and the system of weights and measures. Both coinage and the system of weights and measures serve the needs of trade and facilitate agreement on (explicit or implicit) contracts. The analogy has

1 The views expressed are the author's own, and do not reflect those of the ECB or the Eurosystem. I wish to thank Ignazio Angeloni, Oreste Tristani and Juan-Luis Vega for their comments.

2 J. Tobin, 'Money', in P. Newman et al. (eds), *The New Palgrave Dictionary of Money and Finance* (London, 1992).

3 The oldest reference I am aware of dates back to the seventeenth century: F. Le Blanc, *Traite Historique des Monnaies de France* (Paris, 1690). See also O. Issing, V. Gaspar, I. Angeloni and O. Tristani, *Monetary Policy in the Euro Area: Strategy and Decision-Making at the European Central Bank* (Cambridge, 2001).

4 Tobin 'Money'.

some far-reaching implications, which may be spelled out by quoting from Irving Fisher:

> In every sale where we find the yard as the goods-unit, we find the dollar as the money unit; so many *yards* of carpet are sold for so many *dollars* of money. Likewise every commitment in pounds, bushels, quarts or anything else, involves a commitment in dollars. The dollar is used as much as all other units put together. If, then, we are at such pains to standardize the yard, the pound, and every other goods-unit, having – as we do – official sealers of weights and measures to prevent the cheating of the public because of the changes in the goods-units, how much more important is to stabilize the unit of money applying, as it does, to every purchase and sale.[5]

For Irving Fisher the unit-of-account role of money lies at the root of the case for price stability.[6]

Ioannis Touratsoglou in his article stresses that common currencies result from pressing economic needs and/or reflect an underlying common political will. He also highlighted the public-law character of coin as testified by the authorities' stamp.

Juan Carlos Martinez Oliva provides a fascinating account of how – during the third century AD – the collapse of Roman public finances[7] (brought about by the Parthian and German wars) eventually led to the introduction of fiduciary currency and inflation. This was associated with such discredit of the system that even taxes had to be paid in kind. Oliva interprets the Diocletian monetary reform as involving fiduciary currency, given that his new silver coin – the nummus – had little intrinsic value. In the then prevailing circumstances, it proved impossible to build the confidence, credibility and trust which could have guaranteed the stability of the monetary system.

There is an interesting connection between Martinez-Oliva's contribution and that of Filippo Cesarano on Bretton Woods. Cesarano starts from the premise that the gold standard was 'the crowning achievement of repeated efforts to dispose of the centuries long tampering with currency by the government'. He sees Bretton Woods as a transition from 'commodity money' to 'fiat money'. Here it is – in my view – important to recall that the origins of the 'Great Inflation' that raged from the late 1960s to the late 1980s may be found in the excessive growth of nominal aggregate demand in the United States during the 1960s. These same inflationary pressures were at the source of the demise of the Bretton-Woods monetary order.

Lars Jonung, Marcello de Cecco and Richard Tilly present the experiences, respectively, of the Scandinavian Monetary Union, the Latin Monetary Union and the German Monetary Union. All took place during the nineteenth century under a

5 I. Fisher, *The Money Illusion* (New York, 1928), p. 132.

6 See A. Garcia-Herrero, V. Gaspar, L. Hoogduin, J. Morgan and B. Winkler, 'Introduction', in A. Garcia-Herrero et al. (eds), *Why Price Stability?* (European Central Bank, 2001), for a recent survey and references.

7 There seem to be numerous examples of debauching of currency in connection to public finance profligacy. Another example of the relevance of Public Finances for monetary relations is present in Marcello de Cecco's contribution covering the nineteenth-century Latin Monetary Union. He refers to 'diplomatic squabbles caused by Italian and Pontifical fiscal laxity'.

commodity-money standard. It is argued that consensus around a monetary-policy regime based on a commodity-based standard made monetary unification easier. Jonung makes this point in a particularly clear way, remarking that SMU:

> ... was based on a common view on the conduct of monetary policy. Its aim was a straightforward one: a fixed exchange rate between the domestic currency and gold should be maintained ... Monetary policy was de-nationalized and de-politicized, which made international arrangements easy to accomplish.

Michael Artis sees the experience with the Exchange Rate Mechanism of the European Monetary System (ERM of the EMS) as instrumental in the creation of European Monetary Union. However, he stresses that this role was not always clear in the history of the system from its launch in 1979. Paul de Grauwe covers the motivations of, and possible consequences from, monetary unification, and this ground will also now be addressed.

The process of monetary unification in Europe – the introduction of the euro as the single currency in the euro area – has to be regarded as a unique historical experience. It is the first experience of a monetary union among industrial countries under a 'fiat currency' regime. It led to the creation of the second largest concerted economic and monetary union in the world.

One important theme that cannot be over-emphasized is the interaction between the economic and political aspects of European integration in general, and economic and monetary unification in particular. This has always been crystal clear. In the *Preamble to the Paris Treaty* (1951), establishing the European Coal and Steel Community, the signatories already declared their resolve:

> ... to substitute for age-old rivalries the merger of their essential interests; to create, by establishing an economic community, the basis for a broader community between peoples long divided by bloody conflicts; and to lay the foundations for institutions which will give direction to a destiny henceforth shared.

Almost 40 years later, Jacques Delors and Henning Christophersen wrote: 'While the content of the Community's agenda is both economic and political the whole process will stand or fall on the basis of the functional qualities of economic and monetary union'.[8] To repeat, the processes of monetary, economic and political integration overlap and interact in complex ways. The political aspects of monetary unification are outside the scope of this paper.[9] However, it is important to recognize that the Member States showed determined commitment to the fulfilment of the convergence criteria for participation in the third stage of EMU. Given that this convergence process required a significant adjustment of macroeconomic policies in almost all member countries, it may be seen as revealed preference of political

8 In 10 October 1990, in the Preface to 'One Market, One Money', published in *European Economy*, 44, Commission of the European Communities.

9 See A. Szasz, *The Road to European Monetary Union: A political and economic history* (Basingstoke, 1999). The author offers a fascinating account of the political motivations for monetary unification with a special emphasis on the German perspective. On this it complements and completes the contribution of Paul de Grauwe.

commitment to monetary unification. Artis makes a similar point when commenting on the smoothness of the final transition to EMU. He states: 'the tranquillity of this final phase of transition is testimony to the political commitment of the countries concerned to the realization of monetary union in Europe'.

A second aspect refers to institutional design. The European Union Treaty and the Statute of the European System of Central Banks and the European Central Bank reflect a broad consensus on how to define and implement monetary policy. This includes price stability as the primary goal for monetary policy, independence of the central bank and provisions to ensure transparency and accountability.[10] Broad consensus on monetary policy helped monetary unification in a way that parallels the nineteenth-century experience stressed by Jonung.

A third aspect relates to the transition to the single monetary policy. A brief reference has already been made to the macroeconomic convergence process in the run-up to monetary union. However, given the unique, unprecedented historical character of the start-up of the single monetary policy, it is easy to accept that there were multiple challenges that had to be overcome. First, in central banking, it was key to establish credibility.[11] This was a significant challenge for a newly created institution without the benefits of a reputation build upon an established track record. It is, therefore, remarkable that, since the announcement of the European Central Bank's stability-oriented monetary-policy strategy on 13 October 1998, medium-term inflation expectations have been consistently inside the range compatible with price stability. The stability of inflation expectations is all the more remarkable, given the increase in headline inflation.[12] Second, banks adapted quickly and smoothly to the Eurosystem's operational framework. The transition did not have a major impact on the behaviour of money-market interest rates. Gaspar, Perez-Quiros and Sicilia find that the volatility of money-market interest rates was not particularly high.[13] Specifically, they found that volatility, at the beginning of 1999, was significantly lower than at the end of reserve maintenance periods. After just a few weeks a single – completely unified – money market was already in place. More generally, the Eurosystem's operational framework has worked successfully.[14]

A fourth, and extremely interesting theme, concerns the interaction between monetary union and the single market. This theme can be considered under the

---

10 See Issing et al., *Policy*. For a presentation of the ECB's monetary policy strategy see V. Gaspar, 'The Institutional Design of the ECB and the Eurosystem', comment on J. von Hagen and M. Brückner, 'Monetary Policy in Unknown Territory: the European Central Bank in the Early Years', *mimeo*, 2001, for a more detailed look at the institutional organization of the Eurosystem.

11 A. Blinder, 'Central Bank Credibility: Why Do We Care? How Do We Build It?', NBER Working Paper 7161, 1999; Issing et al., Policy.

12 Headline inflation has been above 2 per cent since June 2000. It reached a peak in May 2001 with a year-on-year rate of 3.4 per cent. These developments were significantly influenced by the behaviour of energy and food prices.

13 V. Gaspar, G. Perez-Quiros and H. Rodriguez, 'The ECB Monetary Policy Strategy and the Money Market', ECB Working Paper, 69, July 2001.

14 M. Manna, H. Pill and G. Quiros, 'The Eurosystem's Operational Framework in the Context of the ECB's Monetary Policy Strategy', *mimeo*, 2001.

headings: 'One Market, One Money' or 'One Money, One Market'. Many authors have stressed the link between monetary unification and the single market. It is clear and well known that full freedom of capital movements is not, in the end, compatible with stable exchange rates and autonomous monetary policies. This is a very fundamental point. It is possible to refer to it as a 'folk theorem' in international macroeconomics.[15] However, its practical implications in form of constraints on feasible policies and institutional design are often overlooked.[16] This remark was key to the making of the Commission's 1990 'One Market, One Money'. The single currency was seen as a complement to the single market. A body of recent research has focused on the reverse link.

An emblematic paper in this line has been that by Andrew Rose, entitled precisely 'One Money, One Market'. He attempted to answer the question: what is the effect of currency unions on trade? For this, he examined a very large macro data set. It covers almost 200 countries and the period from 1970 to 1995, divided into five-year sub-periods. The striking result is that the estimate of the impact on trade from membership in a currency union is simply huge. According to Rose's estimates, trade is multiplied by a factor of three or more. A quote from Rose provides a very clear summing-up:

> In this paper, the gravity model was used to show that two countries with a common currency trade more. The effect is statistically significant and economically large: my point estimate is over three times as much as countries not sharing a single currency. The impact of a common currency is an order of magnitude larger than the effect of reducing moderate exchange rate volatility to zero but retaining separate currencies. The effect takes into account a variety of other factors and seems robust.[17]

In retrospect, it is interesting that in the Commission's 'One Market, One Money', published in 1990, there was not much emphasis given to the impact of monetary unification on the integration of markets. In the Commission's study, monetary unification was seen as the limiting case of reduced exchange-rate volatility. Exchange-rate uncertainty would be eliminated and transaction costs and hedging costs would be reduced. Furthermore, most of the empirical literature quoted by the Commission was based on time-series data. This literature did not offer conclusive results on the impact of exchange-rate volatility on either trade and investment flows – thus the very cautious assessment in 'One Market, One Money'.

Andrew Rose relied instead upon the gravity model from the 1960s.[18] It emphasizes distance as a determinant of trade flows. The importance of distance relates *inter alia*

---

15 See, for example, C. Wyplosz, 'Capital Flow liberalization and the EMS: a French perspective', in *European Economy*, 36, May 1988, pp. 85–104.

16 The argument has been originally made, in the context of European integration by T. Padoa-Schioppa, 'Capital Mobility: Why is the Treaty Not Implemented?' Address to the Second Symposium of European Banks, 1982.

17 A. Rose, 'Currency Unions and Trade; the Effect is Large', in *Economic Policy*, 33, October 2001.

18 See, for example, J. Tinbergen, 'An Analysis of World Trade Flows', in J. Tinbergen (ed.), *Shaping the World Economy* (New York, 1962).

to transport costs. However, more generally, one may regard the gravity model as a natural vehicle for thinking about trading costs in the round. Broadly, trading costs may reflect a plethora of factors, including: tariff and non-tariff regulatory barriers, language, exchange-rate risk, legal systems, market conventions and practices and information asymmetries.[19] Such a perspective may be applied for considering the impact of monetary unification upon patterns of trade and international investment.

Rose's estimates of the impact of currency unions on trade are surprisingly large. They therefore attracted considerable attention and a great deal of scepticism. A number of remarks have been made. First, the number of observations pertaining to countries in currency unions is less than 1 per cent of the total number of observations. Second, there may be a problem of omitted variables. Third, the generalization of the results to, for example, monetary unification in Europe and North America is not clear cut. However, the remarkable finding is that, after further research,[20] although the size of the point estimates have been reduced, they remain highly significant from a statistical viewpoint, and large. The estimates range from an increase of 13 per cent to more than three times. Most results point to increases in trade of more than 50 per cent.

Given less than three years since the start of the single monetary policy, it is too early to offer any definite conclusions building on the euro-area experience. Nevertheless, looking at national money as a possible barrier to economic integration offers an ample field for empirical research on European integration.

The integration of euro banknotes and coin from 1 January 2002 will complete monetary unification in a way that will be apparent to all citizens in the euro area. The euro will become the universal transaction medium and the unit of account for retail transactions. The integration dynamics on goods, services and financial markets will be long lasting.

---

19 J. Anderson and E. van Wincoop, 'Borders, Trade and Welfare', NBER WP 8515, October 2001, is particularly useful in this context. In this paper the authors distinguish trading costs according to whether they are border or non-border costs. The former are further refined to distinguish between those that give rise to economic rents and those that do not.

20 By J. Frankel and A. Rose, 'Estimating the Impact of Currency Unions on Trade and Growth', CEPR DP 2631, 2000; A. Rose and C. Engel, 'Currency Unions and International Integration', CEPR DP 2659, 2000; A. Rose and E. van Wincoop, 'National Money as a Barrier to Trade: the Real Case for Currency Union', in American Economic Review (Papers and Proceedings) 91, 2, 2001; J. Melitz, 'Geography, Trade and Currency Union', CEPR DP 2987, 2001; T. Persson, 'Currency Unions and Trade: How large is the Treatment Effect?', in *Economic Policy*, 33, October 2001; and Rose, 'Currency Unions and Trade'.

Bibliography

J. Anderson and E. van Wincoop, 'Borders, Trade and Welfare', NBER WP 8515, October 2001.

R. Anderton, R. Barrell and J. McHugh, 'Nominal convergence in European wage behaviour: achievements and explanations', in R. Barrell (ed.), *Economic Convergence and Monetary Union in Europe*, (London, 1992).

J. Andreau, 'Declino e morte dei mestieri bancari nel mediterraneo occidentale (II-IV DC)', in A. Giardina (ed.), *Società romana e impero tardoantico: istituzioni, ceti, economie* (Rome, 1986).

J. Andreau, 'Mercati e mercato', in *Storia di Roma, vol. 2: l'Impero mediterraneo, II: I principi e il mondo* (Turin, 1991).

J.W. Angell, 'The General Objectives of Monetary Policy', in A.D. Gayer (ed.), *The Lessons of Monetary Experience* (London, 1937).

M.J. Artis, 'The United Kingdom', in J. Forder and A. Menon (eds), *The European Union and National Macroeconomic Policy* (London, 1998).

—— and W. Zhang, 'The Linkage of Interest Rates within the EMS', in *Weltwirtschaftliches Archiv*, 134, 1, 1998, pp. 117–32.

—— and M. Fratianni, 'The Lira and the Pound in the 1992 Currency Crisis: Fundamentals or Speculation?', in *Open Economies Review* (Special Issue), 7, Supplement, December 1996, pp. 573–600.

—— and P. Ormerod, 'Is there an EMS Effect in European Labour Markets?', in S. Collignon S. and C. Johnson (eds), *The Monetary Economics of Europe: Causes of the EMS Crisis* (London, 1994).

—— and M.P. Taylor, 'Exchange rates, interest rates, capital controls and the European Monetary System: assessing the track record', in F. Giavazzi, M. Micossi and M. Miller (eds), *The European Monetary System* (Cambridge, 1988).

—— and M.P. Taylor, 'The Achievements of the European Monetary System', in *Economic and Social Review*, 20, June 1989, pp. 121–45.

P. Asdrubali, B. Sørensen and O. Yosha, 'Channels of Interstate Risk-sharing: United States 1963–1990', in *Quarterly Journal of Economics*, 111, 1996, pp. 1081–1110.

R. Bagnall, 'Agricultural productivity and taxation in Later Roman Egypt', in *Transactions of the American Philological Association*, 115, 1985, pp. 289–308.

L. Bartolini and A. Prati, 'Soft exchange rate bands and speculative attacks: theory and evidence from the ERM since August 1993', *mimeo*, 1997.

M. Bergman, 'Do monetary unions make economic sense? Evidence from the Scandinavian monetary union 1873–1913', in *Scandinavian Journal of Economics*, 1999.

——, S. Gerlach and L. Jonung, 'The rise and fall of the Scandinavian currency union 1873–1920', in *European Economic Review*, 37, 1993, pp. 507–17.

T. Bertelè, 'Moneta veneziana e moneta bizantina (secoli XII-XV)', in A. Pertusi (ed.), *Venezia e il Levante fino al secolo XVI, vol. 1: Storia-Diritto-Economia* (Venice, 1983).

M. Berthelot and Ch. -E. Ruelle, *Collection des anciens alchimistes grecs*, 3 vols. (Paris, 1888–9, reprint Osnabrück, 1967).

M. Bessec, 'Mean reversion versus adjustment to PPP: the two regimes of exchange rate dynamics uner the EMS, 1979–1998', paper presented at the World Conference Econometric Society, Seattle, 2000.

J. Bidez, *Catalogue des manuscrits alchimistes grecs, vol. 6* (Bruxelles, 1988), p. 26–41. Ital. transl. (with a reproduction of the text publ. by Bidez) by F. Abini, *La Crisopea* (Genua, 1988).

A. Blinder, 'Central Bank Credibility: Why Do We Care? How Do We Build It?', NBER Working Paper 7161, 1999.

K. Borchardt, 'Währung und Wirtschaft', in Deutsche Bundesbank (ed.), *Währung und Wirtschaft in Deutschland 1876–1975* (Frankfurt, 1976).

M. Bordo, 'The Bretton Woods International Monetary System: A Historical Overview', in M.D. Bordo and B. Eichengreen (eds), *A Retrospective on the Bretton Woods System* (Chicago, 1993).

——, 'The Classical Gold Standard: Some Lessons for Today', Federal Reserve Bank of St. Louis Review, 63, 5, 1981.

—— and F. Capie (eds), *Monetary Regimes in Transition* (Cambridge, 1994).

——, C. Goldin and E.N. White (eds), *The Defining Moment. The Great Depression and the American Economy in the Twentieth Century* (Chicago, 1998).

—— and L. Jonung, 'A return to the convertibility principle? Monetary and fiscal regimes in historical perspective. The international evidence', in A. Leijonhufvud (ed.), *Monetary Theory as a Basis for Monetary Policy* (London, 2001).

—— and L. Jonung, 'Lessons for EMU from the History of Monetary Unions?', IEA, Readings 50, London, June 2000.

—— and F.E. Kydland, 'The Gold Standard As a Rule: An Essay in Exploration', in *Explorations in Economic History*, 32, October 1995, pp. 423–64.

—— and H. Rockoff, 'The Gold Standard as a "Good Housekeeping Seal of Approval"', in *Journal of Economic History*, 56, 2, 1996.

—— and H. Rockoff, 'The gold standard as a "good housekeeping seal of approval"', in M. Bordo (ed.), *The gold standard and related regimes* (Cambridge, 1999).

—— and A. Schwartz (eds), *A Retrospective on the Classical Gold Standard* (Chicago, 1984).

J. Braga de Macedo, B. Eichengreen and J. Reis (eds), *Currency Convertibility. The gold standard and beyond* (London, 1996).

W. Buiter, C. Corsetti and P. Pesenti, *Financial Markets and European Monetary Cooperation* (Cambridge, 1998).

A. Burnett, *Coinage in the Roman World* (London, 1987).

M. Buti and A. Sapir, *Economic Policy in EMU: a study* (New York, 1998).

R. Cameron, 'England', in R. Cameron et al. (eds), *Banking in the Early Stages of Industrialization* (New York, 1967).

——, 'France', in R. Cameron et al. (eds), *Banking in the Early Stages of Industrialization* (New York, 1967).

——, 'Scotland', in R. Cameron et al. (eds), *Banking in the Early Stages of Industrialization* (New York, 1967).

R. Cantillon, *Essai sur la nature du commerce en général* (London, 1755 [repr. Paris: INED]).

J.-M. Carrié and A. Rousselle, *L'empire romain en mutation des Sévères à Constantin* (Paris, 1999).

G. Cassel, *The Crisis in the World's Monetary System* (Oxford, 1932a).

——, *The Downfall of the Gold Standard* ([1936], New York, 1966).

——, *The Theory of Social Economy* ([1932b], New York, 1967).

F. Cesarano, 'Hume's Specie-Flow Mechanism and Classical Monetary Theory: An Alternative Interpretation', in *Journal of International Economics*, 45, June 1998, pp. 173–86.

——, 'Monetary Systems and Monetary Theory', in *Kredit und Kapital*, 32, 2, 1999, pp. 192–208.

R. Cessi and P. Sambin, *Le deliberazioni del Consiglio di Rogati (Senato)*, Serie 'Mixtorum', vol. I, p. 105, n. 24.

C. Chase-Dunn and D. Hall, 'Conceptualizing Core/Periphery Hierarchies for Comparative Study', in C. Chase-Dunn and D. Hall (eds), *Core/Periphery Relations in Precapitalist Worlds* (Oxford, 1991).

S.V.O. Clarke, *The Reconstruction of the International Monetary System: The Attempts of 1922 and 1933*, Princeton Studies in International Finance, no. 33 (Princeton, 1973).

C.M. Cipolla, *Money, Prices and Civilisation in the Mediterranean World. Fifth to Seventeenth Century* (Princeton, 1956).

G. Clemente, 'La guerra annibalica', in *Storia di Roma, vol. 2: l'Impero mediterraneo, I: La repubblica imperiale* (Turin, 1990).

'Coin and its use in Byzantium', online exhibit displaying 118 Byzantine coins described, commented and accompanied by explanatory texts on the history of the coinage, its mints and system, its political and economic function and its iconography, http://www.doaks.org/CoinExhibition/First/First1Main3.html

M. Corbier, 'Svalutazioni, inflazione e circolazione monetaria nel III secolo', in A. Giardina (ed.), *Società romana e impero tardoantico: istituzioni, ceti, economie* (Rome Bari, 1986).

M. Crawford, 'Money and Exchange in the Roman World', in *The Journal of Roman Studies*, 60, 1970, pp. 40–8.

——, *La moneta in Grecia e a Roma* (Bari, 1986).

D. Davidson, 'PM rörande den skandinaviska myntkonventionen', report to the Riksbank, 6 February 1917.

J. Day (ed.), *Études d'histoire monétaire* (Lille, 1984).

——, *Monnaies et marchés au Moyen Âge* (Paris, 1994).

M. De Cecco, 'European Monetary and Financial Cooperation before the First World War', in *Rivista di Storia Economica*, 3rd ser., 9, 2, 1992, pp. 55–76.

——, 'Gold Standard', in J. Eatwell, M. Milgate and P. Newman (eds), *The New Palgrave. A Dictionary of Economics* (London, 1987).

——, 'Monetary Theory and Roman History', in *Journal of Economic History*, 45, 4, 1985, pp. 809–22.

——, *Money and Empire. The International Gold Standard, 1880–1914* (London, 1974).

P.C. De Grauwe, *The Economics of Monetary Integration* (3. revised ed., Oxford, 1997).

——, *The Economics of Monetary Union* (Oxford, 2000).

R. De Mattia, *L'unificazione monetaria italiana* (Torino, 1959).

F.E. De Parieu, 'De l'uniformité monétaire', *Journal des économistes*, 3rd ser., 6, (giugno 1867), pp. 321–56.

F. Droulers (ed.), *Histoire de l'écu européen du moyen-âge à nos jours et des précédentes unions monétaires* (Lagny sur Marne, 1990).

I.M. Drummond, *The Gold Standard and the International Monetary System, 1900–1939*, Studies in Economic and Social History (London, 1987).

R. Duncan-Jones, *Money and Government in the Roman Empire* (Cambridge, 1994).

——, *The Economy of the Roman Empire* (Cambridge, 1974).

M.S. Eccles, 'Controlling Booms and Depressions', in A.D. Gayer (ed.), *The Lessons of Monetary Experience* (London, 1937).

B. Eichengreen, *Globalizing Capital. A History of the International Monetary System* (Princeton, 1996).

——, 'Hegemonic Stability Theories of the International Monetary System', in *Can Nations Agree?: Issues in International Economic Cooperation* (Washington, 1989).

——, 'One money for Europe? Lessons from the US Currency Union', in B. Eichengreen (ed.), *European monetary unification* (Cambridge, 1997).

——, 'The EMS Crisis in retrospect', CEPR Discussion Papers, no. 2704, February 2001 (Centre for Economic Policy Research, London).

—— (ed.), *The Gold Standard in Theory and in History* (New York and London, 1985).

—— and M. Flandreau, 'The Geography of the Gold Standard', in J. Braga de Macedo, B. Eichengreen and J. Reis (eds), *Currency Convertibility. The gold standard and beyond* (London, 1996).

—— and C. Wyplosz, 'The Unstable EMS', Brookings Papers in Economic Activity, 1, 1993, pp. 51–124.

L. Einaudi, *Money and Politics: European Monetary Union and the Gold Standard, 1865–73* (Oxford, 2001).

——, 'Teoria della moneta immaginaria nel tempo da Carlomagno alla Rivoluzione francese', in L. Giusso, *Teoria delle unioni monetarie e integrazione europea* (Naples, 1974).

K. Ekholm and J. Friedman, '"Capital" Imperialism and Exploitation in Ancient World Systems', in A.G. Frank and B.K. Gills (eds), *The World System: Five Hundred Years or Five Thousand?* (London, 1993).

W. Eltis, *Britain, Europe and EMU* (London, 2000).

E. Ercolani Cocchi, 'Un'economia monetaria', in V. Castronovo, *Storia dell' economia mondiale, vol. 1: Permanenze e mutamenti dall'antichità al medioevo* (Bari, 1996).

A. Feaveryear, *The pound sterling. A history of English money* (Oxford, 2nd ed. 1963).

M. Feldstein, 'EMU and International Conflict', in *Foreign Affairs*, March–April, 1998.

M.I. Finley, *The Ancient Economy* (London, 1973).

I. Fisher, *100 per cent Money* ([1935], New Haven, 1945).

——, 'The Debt-Deflation Theory of Great Depressions', in *Econometrica*, 1, October 1933, pp. 337–57.

——, *The Money Illusion* (New York, 1928).

——, *The Purchasing Power of Money* ([1911], New York, 1963).

W. Fisher, 'Der Deutsche Zollverein, die Europäische Wirtschaftsgemeinschaft und die Freihandelszone', *Europa Archiv*, 5, 1961.

M. Flandreau, 'Central Bank Cooperation in Historical Perspective: A Sceptical View', in *Economic History Review*, 50, 4, 1998.

——, *L'or du monde, la France et la stabilité du système monétaire international, 1848–73* (Paris, 1995).

——, 'The French crime of 1873: an essay on the emergence of the international gold standard, 1870–1880', in *Journal of Economic History*, 56, 1996.

——, 'Was the Latin Monetary Union a Franc zone?', in J. Reis (ed.), *International Monetary Systems in Historical Perspective* (Houndsmill/London, 1995).

—— and B. Eichengreen, 'The geography of the gold standard', in J. Braga de Macedo, B. Eichengreen and J. Reis (eds), *Currency convertibility. The gold standard and beyond* (London/New York, 1996).

J.M. Fleming, 'Domestic Financial Policies under Fixed and under Floating Exchange Rates', IMF Staff Papers, 9, 3, 1962.

A.G. Frank and B.K. Gills (eds), *The World System: Five Hundred Years or Five Thousand?* (London, 1993).

J. Frankel and A. Rose, 'Estimating the Impact of Currency Unions on Trade and Growth', CEPR DP 2631, 2000.

M. Fratianni and J. von Hagen, *The European Monetary System and European Monetary Union* (Oxford, 1992)

M. Friedman, 'Real and Pseudo Gold Standards', in *Journal of Law and Economics*, 4, October 1961, reprinted in M. Friedman, *Dollars and Deficits. Inflation, Monetary Policy and the Balance of Payments* (Englewood Cliffs, N.J, 1968).

——, 'The Case for Flexible Exchange Rates', in M. Friedman, *Essays in Positive Economics* (Chicago, 1953).

——, 'The Resource Cost of Irredeemable Paper Money', in *Journal of Political Economy*, 94, June 1986, pp. 642–7.

——, 'Why the American Economy is Depression-Proof', in M. Friedman, *Dollars and Deficits. Inflation, Monetary Policy and the Balance of Payments* ([1954], Englewood Cliffs, N.J, 1968).

W. Fritsch and G.H.B. Franco, 'Aspects of Brazilian Experience with the Gold Standard', in P. Martín Aceña and J. Reis (eds), *Monetary Standards in the Periphery. Paper, Silver and Gold, 1854–1933* (London, 2000).

W. Funk, *Wirtschaftliche Neuordnung Europas* (Berlin, 1940).

E. Gabba, 'L'imperialismo romano', in *Storia di Roma, vol. 2: l'Impero mediterraneo, I: La repubblica imperiale* (Turin, 1990).

G.M. Gallarotti, *The Anatomy of an International Monetary Regime. The Classical Gold Standard* (Oxford, 1995).

A. Garcia-Herrero, V. Gaspar, L. Hoogduin, J. Morgan and B. Winkler, 'Introduction', in A. Garcia-Herrero et al. (eds), *Why Price Stability?* (European Central Bank, 2001).

F. Garelli, *La coopération monétaire internationale depuis un siècle* (Geneva, 1946).

V. Gaspar, 'The Institutional Design of the ECB and the Eurosystem', comment on J. von Hagen and M. Brückner, 'Monetary Policy in Unknown Territory: the European Central Bank in the Early Years', *mimeo*, 2001.

——, G. Perez-Quiros and H. Rodriguez, 'The ECB Monetary Policy Strategy and the Money Market', ECB Working Paper, 69, July 2001.

A.D. Gayer (ed.), *The Lessons of Monetary Experience* (London, 1937).

F. Giavazzi and A. Giovannini, *Limiting Exchange Rate Flexibility* (Cambridge, Mass., 1989).

——, and M. Pagano, 'The Advantage of Tying One's Hands. EMS Discipline and Central Bank Credibility', in *European Economic Review*, 32, 1988, pp. 1055–82.

B.K. Gills, 'Hegemonic Transitions in The World System', in A.G. Frank and B.K. Gills (eds), *The World System: Five Hundred Years or Five Thousand?* (London, 1993).

—— and A.G. Frank, 'World System Cycles, Crises, and Hegemonic Shifts, 1700 BC to 1700 A.D', in A.G. Frank and B.K. Gills (eds), *The World System: Five Hundred Years or Five Thousand?* (London, 1993).

R. Gilpin, *War and Change in World Politics* (Cambridge, 1981).

L. Giusso, *Teoria delle unioni monetari e integrazione europea* (Naples, 1974).

R.W. Goldsmith, 'An estimate of the size and structure of the National Product of the early Roman Empire', *Review of Income and Wealth*, 1984, pp. 263–88.

B. Graham, *Storage and Stability* (New York, 1937).

F.D. Graham, 'The Primary Functions of Money and Their Consummation in Monetary Policy', in *American Economic Review. Papers and Proceedings*, 30, March 1940, part 2, pp. 1–16.

——, The Cause and Cure of 'Dollar Shortage'. *Essays in International Finance*, no. 10 (Princeton, 1949).

K. Greene, 'Technological Innovation and Economic Progress in the Ancient World: M.I. Finley Re-Considered', in *Economic History Review*, 53, 1, 2000, pp. 29–59.

P. Grierson and M. Blackburn, *Medieval European Coinage, vol. 1: The Early Middle Ages* (Cambridge, 1986).

D. Gros and N. Thygesen, *European Monetary Integration* (New York, 1998).

T. Guggenheim, 'Some Early Views on Monetary Integration', in H.G. Johnson and A.K. Swoboda (eds), *The Economics of Common Currencies* (London, 1973).

R. Halleux, *Les alchimistes grecs*, vol. 1 (Paris, 1981)

——, *Les textes alchimiques grecs* (Turnhout, 1979).

——, 'Méthodes d'essai et d'affinage des alliages aurifères dans l'Antiquité et au Moyen Age', in C. Morrisson, J.-N. Barrandon et al., *L'or monnayé, vol. 1: Purification et altérations. De Rome à Byzance*, Cahiers Ernest-Babelon 2 (Paris, 1985).

G.N. Halm, 'The International Monetary Fund', in *Review of Economic Statistics*, 26, November 1944, pp. 170–5.

A.H. Hansen, 'Monetary Policy in the Upswing', in A.D. Gayer (ed.), *The Lessons of Monetary Experience* (London, 1937).

J. Hansen, *Gustav von Mevissen. Ein rheinisches Lebensbild*, 2 vols. (Berlin, 1906).

P. Hanson and L. Jonung, 'Finance and growth: The case of Sweden 1834–1991', *Research in Economics*, 51, 1997, pp. 275-301.

G. Hardach and S. Hartig, 'Der Goldstandard als Argument in der internationalen Währungsdiskussion', *Jahrbuch für Wirtschaftsgeschichte*, 1998.

K.W. Harl, *Coinage in the Roman Economy, 300 BC to AD 700* (Baltimore, 1996).

R.G. Hawtrey, 'The Gold Standard', in *Economic Journal*, 29, December 1919, pp. 428–42.

——, 'The Genoa Resolutions on Currency', in *Economic Journal*, 32, September 1922, pp. 290–304.

——, *The Gold Standard in Theory and Practice* ([1927], London, 1947).

——, *The Art of Central Banking* ([1932], London, 1970).

——, *Economic Destiny* (London, 1944).

F.A. von Hayek, *Prices and Production* ([1931], New York, 1967).

——, 'The Fate of the Gold Standard', in R. McCloughry (ed.), *Money, Capital and Fluctuations* ([1932], London, 1984).

——, 'On "Neutral Money"', in R. McCloughry (ed.), *Money, Capital and Fluctuations* ([1933a], London, 1984).

——, *Monetary Theory and the Trade Cycle* ([1933b], New York, 1966).

——, 'A Commodity Reserve Currency', in *Economic Journal*, 53, June–September 1943, pp. 176–84.

E. Heckscher, 'Penningväsendet och penningpolitik', in E. Heckscher (ed.), Bidrag till Sveriges ekonomiska och sociala historia (Stockholm, 1926).

K.T. Helfferich, *Das Geld* (1903, Leipzig, 5th ed. 1921).

M.F. Hendy, *Studies in the Byzantine Monetary Economy, c. 300–c.1450* (Cambridge, 1985).

I. Henriksen and N. Kaergård, 'The Scandinavian currency union 1875–1914', in J. Reis (ed.), *International monetary systems in historical perspective* (London, 1995).

C.L. Holtfrerich, 'The Monetary Unification Process in Nineteenth-Century Germany: relevance and lessons for Europe today', in M. de Cecco and A. Giovannini (eds), *A European Central Bank? Perspectives on Monetary Unification after Ten Years of the EMS* (Cambridge, 1989).

K. Hopkins, 'Taxes and Trade in the Roman Empire', in *The Journal of Roman Studies*, 70, 1980, pp. 101–25.

——, 'Centro e periferia. L'economia politica dell'impero romano', in V. Castronovo, *Storia dell'economia mondiale, vol. 1: Permanenze e mutamenti dall'antichità' al medioevo* (Bari, 1996).

J.K. Horsefield, *The International Monetary Fund 1945–1965: Twenty Years of International Monetary Cooperation, vol. 1, Chronicle* (Washington, 1969a).

——, *The International Monetary Fund 1945–1965: Twenty Years of International Monetary Cooperation, vol. 3, Documents* (Washington, 1969b).

C. Howgego, *Ancient History from Coins* (London, 1995).

——, 'The Supply and Use of Money in the Roman World 200 BC to AD 300', in *The Journal of Roman Studies*, 82, 1992, pp. 1–31.

D. Hume, 'Of The Balance of Trade', in E. Rotwein (ed.), *David Hume. Writings on Economics* ([1752], Madison, 1970).

M. Hutchison and U.M. Bergman, 'Northern Light: Does Optimal Currency Area Criteria Explain Nordic Reluctance to Join EMU?', in J. von Hagen and M. Widgren (eds), *Regionalism in Europe: Geometries and Strategies After 2000* (Amsterdam, 2001).

O. Issing, V. Gaspar, I. Angeloni and O. Tristani, *Monetary Policy in the Euro Area: Strategy and Decision-Making at the European Central Bank* (Cambridge, 2001).

H.G. Johnson, 'The Monetary Approach to the Balance of Payments Theory', in J.A. Frenkel and H.G. Johnson (eds), *The Monetary Approach to the Balance of Payments* (London, 1976).

A.H.M. Jones, *L'economia romana* (Turin, 1984).

L. Jonung, 'EMU – the first 10 years. Challenges to the sustainability and price stability of the Euro-area – What does history tell us?', in M. Buti (ed.), *The functioning of EMU. Challenges of the early years* (London, 2002).

——, 'Swedish experience under the classical gold standard 1873–1913', in: M. Bordo and A. Schwartz (eds), *The Classical Gold Standard in Retrospective* (Chicago, 1984).

—— and F. Sjöholm, 'Should Sweden and Finland Form a Monetary Union?, in *The World Economy*, 22, 5, July 1999.

P.B. Kenen, *Managing Exchange Rates* (London, 1988).

P.B. Kenen, 'What have we learned from the EMS Crises?', in *Journal of Policy Modeling*, 17, 1995, pp. 449–61.

R.O. Keohane, 'The Theory of Hegemonic Stability and Changes in International Economic Regimes', in C. Roe Goddard, J.T. Passe-Smith and J.G. Conklin (eds), *International Political Economy: State-Market Relations in the Changing Global Order* ([1980] London, 1996).

J.M. Keynes, 'Activities 1940–1944. Shaping the Post-War World: The Clearing Union', in D. Moggridge (ed.), *The Collected Writings of John Maynard Keynes*, vol. 25 (London, 1980a).

——, 'Activities 1941–1946. Shaping the Post-War World: Bretton Woods and Reparations', in D. Moggridge (ed.), *The Collected Writings of John Maynard Keynes*, vol. 25 (London, 1980b).

——, *Consequences of the Peace* (1920).

——, *A Tract on Monetary Reform* (London, 1923).

——, *A Treatise on Money* (London, 1930).
——, 'Poverty in Plenty: Is the Economic System Self-Adjusting?', in D. Moggridge (ed.), *The Collected Writings of John Maynard Keynes*, vol. 9 ([1934], London, 1973).
——, 'The Future of the Foreign Exchanges', in D. Moggridge (ed.), *The Collected Writings of John Maynard Keynes, vol. 21* ([1935], London, 1982).
——, 'The Means to Prosperity', in D. Moggridge (ed.), *The Collected Writings of John Maynard Keynes, vol. 13* ([1933], London, 1972).
——, 'The Objective of International Price Stability', in *Economic Journal*, 53, June–September 1943, pp. 185–7.
C. Kindleberger, *A Financial History of Western Europe* (London, 1984).
S. Kingsley and M. Decker (eds), *Economy and Exchange in the East Mediterranean during Late Antiquity. Proceedings of the conference held at Somerville College*, Oxford, 29 May 1999 (Oxford, 2001).
G.F. Knapp, *Staatliche Theorie des Geldes* (Leipzig, 1905).
C. Kraay, *Archaic and Classical Greek Coins* (London, 1976).
O. Krantz, 'Den svensk-norska unionens betydelse för Sveriges ekonomiska utveckling' ('The impact of the union between Sweden and Norway on the economic development of Sweden'), *Meddelande från Ekonomisk-historiska institutionen*, Lunds universitet, 49, 1987.
J. Kremers, 'Gaining Policy Credibility for a Disinflation: Ireland's experience in the EMS', IMF Staff Papers, 37, March 1990, pp. 116–45;
P. Krugman, 'Target zones and exchange rate dynamics', in *Quarterly Journal of Economics*, 106, 1991, pp. 311–25.
D. Laidler, 'Rules, Discretion and Financial Crises in Classical and Neoclassical Monetary Economics', ms., April 2001.
A. Laiou, 'Byzantine Trade with Christians and Muslims and the Crusades', in A. Laiou and R.P. Mottahedeh (eds), *The Crusades from the Perspective of Byzantium and the Muslim World* (Washington, 2001).
—— (ed.), *Economic History of Byzantium* (Washington, 2002) (Greek edition, Athens: National Bank of Greece Cultural Foundation).
F.C. Lane and R.C. Mueller, *Money and Banking in Medieval and Renaissance Venice* (Baltimore, 1985).
—— and J.C. Riemersma (eds), *Enterprise and Secular Change* (London, 1953).
K. Lannoo D. and Gros, *Capital markets and EMU*, Report of a CEPS Working Party, Centre for European Policy Studies (Brussels, 1998).
F. Le Blanc, *Traite Historique des Monnaies de France* (Paris, 1690).
Liudprand of Cremona, *The Embassy to Constantinople*, trans. J.J. Norwich (London, 1993).
G. Le Rider, *La naissance de la monnaie. Pratiques monétaires de l'Orient ancien* (Paris, 2001).
J. Ljungberg and L. Schön, 'Domestic markets and international integration. Paths to industrialization in the Nordic countries', paper presented at the IVth EHES conference, Oxford, 20–23 September (Lund: Department of Economic History, 2001).

A. Llona, 'Chile during the Gold Standard. A Successful Paper Money Experience', in P. Martín Aceña and J. Reis (eds), *Monetary Standards in the Periphery. Paper, Silver and Gold, 1854–1933* (London, 2000).

E. Lo Cascio, 'State and Coinage in the Late Republic and Early Empire', in *The Journal of Roman Studies*, 71, 1981, pp. 76–86.

T.M. Lucchelli, *La moneta nei rapporti tra Roma e l'Europa barbarica: aspetti e problemi, La Nuova Italia* (Florence, 1998).

R.E. Lüke, 'The Schacht and the Keynes Plans', *Banca Nazionale del Lavoro Quarterly Review*, March 1985, pp. 65–76.

P. Ludlow, *The Making of the European Monetary System* (London, 1982).

F.A. Lutz, *The Keynes and White Proposals*, Essays in International Finance, no. 1 (Princeton, 1943).

A. Maddison, *The World Economy: A Millennial Perspective* (Paris, 2001).

G. Mankiw, 'The Inexorable and Mysterious Trade-Off Between Inflation and Unemployment', in *Economic Journal*, 111, May 2001, pp. C45–C61.

M. Manna, H. Pill and G. Quiros, 'The Eurosystem's Operational Framework in the Context of the ECB's Monetary Policy Strategy', *mimeo*, 2001.

P. Martín Aceña, 'The Spanish Monetary Experience, 1848-1914', in P. Martín Aceña and J. Reis (eds), *Monetary Standards in the Periphery. Paper, Silver and Gold, 1854–1933* (London, 2000).

P. Martín Aceña and J. Reis (eds), *Monetary Standards in the Periphery. Paper, Silver and Gold, 1854–1933* (London, 2000).

S. Mastropasqua, M. Micossi and R. Rinaldi, 'Interventions, sterilization and monetary policy in European Monetary System countries, 1979–87', in F. Giavazzi, J. Mélitz, 'Geography, Trade and Currency Union', CEPR DP 2987, 2001.

J. Mélitz and F. Zumer, 'Interregional and International Risk Sharing and Lessons for EMU', CEPR Discussion Paper, no. 2154, May 1999.

C.E. Meyer, 'Excavations undertaken by the university of Chicago at Bir Umm Fawakhir', in *Journal of Roman Archaeology*, 2000.

R.I. McKinnon, 'The Rules of the Game: International Money in Historical Perspective', in *Journal of Economic Literature*, 31, March 1993, pp. 1–44.

W.H. McNeill, 'Foreword', in A.G. Frank and B.K. Gills (eds), *The World System: Five Hundred Years or Five Thousand?* (London, 1993).

H. Michell, 'The Edict of Diocletian: a Study of Price Fixing in the Roman Empire', in H. Rockoff (ed.), *Price Controls*, Elgar Reference Collection [1947].

M. Micossi, and M. Miller (eds), *The European Monetary System* (Cambridge,1988).

J.S. Mill, *Principles of Political Economy*, W. Ashley (ed.), ([1848], New York, 1987).

A. Milward, 'The Origins of the Gold Standard', in J. Braga de Macedo, B. Eichengreen and J. Reis (eds), *Currency Convertibility. The Gold Standard and beyond* (London/New York, 1996).

L.von Mises, *The Theory of Money and Credit* ([1912], Indianapolis, 1980).

F. Mlynarsky, 'Proportionalism and Stabilization Policy', in A.D. Gayer (ed.), *The Lessons of Monetary Experience* (London, 1937).

O. Morkholm, *Early Hellenistic Coinage. From the Accession of Alexander to the Peace of Apamea, 336–188BC* (Cambridge, 1991).

C. Morrisson, 'La diffusion de la monnaie de Constantinople: routes commerciales ou routes politiques?', in C. Mango and G. Dagron (eds), *Constantinople and its Hinterland* (Aldershot, 1995).

——, 'La monnaie fiduciaire à Byzance ou "Vraie monnaie", "monnaie fiduciaire" et "fausse monnaie" à Byzance', in *Bulletin de la Société française de Numismatique*, 34, 1979, pp. 612–6.

——, *Monnaie et finances à Byzance: analyses, techniques* (Aldershot, 1994).

—— et al., *Museum Notes*, American Numismatic Society, 32, 1987.

——, J.-N. Barrandon et al., *L'or monnayé, vol. 1: Purification et altérations. De Rome à Byzance*, Cahiers Ernest-Babelon 2 (Paris, 1985).

R. Mundell, *International Economics* (New York, 1963).

——, 'The Future of the International Financial System', in A.L.K. Acheson, J.F. Chant and M.F.J. Prachowny (eds), *Bretton Woods Revisited* (London, 1972).

——, 'The Redundancy Problem and the World Price Level', in R.A. Mundell, *International Economics* (New York, 1968).

D. Nash, 'The Celts', in M. Price (ed.), *Coins. An Illustrated Survey, 650BC to the Present Day* (London, 1980).

G.B. Nilsson, 'Drömmen om universalmyntet', in *Pecunia*, 1, 1990, pp. 59–74.

R. Nurkse, *International Currency Experience. Lessons of the Inter-War Period* (Geneva, 1944).

M. Obstfeld, 'EMU, Ready or not?', Princeton Essays in International Finance, July 1998.

M. Obstfeld and A.M. Taylor, 'The Great Depression as a Watershed: International Capital Mobility over the Long Run', in M.D. Bordo, C. Goldin and E.N. White (eds), *The Defining Moment. The Great Depression and the American Economy in the Twentieth Century* (Chicago, 1998).

J.A. Ocampo, 'Variable Monetary Regimes in a Preindustrial Economy: Colombia, 1850–1933', in P. Martín Aceña and J. Reis (eds), *Monetary Standards in the Periphery. Paper, Silver and Gold, 1854–1933* (London, 2000).

S. Oppers, 'Recent Developments in Bimetallic Theory', in J. Reis (ed.), *International Monetary Systems in Historical Perspective* (Houndsmill/London, 1995).

J. Oswald of Dunnikier, 'Letter to Hume, 10 October 1750', in E. Rotwein (ed.), *David Hume. Writings on Economics* ([1750], Madison, 1970).

S.F. Overturf, *Money and European Union* (New York, 1997).

G. Pachymérès, Relations historiques, in A. Failler (ed.), *Corpus Fontium Historiae Byzantinae XXIV/1-4, 4 vols.* (Paris, 1984–1999), p. 540 (= Bonn II, pp. 493–4).

T. Padoa-Schioppa, 'Capital Mobility: Why is the Treaty Not Implemented?' Address to the Second Symposium of European Banks, 1982.

T. Persson, 'Currency Unions and Trade: How large is the Treatment Effect?', in *Economic Policy*, 33, October 2001.

A.C. Pigou, *Industrial Fluctuations* (London, 1927).

B. Pitarakis, 'Mines anatoliennes exploitées par les Byzantins : recherches récentes', in *Revue Numismatique*, 1998, pp. 141–185.

Plutarch, *The Lives of the Noble Grecians and Romans. Alexander* (translated by John Dryden) available at http://www.ellopos.net/elpenor/greek-texts/ancient-greece/plutarch_alexander_gymnosophists.asp.

'presveis' Numismatic site of the Greek Ministry of Culture, http://www.culture.gr

M. Psellos, *Chronography*, ed. Leib, B., II, 173, transl. E.R.A. Sewter (London, 1953).

J. Reis, 'Financial Institutions and Economic Growth: A Comparative Analysis of Scandinavia and Southern Europe', paper presented at the IVth EHES conference, Oxford, 20–23 September (Florence: European University Institute, 2001).

J. Reis, 'The Gold Standard in Portugal, 1854–91', in P. Martín Aceña and J. Reis (eds), *Monetary Standards in the Periphery. Paper, Silver and Gold, 1854–1933* (London, 2000).

H. Rittmann, *Deutsche Geldgeschichte 1484–1914* (Munich, 1975).

D.H. Robertson, *Money* ([1928], Cambridge, 1970).

A. Rose, 'Currency Unions and Trade; the Effect is Large', in *Economic Policy*, 33, October 2001.

——, 'One money, one market: the effect of common currencies on trade', in *Economic Policy*, 30, 2000.

—— and C. Engel, 'Currency Unions and International Integration', CEPR DP 2659, 2000.

—— and E. van Wincoop, 'National Money as a Barrier to Trade: the Real Case for Currency Union', in *American Economic Review* (Papers and Proceedings) 91, 2, 2001.

M.I. Rostovtzeff, 'Les classes rurales et les classes citadines dans le Haut Empire romain', in J. Andreau, 'Mercati e mercanto', in *Storia di Roma, vol. 2: l'Impero mediterraneo, II: I principi e il mondo* (Turin, [1926] 1991), pp. 369–70.

——, *The Social and Economic History of the Roman Empire* (Oxford, 1926).

J. Russell, 'Late Ancient and Medieval Population', *Transactions of the American Philosophical Society*, n. s., 48, 3, 1958, pp. 1–152.

W. Salter, 'Internal and External Balance: The Role of Price and Expenditure Effects', *Economic Record*, 36, 1959.

T.J. Sargent and F.R. Velde, 'The Big Problem of Small Change', paper prepared for the 4th EHES Conference, Oxford, September 2001.

L. Sarno, 'Exchange rate and interest rate volatility in the European Monetary System: some further results', in *Applied Financial Economics*, 7, 1997, pp. 255–63.

J. Schneider, 'Was There a Precapitalist World-System?', in C. Chase-Dunn and D. Hall (eds), *Core/Periphery Relations in Precapitalist Worlds* (Oxford, 1991).

—— and O. Schwarzer (eds), *Statistik der Geld- und Wechselkurse in Deutschland, 1815–1913* (St. Katharinen, 1990).

J.A. Schumpeter, *History of Economic Analysis* (Oxford, 1954).

Select Committee of the House of Lords, *The European Monetary System* (London, 1983), HMSO.

J.-P. Sodini and C. Morrisson, 'The Sixth Century', in A. Laiou (ed.), *Economic History of Byzantium* (Washington, 2002).

A. Soetbeer, *Edelmetallproduktion und Wertverhältnis zwischen Gold und Silber* (Gotha, 1879).

——, *Materialien zur Erläuterung und Beurteilung der wirtschaftlichen Edelmetallverhältnisse und der Währungsfrage* (Berlin, 2nd edn. 1886).

B. Sprenger, *Geldmengenänderungen in Deutschland im Zeitalter der Industrialisierung* (Cologne, 1982).

——, 'Harmonisierungsbestrebungen im Geldwesen der deutschen Staaten zwischen Wiener Kongress und Reichsgründung', in E. Schremmer (ed.), *Geld und Währung vom 16. Jahrhundert bis zur Gegenwart*, supplement, Vierteljahrschrift für Sozial- und Wirtschaftsgeschichte, 106 (Stuttgart, 1993).

P. Spufford, *Money and its use in Medieval Europe* (Cambridge, 1988).

L.O. Svensson, 'Assessing target zone credibility. Mean reversion and devaluation expectations in the ERM 1979–92', in *European Economic Review*, 1993, pp. 763–802.

——, 'The Simplest Test of Target Zone Credibility', IMF Staff Papers, 38, September 1991, pp. 655–65.

A. Szasz, *The Road to European Monetary Union: A political and economic history* (Basingstoke, 1999).

K. Talia, 'Monetary integration and disintegration. Studies in the Scandinavian Currency Union', *licentiat thesis* (Stockholm School of Economics, 2001).

G. Tattara, 'Was Italy Ever on Gold', in P. Martín Aceña and J. Reis (eds) *Monetary Standards in the Periphery. Paper, Silver and Gold, 1854–1933* (London, 2000).

P. Temin, 'A Market Economy in the Early Roman Empire', Discussion Papers in Economic and Social History, n. 39 (University of Oxford, March 2001).

T. Theurl, *Eine gemeinsame Währung für Europa. 12 Lehren aus der Geschichte* (Innsbruck, 1992).

——, 'Erfolgsbedingungen für monetäre Union souverän bleibender Staaten: die Beispiele des 19. Jahrhunderts', in A. Mosser (ed.), *Österreichs Weg zum Euro. Aspekte-Perspektiven-Handlungsspielräume* (Vienna, 1998).

R. Tilly, *Geld und Kredit in der Wirtschaftsgeschichte* (Stuttgart, 2003).

——, Financial institutions and industrialization in the Rhineland, 1815–1870 (Madison, 1966).

——, 'Germany', in R. Cameron et al. (eds), *Banking in the Early Stages of Industrialization* (New York, 1967).

J. Tinbergen, 'An Analysis of World Trade Flows', in J. Tinbergen (ed.), *Shaping the World Economy* (New York, 1962).

'To Byzantio os oikoumene', catalogue of the exhibition, Byzantine and Christian Museum, Oct. 2001–Jan. 2002 (Athens: Hypourgeio Politismo, 2001).

J. Tobin, 'Money', in P. Newman et al. (eds), *The New Palgrave Dictionary of Money and Finance* (London, 1992).

R. Triffin, *Gold and the Dollar Crisis* (New Haven, 1960).

——, *The Evolution of the International Monetary System: Historical Reappraisal and Future Perspectives* (Princeton 1964).

H. Ungerer, O. Evans P. and Nyberg, 'The European Monetary System – recent developments', International Monetary Fund Occasional Papers, no. 48, 1986.

H. Ungerer, O. Evans and P. Nyberg, 'The European Monetary System: the experience 1979–82', International Monetary Fund Occasional Papers, no. 19, May 1983.

W. Vanthoor, *European Monetary Union since 1848, a Political and Historical Analysis* (Cheltenham, 1996).

J. Viner, 'Two Plans for International Monetary Stabilization', in J. Viner, *International Economics* ([1943], Glencoe, Ill., 1951).

——, *The Customs Issue* (New York, 1950).

A. Watson, 'Back to Gold – and Silver', in *Economic History Review*, 20, 1, 1967, pp. 1–34.

A. Weber, 'Policy-makers' reputation in the EMS disinflation', in *European Economic Review*, 36, 1992, pp. 1473–92.

K. Wicksell, 'Den skandinaviska myntunionens återställande', unpublished manuscript from 1923, in L. Jonung, T. Hedlund-Nyström and C. Jonung (eds), *Att uppfostra det svenska folket. Knut Wicksells opublicerade manuskript* (Stockholm, 2001).

——, *Interest and Prices* ([1898], New York, 1965).

——, 'The monetary problems of the Scandinavian countries', 1925, translated and reprinted in K. Wicksell, *Interest and Prices*, translated by R.F. Kahn (New York, 1965).

——, 'The Scandinavian Monetary System after the [First World] War', orginally published as "Det skandinaviska penningväsendet efter kriget" i Bidrag till frågan om ett ekonomiskt närmande mellan de skandinaviska länderna. Inlägg av skandinaviska ekonomer (1917), translated and published in B. Sandelin (ed.), *Knut Wicksell. Selected essays in economics, vol. 2* (London and New York, 1999).

E. Wilhelmsson, 'Den skandinaviska myntunionen', in *Bancoposten, utgiven av Riksbankstjänstemännens förening*, 8, 6, 15 Dec. 1923, pp. 155–61.

D. Williams, 'The 1931 Financial Crisis', Yorkshire Bulletin of Economic and Social Research, 15, November 1963, pp. 92–110, reprinted in M. Thomas (ed.), *The Disintegration of the World Economy Between the World Wars, vol. 2* ([1963], Cheltenham and Brookfield, 1996).

J. Williams, J. Cribb and E. Errington (eds), *Money. A History* (London, 1997).

J.H. Williams, 'International Monetary Organization and Policy', in A.D. Gayer (ed.), *The Lessons of Monetary Experience* (London, 1937).

J. Williamson, 'Crawling Bands or Monitoring Bands: how to manage exchange rates in a world of capital mobility', in *International Finance*, October 1998, 1, pp. 59–79.

——, 'On the System in Bretton Woods', in *American Economic Review*, Papers and Proceedings, 75, May 1985, pp. 74–9.

H.P. Willis, *A History of the Latin Monetary Union*, Economic Studies Series no. 5 (Chicago, 1901).

E.O. Winstedt (ed.), *Christian Topography* (Cambridge, 1909).

C. Wyplosz, 'Capital Flow Liberalization and the EMS: a French perspective', in *European Economy*, 36, May 1988, pp. 85–104.

L.B. Yeager, 'Fluctuating Exchange Rates in the Nineteenth Century: The experience of Austria and Russia', in R.A. Mundell and A.K. Swodoba (eds), *Monetary Problems of the International Economy* (Chicago, 1969).

——, *International Monetary Relations. Theory, History and Policy* (New York, 1976).

D. Ziegler, 'Der "latecomer" lernt. Der Peel's Act und die preußische Währungsgesetzgebung im Zeitalter der Industrialisierung', in H. Berghoff und D. Ziegler (eds), *Pionier und Nachzügler. Vergleichende Studien zur Geschichte Großbritanniens und Deutschlands im Zeitalter der Industrialisierung* (Bochum, 1995).

Index

(References to illustrations are in **bold**)

For Product Safety Concerns and Information please contact our EU representative GPSR@taylorandfrancis.com Taylor & Francis Verlag GmbH, Kaufingerstraße 24, 80331 München, Germany

Batch number: 10726288

Printed by Printforce, the Netherlands